Social Skills in Interpersonal Communication

Second Edition

Owen Hargie, Christine Saunders and David Dickson

CROOM HELM
London & Sydney

BROOKLINE BOOKS
Cambridge, Massachusetts

Croom Helm Ltd, Provident House, Burrell Row, Beckenham, Kent BR3 1AT
Croom Helm Australia, 44-50 Waterloo Road, North Ryde, 2113, New South Wales

British Library Cataloguing in Publication Data

Hargie, Owen
Social skills in interpersonal communication — 2nd ed.
1. Interpersonal communication
I. Title II. Saunders, Christine
III. Dickson, David, *1930–*
302.2 BF637.C45

ISBN 0-7099-4774-7

Brookline Books, PO Box 1046, Cambridge, MA 02238.

Library of Congress Cataloging-in-Publication Data

Hargie, Owen.
Social skills in interpersonal communication.

Bibliography: p.
Includes index.
1. Social skills. 2. Interpersonal communication.
I. Saunders, Christine. II. Dickson, David. III. Title.
[DNLM: 1. Communication. 2. Interpersonal Relations.
3. Social Behavior. HM 299 H279s]
HM299.H36 1987 302.3'4 87-18265
ISBN 0-914797-41-7 (pbk.)

Printed and bound in Great Britain by Mackays of Chatham Ltd, Kent

Contents

Preface to the Second Edition

1.	Introduction	1
2.	Nonverbal Communication	8
3.	Reinforcement	35
4.	Questioning	58
5.	Reflecting	87
6.	Set Induction and Closure	108
7.	Explanation	143
8.	Listening	162
9.	Self-disclosure	187
10.	Assertiveness	209
11.	Group Interaction and Leadership	227
12.	Concluding Comments	253
Bibliography		255
Subject Index		280
Author Index		284

FOR:
PATRICIA, ETHEL, ERIC, ROB, ANNE and MARY

Preface to the Second Edition

The importance of effective interpersonal communication in professional contexts is now widely recognised. Interpersonal skills training programmes have been reported in the literature for doctors, dentists, nurses, health visitors, psychiatrists, pharmacists, speech therapists, occupational therapists, physiotherapists, social workers, teachers, clergymen, counsellors, careers advisers, youth workers, policemen, librarians, psychologists, selection interviewers, engineers, and business managers. In all of these occupations, the ability to communicate effectively at an interpersonal level is a vital part of the job, and it is therefore reasonable to expect that these professionals should have a knowledge of various types of social skills, and of their effects in social interaction. It is for this reason that interest in the study of social skills in professional contexts has mushroomed in the past few years.

It is six years since the first edition of this book was published, and during this time we have received a considerable amount of feedback from tutors and trainees involved in interpersonal skills programmes, both within and without the University of Ulster. We have also received feedback from practising professionals. As a result of this feedback we have extended the coverage of skills to include chapters on assertiveness, and on group interaction. Both of these areas would seem to be of vital importance to the work of many professionals. As well as updating research information on all of the skills, we have also provided wider coverage of the skills of listening and self-disclosure by devoting a chapter to each.

These are the main changes which have been made to this edition. The function of the book remains exactly the same, however, in that it has been designed and presented in such a fashion as to provide a useful reference for the study of social skills *per se* by interpersonal professionals. It is concerned with the identification, analysis and evaluation of a range of social skills which are employed widely in professional interaction. As such, this text should be of interest both to qualified personnel and to trainees in many fields. Detailed accounts are provided of 12 social skill areas, namely: nonverbal communication, reinforcement, questioning, reflecting, set induction, closure, explaining, listening, self-disclosure, assertiveness, and interacting in, and leading, small group discussions.

In writing this book, the authors would like to acknowledge the assistance provided by the Faculty of Social and Health Sciences, University of Ulster. We would also like to thank all those members of staff at the University, and at other Centres in Northern Ireland, who have been involved in, and contributed to, the evolution of our skills training programmes. The support, advice and encouragement of these colleagues is reflected in this second edition. The stimulation and invaluable feedback provided by trainees on our skills programmes is also recognised. A special word of thanks is given to Tim Hardwick, Senior Editor at Croom Helm, for his continued help and expertise. Words of appreciation are due to Mrs Sadie Faulkner for her diligence, and forbearance, in typing the manuscript. Finally, we are indebted to our families who provided the necessary motivation throughout the production of this book.

(It should be noted that where either the masculine or feminine gender is referred to throughout this text, this should be taken as encompassing both genders as appropriate.)

Owen Hargie
Christine Saunders
David Dickson
Jordanstown, 1987

1

Introduction

In recent years increasing attention has been devoted to the entire spectrum of socially-skilled interaction. The fairly obvious observation that some individuals are better social interactors than others, has led to carefully formulated and systematic investigations into the nature and function of interpersonal interaction. This has occurred at three levels. Firstly, theoretical analyses of how and why people behave as they do have resulted in various conceptualisations of socially-skilled behaviour (see for example Ellis and Whittington, 1983; Trower, 1984). Secondly, research has been conducted into the identification and effects of different types of social behaviour. It is at this level that this book is concentrated. Thirdly, a number of different approaches to training in social skills have been introduced in order to ascertain whether it is possible to improve the social performance of the individual (for a review of these see L'Abate and Milan, 1985).

THE NATURE OF SOCIAL SKILLS

At this stage, it is useful to examine exactly what is meant by the term 'social skill'. At first sight this may appear unnecessary, since the term has already been referred to and presumably the reader has understood what was meant by it. In this global sense, social skills are the skills employed when interacting at an interpersonal level with other people. This definition of social skill is not very informative, however, since it really indicates what social skills are used for rather than what they are.

Attempts to define the term 'social skill' proliferate within the psychological literature. In order to illustrate this point it is useful to examine some of the definitions which have been put forward by different theorists.

Phillips (1978), in reviewing a number of approaches to the analysis of social skill, concludes that a person is socially-skilled according to:

> the extent to which he or she can communicate with others, in a manner that fulfills one's rights, requirements, satisfactions, or obligations to a reasonable degree without damaging the other person's similar rights, requirements, satisfactions, or obligations, and hopefully shares these rights etc. with others in free and open exchange (p. 13).

This definition emphasises the macro-elements of social encounters, in terms of reciprocation between participants (although Phillips does point out that 'knowing how to behave in a variety of situations' is part of social skill). This theme is also found in the definition given by Schlundt and McFall (1985) who define social skills as 'the specific component processes that enable an individual to behave in a manner that will be judged as "competent". Skills are the abilities necessary for producing behaviour that will accomplish the objectives of a task' (p. 23).

These definitions tend to view social skill as an ability which the individual may possess to a greater or lesser extent. A somewhat different focus has been offered by other theorists, who define social skill in terms of the *behaviour* of the individual. Thus McGuire and Priestley (1981) regard social skills as 'those kinds of behaviour which are basic to effective face-to-face communication between individuals' (p. 6). Argyle (1981) extends this behavioural emphasis, to encompass the *goals* of the individual, when he states 'By socially skilled behaviour, I mean social behaviour which is effective in realising the goals of the interactors' (p. 1). Kelly (1982) adds the dimension of *learning* by defining social skills as 'those identifiable, learned behaviours that individuals use in interpersonal situations to obtain or maintain reinforcement from their environment' (p. 3).

Michelson *et al.* (1983), in evaluating the defining features of social skill, derive six main elements which they regard as being central to the concept. They point out that social skills:

(1) are primarily acquired through learning;
(2) comprise specific, discrete verbal and nonverbal behaviours;
(3) entail effective, appropriate initiations and responses;
(4) maximise social reinforcement from others;

(5) are interactive in nature, and require appropriate timing and reciprocity of specific behaviours;
(6) are influenced by environmental factors such as the age, sex, and status of the other person.

In a recent review of definitions of skilled behaviour, Hargie (1986a) also identified six main facets of social skill as comprising 'a set of goal-directed, inter-related, situationally appropriate social behaviours which can be learned and which are under the control of the individual' (p. 12). This is the definition adopted in this book. It emphasises six separate components of social skill:
(1) Socially-skilled behaviours are *goal-directed*. They are those behaviours which the individual employs in order to achieve a desired outcome, and are therefore purposeful behaviours, as opposed to chance, or unintentional, behaviours. For example, if person A wishes to encourage person B to talk freely, he will look at B, nod his head when B speaks, refrain from interrupting B, and utter what Richardson *et al.* (1965) term 'guggles' ('hmm hmm'; 'uh, hu'; etc.) periodically. In this instance these *behaviours* are *directed* towards the *goal* of encouraging participation.
(2) Socially-skilled behaviours should be *interrelated*, in that they are synchronised behaviours which are employed in order to achieve a *common* goal. Thus the individual may employ two or more of these behaviours at the same time. As mentioned previously, when encouraging B to talk, A may smile, nod his head, look directly at B, and utter a guggle — all at the same time, and each of these signals will be interpreted by B as signs of encouragement to continue speaking. Each behaviour relates to this common goal, and so the behaviours are in this way interrelated and synchronised.
(3) Social skills should be *appropriate* to the *situation* in which they are being employed. The socially-skilled individual will be able to adapt his use of behaviours to meet the demands of particular individuals in specific social contexts. There is some evidence that professionals who develop a style of interacting for one aspect of their work, find it difficult to change this style if they have to move to another professional context. For example teachers with considerable classroom experience may encounter such problems if they are then required to undertake a counselling role with pupils (Hargie, 1986b).
(4) Social skills are defined in terms of identifiable units of *behaviour* which the individual displays. As Argyle (1983) points out, socially-skilled responses are hierarchically organised in such a way that large elements, like being interviewed, are comprised of smaller behavioural

units such as looking at the interviewer and answering questions. Argyle argues that the development of social skills can be facilitated by training the individual to acquire these smaller responses (this technique is also used in the learning of many motor skills).

(5) The fifth aspect of the definition adopted in this book is that social skills are comprised of behaviours which can be *learned*. It is now generally accepted that most forms of behaviour displayed in social contexts are learned by the individual. This is evidenced by the general finding that children reared in isolation from other humans display distorted, socially unacceptable forms of behaviour, and do not acquire a language. At a less extreme level, there is evidence to suggest that children from a socially deprived home environment may also develop unacceptable social behaviours while children from a culturally richer home environment tend to develop more appropriate social behaviours (Eisler and Frederiksen, 1980).

Bandura (1971) has developed a social learning theory, which purports that all repertoires of behaviour, with the exception of elementary reflexes (such as eye blinks), are learned. This process of social learning involves the *modelling* and *imitation* of the behaviour of significant others, such as parents, teachers, siblings or peers. By this process, from an early age, children may walk, talk and act like their same-sex parent. At a later stage, however, the child may develop the accent of his, or her, peers and begin to talk in a similar fashion — despite the accent of parents. The second major element in social learning theory is the *reinforcement* of behaviours which the individual displays. In childhood, for example, the parents will encourage, discourage or ignore various behaviours which the child displays. As a general rule, the child will tend to learn, and employ more frequently, those behaviours which are encouraged, while tending to display less often those behaviours which are discouraged or ignored.

(6) The final element in the definition of social skills is that they should be under the *control* of the individual. Thus a socially inadequate individual may have learned the basic elements of social skills but may not have developed the appropriate thought processes necessary to control the utilisation of these elements in social interaction. An important dimension of control relates to the timing of social behaviours. If the use of a social skill is to achieve its desired effect, then the timing of the use of skilled behaviours is a very important consideration, in that socially-skilled behaviours need to be employed at the most suitable juncture. For instance, verbal statements of encouragement should be uttered immediately in response to the utterances by the other person that they are intended to encourage

— otherwise they may not be viewed as encouragement. Indeed 'saying the right thing at the wrong time' would seem to be a characteristic of some social inadequates (Hargie and McCartan, 1986). It would, therefore, seem that learning *when* to employ social behaviours is just as crucial as learning *what* these behaviours are and *how* to use them.

EXAMPLE OF SOCIAL SKILL

In order to understand more fully these six basic elements of social skill, the skill of reinforcement (which will be reviewed in more detail in Chapter 3) can serve as a useful example. This skill is subdivided into verbal and nonverbal reinforcement techniques which can be employed in social interaction. These two subdivisions are in turn analysed in terms of the operational behaviours which are used to define and chart the use of the skill itself (see Figure 1.1).

Figure 1.1: The social skill of reinforcement

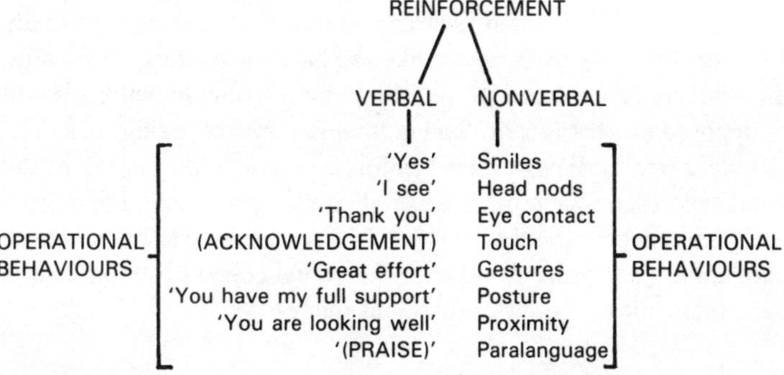

Verbal reinforcers

These are the utterances made by individuals which serve the purpose of encouraging another person to continue with a certain behaviour or activity. There are two main categories of verbal reinforcement:

Acknowledgement

This refers to utterances which acknowledge or agree with what has been said or done by another. Examples of such reinforcers include:

'Yes'; 'That's right'; 'OK'. These words or phrases indicate to the speaker that his message has been received and comprehended.

Praise

This type of verbal reinforcement is stronger than the simple acknowledgement of what has been said, since it indicates overt support and encouragement for the speaker. Examples of such verbalisations are: 'You have done very well'; 'I agree with you entirely'; 'I love your dress'.

Nonverbal reinforcers

These include most of the features of nonverbal behaviour (see Chapter 2) when used in a positive or encouraging fashion. Thus *smiling, nodding* and *looking* at the other person can usually be taken as signs of nonverbal reinforcement. Similarly, certain forms of *touch* can be used to convey support or encouragement (e.g. shaking hands to congratulate someone, or hugging a loved one), as can certain gestures (e.g. 'thumbs-up'), or a forward-leaning posture when seated. Similarly body *proximity* is often regarded as reinforcing since we usually stand or sit closer to those we like, or have an interest in. Finally, the whole area of *paralanguage* is important — how something is said as opposed to what is said. Saying 'that is very interesting' in a dull, flat voice may well negate any reinforcing value of the statement and would represent inappropriate use of paralanguage. In other words, oral statements should always be accompanied by apposite paralanguage in order to enhance the verbal content (saying 'that is very interesting' should itself sound interesting!).

OVERVIEW

The factors discussed in this chapter, relating to the nature of social skills, should be borne in mind when examining each of the skills reviewed in the remainder of this text. It is recognised that the fluent application of these skills is a crucial feature of effective social interaction. However, the appropriateness of social behaviour is determined by a number of variables relating to the context of the interaction, the roles of the interactors and their goals, and personal features of the interactors (e.g. age, sex, personality, etc.). It is, therefore, impossible to legislate in advance for every possible social situation, in terms of what behaviours will be most successful to employ. The information about social skills contained in this book may therefore be regarded as providing resource material for the reader. How these resources are employed is a decision for the reader, given the situation in which any particular interaction is taking place.

There are twelve main skill areas covered in this text, beginning with nonverbal communication in Chapter 2. This aspect of social interaction is the first to be examined, since each of the social skills which follows contains nonverbal elements and so an understanding of the main facets of this channel facilitates the examination of all of the social skills. Chapter 3 incorporates an analysis of the skill of reinforcement, while the skill of questioning is reviewed in Chapter 4. In Chapter 5, an alternative strategy to questioning, namely reflecting, is investigated. Reflection consists of concentrating on what another person is saying and reflecting back to him the central elements of his statements. Two important episodes in any action — the opening and closing sequences — are reviewed in Chapter 6, while the skill of explaining is focused upon in Chapter 7. The skill of listening is explored in Chapter 8, where the active nature of listening is emphasised. In Chapter 9, self-disclosure is examined from two perspectives; firstly, the appropriateness of self-disclosure by the professional, and secondly, methods for promoting maximum self-disclosure from clients. Techniques for protecting personal rights are discussed in Chapter 10 in terms of the skill of assertiveness. Finally, in Chapter 11 the skills involved in interacting in, and leading, small group discussions are examined.

It should be realised that research in the field of social interaction is progressing rapidly and it is anticipated that, as our knowledge of this area increases, other important skill areas will be identified. The skills contained in this book do not represent a completely comprehensive list of all of the skills which have been identified to date, but they are generally regarded as being the central skills of interpersonal communication. In addition, it is recognised that, while these skills are studied separately, in practice they often overlap and seldom occur in isolation. Rather, the skills complement one another, and a knowledge of the repertoire of skilled behaviours outlined should enable the reader to extend and refine his own pattern, or style of interaction.

2

Nonverbal Communication

INTRODUCTION

Up until the early 1960s there were relatively few texts which were directly concerned with nonverbal aspects of human communication. However, more recently, a number of authors (Birdwhistell, 1970; Knapp, 1972; Argyle, 1975; Scherer and Ekman, 1982; and Bull, 1983) have recognised that any study of the complete communication process must take account of both verbal and nonverbal channels which are found to a greater or lesser extent in all forms of communication. In practice, therefore, observations of everyday interactions in the home, street, classroom or at work profit from a detailed consideration of the verbal and nonverbal messages that govern and influence behaviour in different social settings.

In this chapter it is intended to map out briefly elements of nonverbal behaviour which should provide the reader with greater insight into and, therefore, some measure of control over communication processes. The selection of material, from what is now becoming a widely researched area, has been governed by its direct relevance to increasing the awareness, sensitivity and eventual skill preferences of people whose daily job is largely made up of 'dealing with others'.

The importance of appreciating the key role of nonverbal processes in communication is persuasively put by Birdwhistell (1970), one of the authorities in the field, who claims that the average person actually speaks for a total of only ten to eleven minutes daily; the standard spoken sentence taking only about 2.5 seconds. In addition, he estimates that in a typical dyadic encounter the verbal components carry about one-third of the social meaning of the situation while the nonverbal channel conveys approximately two-thirds. Thus in the words of the song, 'It's not what she says but the way that she says it!', much of the information we are transmitting and receiving is being conveyed via the nonverbal channel.

WHAT IS NONVERBAL COMMUNICATION?

In order to define the concept 'nonverbal', it is useful to examine two important distinctions identified by Laver and Hutcheson, 1972; verbal and nonverbal, and vocal and nonvocal. Vocal behaviour refers to all aspects of speech, that is, actual language used and accompanying verbal expressions such as tone of voice, rate of speech and accent, etc., whereas nonvocal behaviour refers to all other activities which have a communicative function such as facial expressions, gestures and bodily movements. Verbal behaviour, on the other hand, is taken to mean only the actual words or language used while nonverbal behaviour refers to all vocal and nonvocal behaviour which is not verbal in the sense defined above. Thus quite apart from the verbal content of what a person says, meaning is communicated by tone of voice, talk speed, volume of speech and intonation. In addition to the nonverbal aspects of speech, information is transmitted and received through a whole range of body movements such as the posture adopted when sitting in a chair — is it one of stiffness and uprightness perhaps suggesting tension or anxiety or is the person slumped down in the chair with perhaps his feet on a small table suggesting a feeling of relaxation or familiarity? Faces, too, play an important role in social encounters by giving expression to our inner thoughts as, for instance, they show delight when we are presented with an unexpected gift or perhaps display sadness when we are told about the death of a close friend.

Before we open our mouths to speak our physical appearance conveys a great deal of information about our age, sex, occupation and status (if a certain uniform is worn) and personality. Social class too can be represented by distinctive clothing although as Goffman (1956) has observed people often try to conceal their true origins by wearing fake jewellery or cheap imitations of *haute couture* garments.

Not only are we concerned with the appearance and behaviour of the person involved in communication, but in addition, environmental factors such as architecture, furniture, decoration, smells, colour, texture and noise are extremely influential on the outcome of interpersonal relationships. These are only a few of the categories which nonverbal behaviour attends to. A more comprehensive range of nonverbal categories will be presented later in the chapter.

PURPOSES OF NONVERBAL COMMUNICATION

Nonverbal communication serves a number of purposes depending upon the context in which it is utilised. One of the most obvious functions it has is that it can totally replace speech. Consider, for instance, at one extreme the person who is deaf and dumb. He relies entirely on the use of hand and arm movements which have been developed universally to allow communication to take place. Sometimes, on the other hand, individuals are temporarily cut off from being able to communicate through speech, and so resort to using some form of body movements. This is particularly evident among deep sea divers, mime artists, race-course touts, and individuals who suffer a temporary loss of voice. At a less extreme level, there are occasions when we do not always have to put into words what we want to convey and indeed to do so would be pretentious and too formal or forward. Consider the girl who meets a boy for the first time. She can give off signals through smiling or eye contact that she 'fancies' him and would like to explore this relationship further. 'Actions can speak louder than words'. By and large, therefore, perceptive individuals can identify and interpret a wide range of nonverbal cues with a fair degree of accuracy and in so doing get the message over more effectively.

Nonverbal behaviour is also used to complement the spoken word. More particularly, specific nonverbal acts give the listener some idea of the affective state of the talker. Obviously not all oral statements are charged with the same degree of emotional content. For example there is every likelihood that a person will not put the amount of feeling into the statement, 'It's lunchtime!' that she would into the phrase, 'My father has just died!' However, the words uttered by individuals experiencing some kind of emotional state, be it sadness, anxiety, fear, anger, frustration or affection, are usually elaborated on by the utilisation of accompanying nonverbal behaviour. We stamp our feet when we are angry, grin broadly when pleased, and gasp when we are unexpectedly surprised.

It is also interesting to note, on the other hand, that nonverbal behaviour can on occasions contradict the verbal message. Consider, for example, the teacher who verbally invites pupils' questions and critical comments regarding the content of the lesson but who, in effect, makes it quite clear, via his nonverbal behaviour, that he will not be receptive to criticism. These subtleties can also be observed on TV. Witness the political leader who announces that he has every confidence in the measures he has taken for the good of the nation, while at the same time displaying a stream of nonverbal behaviour which indicates anxiety and lack of confidence. Where this contradiction exists it is generally thought that listeners place more credence on the nonverbal behaviours as they are considered harder to falsify (Shapiro, 1968). Such behaviours include blushing, sweating, trembling and tensing — which are spontaneous and outside the control of the individual. However, it is also recognised that with practice some people become extremely proficient at most forms of nonverbal deception as testified by the performances of top-class stage actors. Generally, though, complementary functions of nonverbal behaviour indicate attitudes, emotions and dispositions towards another person.

A third purpose of the nonverbal channel, and in a way related to the previous function, is that by accompanying speech it serves to reinforce more graphically what has been said although not necessarily linked with the emotional state. Friesen, Ekman and Wallblatt (1980) refer to these gestural acts as illustrators and they will be examined later in the chapter under gestures. For instance, when a person is asked to give an explanation to another concerning a route to travel, the shape of an object or the description of a particular job, he often illustrates what he is saying with movements and gestures. By observing people in conversations it can be noted that these accompanying movements actually facilitate speech where it is difficult to describe aspects of space and shape in purely verbal terms.

Fourthly, nonverbal behaviour can help to emphasise parts of the verbal messages by being an integral part of the total communication process. When a speaker puts more stress on certain words than others, uses pauses between words to convey gravity or interest, varies the tone and speed of his utterances, he is underlining the importance of certain words or phrases in the mind of the listener. In a sense it is analogous to the writer who puts words in italics, underlines them or gives chapter headings. In addition, body movements are frequently used to add more weight to the verbal message. Take, for example, the teacher who tells the class there are four aspects of the lesson that are important to remember and emphasises this in the form of holding up four fingers; or the mother who wants to ensure and stress that her son is listening closely to what she is saying may, in addition to the words, 'Listen to me', swing him round to face her closely and put both arms on his shoulders. These actions are all designed to add weight to the verbal message.

A fifth and equally important purpose of nonverbal behaviour is that it helps to regulate the flow of communication between speaker and listener. It becomes apparently clear when observing two persons interacting, that they somehow seem to know when it is their turn to either speak or listen without actually stating to the other, 'Go on it's your turn now'.

Duncan and Fiske (1977) have identified a number of nonverbal cues which offer a speaking turn to the other person. These are a rise or fall in pitch at the end of a clause, a drop in voice volume, and termination of hand gestures. In addition, they found that if a speaker continued to use gestures such as hand gesticulation, it essentially eliminated attempts by the listener to take over the turn. Another line of research on turn-taking focused on the regulating functions of gaze (Kendon, 1967). Kendon's findings, supported by later studies by Duncan and Fiske (1977), show that turning the head away from the listener functioned as a turn-yielding cue. This aspect will be dealt with later in the chapter under the heading 'eye gaze'.

Linked with this fifth purpose is a sixth which contends that nonverbal behaviour can both initiate and sustain communication by providing an important source of feedback to the interactors. For individuals to proceed to interact with each other they need to be able to reach some kind of common understanding between them. To do this they must acquire as much information about each other as possible in order to be sensitive to the views and feelings of the other person. Interactors are constantly adapting and modifying their subsequent behaviour in the light of how they think their messages are being received. So the interviewer, entreating the client to describe how he feels about a controversial issue, who detects aspects of discomfort in his client's behaviour may quickly change the subject or develop his line of questioning towards a less controversial aspect in order to ease any tension that might arise between them.

A seventh purpose of nonverbal behaviour is that it can have a considerable influence on other people by defining relationships without making them too explicit. If a person wants to influence another by being dominant over him he can manipulate his nonverbal behaviour in order to bring this about. Consider the following behaviours as aspects of dominant nonverbal cues: a louder voice, greater amount of talk, choosing a focal position in a room, standing on a raised dais, sitting behind a desk, sitting at the head of the table, occupying a more impressive chair, interrupting successfully when another person talks, and using long glances to establish a dominant relationship. When individuals are negotiating and sustaining personal relationships it would be too disturbing for one to state openly that he did not like the other very much or that he thought he was more important than the other. Yet nonverbal cues can be emitted regarding these states without the sender being explicit. In addition, initial relationships can change over time so that an original dominant-submissive relationship can become one more equal in nature. Change would not come about as readily if persons had explicitly stated at the beginning how they felt towards each other. This alternative channel allows individuals to make up their minds slowly about others and change their views without being committed to define verbally a relationship which may vary with time.

Finally, nonverbal behaviour can help to define acceptable patterns of behaviour in a variety of social settings. All social settings, from the simple, such as Sunday lunch, the office Christmas party, or a visit to the dentist, to the more elaborate, such as a graduation ceremony, or a funeral, carry with them acceptable codes of conduct. If a person deviates from these common patterns of behaviour and so upsets the social scene, he is usually called upon either to apologise or offer an excuse or explanation for his deviant behaviour (Goffman, 1972).

The remainder of this chapter will look more closely at the various components of behaviour which make up the nonverbal channel. Since the challenge of the present chapter is to present and discuss these aspects of nonverbal behaviour which serve a communicative function it is decided to classify the various behavioural elements into six dimensions, namely physical contact, kinesics (commonly referred to as 'body language'), proxemics (interpersonal spacing), physical characteristics, environmental factors and paralanguage (vocal part of speech such as voice pitch, volume and silences, etc.).

PHYSICAL CONTACT

This category of nonverbal communication has been included first because it is the earliest form of social communication we experience. Our first contact with the outside world and what it is going to be like comes through tactile experiences. Some of these touch experiences include: the doctor's hands as a baby is delivered and the mother's hands which feed, bathe, cradle, nurse and comfort the baby throughout his waking hours. These early tactile explorations appear to be of crucial importance to subsequent healthy behavioural development of young adults (Montagu, 1971). As a child grow ups and enters adult life, touching is an area of behaviour that is susceptible to multiple interpretations since as Heslin and Alper (1983) note, 'It [touch] is complicated by social norms regarding who has permission to touch whom and what is considered to be an appropriate context for such behaviour' (p. 47). For instance, Dickson (1985) has noted that touching between women and men and also between women in our society is acceptable but touch among men is frowned upon.

Touching serves a number of functions which are related to both the context in which touching occurs and to the relationship of the interactors. Heslin (1974) identifies these functions, ranging from the most distant to the most intimate, as: functional/professional, social/polite, friendship/warmth, love/intimacy and sexual arousal. The first three categories only of this taxonomy will be discussed in this chapter since they are the most relevant to professional contexts. A number of professionals touch people in the normal course of their work: nurses, dentists, doctors, physical education teachers, health visitors, hairdressers and physiotherapists to name but a few. However, touch in this sense does not carry connotations of social relationships but rather is seen as a necessary function of a particular job. Sometimes there is a tendency to decry the 'cool' manner in which professionals relate to their clients. However, such a manner is necessary if misinterpretations of touch contacts are not to be made.

Social/polite touching (especially hand shaking) is an act that attempts to equalise status by signalling that the interactors are intending to acknowledge the 'human element' of the interaction rather than status differences. Friendship/warmth touch contacts such as a friendly pat, arm-linking, a comforting touch on the arm, aimed at establishing friendly relationships with others, can be very rewarding to individuals in terms of giving encouragement, expressing cares and concerns and showing emotional support and understanding. Research into the influence that touch contacts can have on individuals shows that touching can help recipients talk to other people especially about themselves and their problems (Pattison, 1973). In addition, it can be found that persons are more likely to comply with requests and perform favours more readily when they are touched by the requester than when they are not (Kleinke, 1980; Willis and Hamm, 1980). This finding must surely have implications for the medical profession who find it a constant struggle to get patients to comply with their instructions for the taking of medications. Finally, touching can communicate a feeling of warmth and caring and at the same time can make the recipient have a more positive attitude towards the toucher and the physical setting in which the touch contact took place. In an interesting study by Fisher *et al.* (1975) it was found that when men and women clerks in a university library touched the hand of a reader returning identification cards, this less than half-second contact caused the women readers not only to like the librarian but also the library better than those who were not touched.

Finally, it is important to be aware that there are groups within the community who very rarely touch other individuals; elderly people with no close relatives and widowed people receive little or no bodily contact designed to cater for their emotional needs. Professional helpers, such as teachers, social workers, nurses, health visitors and doctors, aware of this void, could employ appropriate touch contacts to redress this imbalance. Alternatively a number of encounter groups have been deliberately set up to fulfil the need for bodily contact — which appears to be becoming a less frequent form of nonverbal communication, particularly in Western cultures (Schutz, 1967).

KINESICS

Kinesics or body motion, as the name suggests, includes all those movements of the body such as gestures, limb movements, head nods, facial expressions, eye gaze and posture. When we look at individuals or groups interacting, one aspect which is immediately striking is the amount of movement being displayed. People do not remain motionless when they are communicating. Instead, in general terms information, attitudes, affective states or moods and status cues are being communicated through body movements. More specifically, Patterson (1983) suggests there are five basic functions of body movements, namely, information giving, regulating interaction, expressing affective states, indicating social control, and facilitating task goals. This typology is somewhat similar to that of Ekman and Friesen (1969) developed 15 years earlier in which three categories, namely illustrators, affect displays and regulators, are directly related to Patterson's, facilitating task goals, expressing affect displays and regulating interaction. However, two other functions of Ekman and Friesen, emblems and adaptors, are alternative classification groupings. Emblems are those nonverbal behaviours which have a direct verbal translation, such as pointing to your wrist when you wish to 'know the time' or putting the thumbs in the air when you want to signify a win or some other success. These gestures are frequently used when the normal verbal channels are blocked or inadequate. According to Ekman and Friesen, adaptors are developed in childhood and tend to reveal personal orientations or characteristics towards the verbal messages. For instance, many of the restless movements of the hands and fingers, and kicking movements of the legs and feet, may be acts of tension or anxiety, revealing more intense affective states than that portrayed merely by speech utterances. The remainder of this section will analyse these various functions in relation to the five main areas of kinesics: gestures, posture, head nods, eye gaze, and facial expression.

Gestures

Kendon (1983) distinguished between gestures which totally replace speech (gestural autonomy) and gestures which complement speech (illustrators). Autonomous gestures or emblems, to use Kendon's label, are employed everyday where speech would be inadequate, for example in noisy environments (the floor of a busy factory) or over greater distances (policemen on point duty). Some instances of the vast range of hand and arm movements which are utilised everyday and to which meaning is attached are:

Gesture	*Inference*
hands outstretched	appealing
feet shuffling	impatience
moving hand	goodbye
shoulder shrugging	I don't know
drumming table with fingers	anxious
shaking clenched fist	angry
palms up and facing forward	stop, wait
thumbs up	success
thumbs down	loss
clenched fists	fear
rubbing eyes	bored
pointing arm and hand	go
clapping (fast)	approval
clapping (slow)	disapproval

It is interesting to note that forms of autonomous gestures tend to be different from one culture to another (Kendon, 1981) and that the cultures of the Mediterranean appear to be far richer in autonomous gestural forms than are the cultures of northern Europe (Morris *et al.*, 1979). Further comparative studies are needed, however, to reveal the origins of these systems and what purposes they serve.

Friedman and Hoffman (1967) distinguish between gestures which are linked with speech (illustrators) and directed towards objects or events and those which are oriented towards the self. They suggest that the speech-linked hand gestures are intended to communicate, while the second group act as a form of tension release. Let us look more closely at the speech linked hand gestures first. Hand gestures can be used to provide points of emphasis. For example teachers, when they are asking pupils to remember some important information, enumerate with their fingers the number of points to be remembered. In addition, hand gestures can provide illustrations of the verbal content of a message. These illustrations can take the form of shaping with the hands actual objects or events being discussed, outlining pathways or directions which represent thought patterns, or employing some of the more generally agreed upon gestures listed previously in this section in conjunction with speech. Equally important, is the need on occasions to use hand gestures in order to facilitate speech. It is fairly commonplace to observe speakers, struggling to find the appropriate words and phrases, using their hands to stimulate more rapid thought processes. Teachers, interviewers, public speakers and salesmen, who supplement their dialogue with good use of hand and arm movements, usually arouse and maintain the attention of their listeners, indicate their interest and enthusiasm, and tend to make the interaction sequence an interesting and enjoyable experience for all participants.

Evidence that clarity and comprehension of an explanation or description can be increased by the use of gestural cues comes from a study by Rogers (1978) in which eight male and female students were asked to view various actions on a silent film, such as a tennis ball bouncing, or a car swerving, and then describe them to another person who was unable to view the film. These descriptions were subsequently video-taped and shown to another group of students either with sound and vision or with sound only. Results showed that comprehension was significantly increased in the audio-visual as opposed to the sound only condition.

Further evidence that accuracy of understanding can be increased when gestural acts are used to complement the spoken word is provided in three studies by Riseborough (1981). Firstly, she showed that persons were more able to identify objects from descriptions accompanied by appropriate gestures than those without gestures. Secondly, she found that subjects could recall a story more accurately when accompanying gestural behaviours were employed. Thirdly, when the sound channel was obstructed by white noise, illustrative gestures increased comprehension.

If illustrators do complement speech acts, then it could be hypothesised that when people are restrained or restricted from using gestures, speech patterns would be hesitant and dysfluent. Graham and Heywood (1976) asked a group of British male students to communicate information about two-dimensional shapes, firstly with free use of hands and arms and secondly keeping their arms folded. The only significant result obtained was that pausing increased under the no-gesture condition.

Hand movements can also convey emotional states, although these are usually unintentional. The most common example is the highly nervous and anxious interviewee at a selection interview who exhibits his inner state by nervous wringing movements of the hands, fiddling with small objects, or constantly moving the fingers and hands on his lap. These are all forms of 'social leakage' which can be avoided if interviewees are encouraged to 'anchor' their hands on either the arms of the chair or on their lap and only use the hands to illustrate or facilitate their speech content. (Alternate methods of ventilating tension during selection interviews include wriggling or curling of the toes, or tightening of the calf muscles on the legs. Such forms of 'leakage' are not so immediately apparent.) Hand gestures can also reveal other emotional dispositions such as, embarrassment — hand over the mouth; anger — knuckles showing white; aggression — fist clenching; shame — hands covering the eyes; nervousness — nail and finger biting. Teachers, interviewers, nurses, health visitors, social workers, etc., should be sensitive to these hand signals which, because of their often spontaneous nature, may reveal more about the client's feelings than words would permit.

Posture

Although there are three main categories of human posture, standing, sitting or squatting, and lying, we are predominantly concerned with the position of the body when mainly sitting and standing. Posture itself can signify differential status, a positive or a negative attitude, emotional level and persuasion.

Turning first to the role of status in posture communication, we need to differentiate between status related to subjects when they are standing and conversely when they are sitting. It has been noted that high-status individuals adopt a more relaxed position when they are seated (e.g. body tilting sideways; lying slumped in a chair) than low-status subjects who sit more upright and rigid in their chairs.

In a standing position, the high-status subject again will appear more relaxed, often with arms crossed or hands in pockets, than low-status subjects who are generally 'straighter' and 'stiffer' (Mehrabian, 1972). To observe this factor the reader might like to switch the sound off next time when watchng two individuals on an interview programme on television. Try to deduce from their postural positions which one is controlling the interview and which one is being interviewed.

With regard to attitudinal state, a seated person who leans forward towards the other is deemed to have a more positive attitude towards both the subject and the topic under discussion than when he leans backwards, away from the subject he is addressing (Siegel, 1980). When the subjects are standing, on the other hand, a more positive attitude is conveyed when an individual directly faces another rather than turns away. It is also interesting to note that most prolonged interactions are conducted with both participants either sitting or standing, not where one is standing, the other sitting. Where this situation does occur, communication usually is of a cursory (e.g. information desks) or strained (e.g. interrogation sessions) nature.

We should also be alert to the different, more intense, emotions that can be conveyed directly by postural positions. While earlier in the chapter we noted that the face displayed information regarding specific emotions, bodily posture conveys the intensity of that emotion (Ekman and Friesen, 1967). Clients who are temporarily emotionally aroused can adopt specific postures which speak louder than words. For instance, extreme depression can be shown in a drooping, listless pose while, on the other hand, extreme anxiety can be seen in the muscularly tense, stiff, upright person. Focusing on patient behaviour, Fisch, Frey and Hirsbrunner (1983) found that posture was a significant indicator when differentiating between severely depressed and nearly recovered patients during doctor-patient interviews.

Finally, in an attempt to identify those nonverbal behaviours which had a persuasive impact on others, it was found that more upright postural positions or 'reduced reclining angles' along with intensity of voice and increased head nodding were instrumental in achieving this goal (Mehrabian, 1972; Washburn and Hakel, 1973).

Head nods

Head-nodding and shaking are in constant use during the interactive process and are related both to the role of the speaker and of the listener.

In relation to the listener's role, there are two ways in which interest and enthusiasm for the speaker's message can be conveyed. Ekman and Oster (1979) suggest that interest shown towards a speaker is communicated by a tilting of the head to one side rather than conveyed from facial expressions. Additionally, head-nodding is a signal to others that you wish them to continue talking and it is widely used by interviewers to encourage and motivate interviewees to speak at length. Duncan (1972) identified five cues, namely, sentence completions, requests for clarification, brief phrases such as 'uh-huh', 'yeah' and 'right', and head-nods and head shakes, which indicated continuing attentiveness towards the speaker.

Examining the role of the speaker, Duncan and Fiske (1977) found that two cues, notably the head turning away from the other person and beginning to gesture, were significantly associated with wanting to take a turn to speak. Thomas and Bull (1981), examining conversations between mixed-sex pairs of British students, confirm the findings of the previous two studies. They found that prior to asking a question, the students typically either raised the head or turned the head towards the listener; while just before answering a question the speaker turned his head away from the listener. This last finding may be due, as Beattie (1979) notes, to the effects of cognitive planning on the part of the listener prior to taking up the speaker's role.

When persons wish to bring a conversation to a close, there is evidence that head movements are instrumental in bringing this about in a smooth and synchronised way. Knapp *et al.* (1973) examined the behaviour of interacting pairs 45 seconds prior to leave-taking and found four frequently occurring nonverbal cues; breaking eye contact, pointing the legs and feet towards the door, leaning forward and head-nodding. The above authors conclude that, 'Nodding, smiling, and reinforcement may be viewed as behaviours which "politely" signal inattentiveness and lack of responsiveness on the part of the leaver' (p. 197). This latter point is dealt with more fully in Chapter 6.

Finally, the movements of the head also signify inner feeling states, such as cocked to one side showing interest or puzzlement, bowed low displaying depression or sadness, and tossed high in the air as a sign of defiance.

Eye gaze

Man's obsession with the eyes and their potent effects on human behaviour has been graphically documented down through the ages. This is also exemplified by a number of phrases which are in common usage, including 'He's making eyes at me'; 'She gave him a look to kill'; 'His eyes seemed to bore right through me'; 'Don't look at me like that'; 'There's something about his eyes'. Musicians, artists and choreographers, too, have captivated the magic and mystique of the eyes in their various art forms. Indeed the epitomy of the effects the eyes can have on man is the eye gaze of the Mona Lisa which has fascinated man for centuries. However, as students of human interaction, we are less concerned with the subjective impression which individuals make regarding the eye region of the face and more with the patterned movement made by the eyes as forms of signals or cues in any given interaction.

In what has almost become a classic in the literature on visual communication, Kendon (1967) found that, in general, people looked more as they listened than as they spoke, and the duration of looking was longer during listening than talking. Kendon also examined mutual looking, that is eye-to-eye contact, and found that looking came in short bursts, so that as soon as eye-to-eye contact was made one or other of the interactors broke it. A typical interactive sequence would be: When person A comes towards the end of his utterance he looks at person B to signal that it is B's turn to speak. Person B, in turn, will tend to look away after he begins his response, especially if he intends to speak for a long time, or the material he is dealing with is difficult to understand. It is necessary, according to Beattie (1981), for the speaker under these conditions to blot out as many distractions as possible. Therefore, he effectively closes the visual channel. The listener, on the other hand, generally continues to look at the speaker unless the speech is very long, in which case he will look at the speaker only intermittently. It would appear that this pattern of gazing is a useful device to synchronise and control the flow of conversation between individuals and eliminates both the need verbally to state whose turn it is to speak and the habit of constantly interrupting each other.

However, since this research was carried out almost 20 years ago now, a number of studies have raised doubts about the initial findings (see Beattie, 1978; Rutter *et al.*, 1978, and Kendon, 1978). From these more recent studies it would appear that further research is needed into the effects of status, interpersonal relationship and interactional situation on the regulation of turn-taking.

A number of studies (Argyle and Ingham, 1972; Russo, 1975; and Rutter *et al.*, 1978) have confirmed that women tend to look more than men. Two possible explanations for this phenomenon appear to be that women display a greater need for affiliation than do men, and that desire for affiliation promotes more looking (Argyle and Cook, 1976). Alternatively, it is contended that eye contact is seen as less threatening to women than men, with the result they are less likely to break eye contact than men in similar situations.

Eye contact is also a means by which we communicate the intensity of our emotions towards the other person, either of an affiliative nature or conversely of a threatening nature. We appear to make more and longer eye contact with people we like but this varies between males and females (Harper *et al.*, 1978). Courting couples for instance will spend a long time 'making eyes' at each other. Persons who are showing a great deal of hostility to each other will also persist in engaging in long periods of mutual gaze. However, it is usually easy to distinguish the two kinds of behaviour since subsidiary facial expressions, such as smiling in the affiliative situation and teeth baring in the threatening behaviour, are in evidence.

It is also important to add that individuals are also looking for feedback on how their messages are being received: signs of approval and disapproval. This then makes it possible for interactors to modify their social behaviour so as to maximise approving feedback. Kendon (1967) refers to this as the 'monitoring' function of gaze.

Finally, if you want to avoid communication you will generally be successful as long as you avoid eye contact in a seemingly natural way. School children become adept at this when they do not know the answer to a question which the teacher has posed to the whole class.

Facial expressions

The face conveys a rich source of information regarding the emotional state of an individual. In fact, some theorists regard facial expressions as the next most important source of information to language itself. Some evidence of this can be found in the amount of time and space authors, playwrights and script writers give to describing in detail the facial movements of their characters.

Although facial cues are readily visible to us we frequently find it difficult to judge the emotional states being displayed. Ekman *et al.* (1971) draw our attention to the fact that we are dealing with a very complex phenomenon, pointing out that:

(1) one emotion is shown in one facial area and another is shown

> in another area — e.g. brows raised as in surprise, and lips pressed as in anger; (2) two different emotions shown in one part of the face — e.g. one brow raised as in surprise and the other lowered as in anger; and (3) a facial display produced by muscle action associated with two emotions but containing specific elements of neither (p. 53).

One more recent study, however, found that judgements about the content of a conversation could be made merely by observing and analysing the facial expressions of the participants. Dabbs (1985) asked two judges to view a video-tape, with the sound turned off, of 13 male and 13 female university students who had not previously met and who conversed in opposite-sex pairs for half an hour each. The subjects' faces were recorded and, from the findings, it was significant that judges could assess from facial expressions shown whether the respondents were talking at a social level (displaying nods, smiles or pleasing expressions) or an intellectual level (displaying thoughtful expressions and markedly less attention to each other).

It is commonly believed that facial expressions are a combination of innate and socially learned behaviour (Knapp, 1972). Some evidence seems to support the innate behaviour theory. For instance, a number of behaviours appear to be common across the different cultures of the world; behaviours such as one eyebrow raised, both eyebrows raised, yawning or lip biting which suggest, in turn, concern, surprise, tiredness or boredom, and anxiety.

Often facial expressions and speech are at variance with each other, in which case we are apt to place more credence on what we see rather than what we hear (Zaidel and Mehrabian, 1969), although this varies with age, children and young adolescents paying more attention to visual components than older adolescents and adults (Bugental *et al.*, 1970). In addition, it is much easier to control speech behaviour than it is facial behaviour. A nervous twitch of the mouth in a crucial interview situation, blushing when attempting to hide embarrassment, and seething with anger while trying not to show it, are only some of the many examples which account for this occurrence, particularly strong emotions being the most difficult to conceal. Recognising and understanding the various facial expressions would seem to be a useful skill for any student of human behaviour.

Finally, two studies have focused on sex differences related to facial expressions (Duncan and Fiske, 1977; Bond and Ho, 1978). These studies found that when subjects conversed with a person of the same sex or the opposite sex, female subjects smiled significantly more frequently and spent a significantly higher proportion of time smiling than did males.

PROXEMICS

Proxemics refers to the role of space in man's behaviour. In particular there are three aspects, namely territoriality, proximity and orientation, which all have a direct bearing on the communication process. Each will be discussed in turn.

Territoriality

Spatial behaviour is connected with 'territory', establishing it, invading it, and defending it. Personal space is that space immediately surrounding the body, and it can be disturbing for individuals if this personal space is invaded. Social workers, teachers, doctors and interviewers should normally avoid moving too close to their clients. If they do move too near to an individual this may result in a tendency for that person to move his head or body backwards. Personal territory, on the other hand, is a much larger area in which a person moves. This space often provides the individual with privacy or social intimacy. Examples of individuals creating their personal territory can be found everyday in our general lives. Thus members of a family usually occupy the same seats at meal-times, or specific seats when driving in the family car. Staff-rooms in schools, too, contain chairs which seemingly 'belong' to individual members of staff, as the student teacher often finds out to her embarrassment after occupying one of them on school placement! People in offices which are shared go to great lengths to place their desks in such a way as to create social barriers, or alternatively establish a status difference between themselves and clients. Booking personal territory in the form of leaving bags and coats on seats in libraries, restaurants and trains, etc., are common everyday occurrences which we accept. Teachers arrange the desks in their classroom on occasion to establish a personal territory; rows of desks for pupils facing, at some distance, their own desk. However, if a teacher wants to break down the barriers between himself and the class it can often be achieved by rearranging the furniture. For example, he can arrange the chairs in a circle or semicircle to encourage whole-class discussion, or set up small groups of tables and chairs to encourage group co-operation exercises.

Alternatively, he can remove the furniture completely to encourage free movement and drama lessons.

Finally, as with personal territory, individuals can sometimes feel threatened when their home territory is invaded. Examples of home territory are the house itself, cafés taken over by particular groups, pubs taken over by a sports team, or even street corners frequented by gangs of youths. Social workers may be told very forcibly by their clients that they are not welcome in their home and any attempt by the social worker to establish entry may be severely criticised. Teachers, too, look upon their classrooms as private places and feel threatened and anxious on occasions when they are observed by other teachers, the headmaster, the inspectorate or educational researchers. Violence can often be the order of the day when home territories are invaded by rival groups. Witness two groups of rival supporters who have established their territory behind the 'home' team's goal. If the rival side attempts to invade their territory, the home side will defend it with violence. There is no doubt, therefore, that spatial behaviour is considered one of the important nonverbal social skills since seating positions, furniture arrangements, availability of space and positions of the interactors play an integrated part in determining both the amount and kind of interaction that will ensue.

Proximity

If individuals have freedom of choice regarding the position they take up in relation to each other, it can convey information about their relationship. More specifically, proximity refers to the interpersonal distance that individuals maintain when they are involved in interaction. The first distinction we can make is that generally we interact at a closer distance to people when we are standing rather than sitting. A sitting distance of five to six feet is common for discussion in a work situation while eight to ten feet appears to be the norm in a sitting-room or lounge. On the other hand, the usual nose-to-nose distance for ordinary conversation when we are standing is three to four feet. If a person violates these patterns of interpersonal distance by either placing himself within two feet or beyond ten feet of our face when conversing we would feel uncomfortable and move ourselves either away from him or towards him until the appropriate distance is established. It is not difficult to appreciate that the narrowing of distance indicates a claim to a higher degree of intimacy and by deposition the increasing of the distance suggests coldness and aloofness (thus the expression 'he is very stand-offish').

(Hall 1959, 1966) put forward, from his observation of North American society, that distance could be classified into four main zones depending on the purposes set for the interaction.

Intimate Zone	— Those who have an intimate relationship with each other will interact at a distance of approximately 18 inches
Personal Zone	— Those who have a close personal relationship with other individuals will take up a distance of 18 inches to 4 feet
Social/Consultative Zone	— Nine to 12 feet is an appropriate distance for professionals to interact with their clients and it can often be from behind a desk
Public Zone	— Speakers on public occasions are usually placed at a distance of 12 feet or greater from their audience

A study carried out by Baxter and Rozelle (1975) focused on a simulated police-citizen interview in which the distance between the officer and citizen was systematically varied according to Hall's first three distance categories. Briefly, as the interpersonal distance was decreased to within two feet of the two interactors, the citizen's speech time and frequency became disrupted and disorganised, eye movements and gaze aversion increased, more head movements (particularly rotating) increased, while foot movements decreased. Thus these nonverbal behaviours, produced by manipulating the interpersonal distance zone were strikingly similar to those identified by 'real' police officers as describing behaviours indicating guilt, suspicion and deception. Thus it is important to be aware that the initiator can influence the other person's nonverbal behaviour and misconstrue the resulting consequences. Although this research was related to one professional group only, it has implications for other professonal situations, such as selection, survey and counselling interviews.

In addition, status differences between individuals must also be taken into account when observing interpersonal distances. People of equal status tend to take up a closer distance between each other than people of unequal status (Lott and Sommer, 1967). In fact, where a status differential exists the lower status individual will allow the higher status individual to approach quite closely, but will rarely approach the high statgus individual with the same degree of closeness. Witness the teacher who invariably moves round the classroom helping individual pupils with learning difficulties. In some subjects like physical education, drama, and art, the teacher may actually physically help a pupil to accomplish a task. Yet we would struggle to find instances where the pupil voluntarily approaches close to the teacher. Indeed, in a number of situations pupils prefer the greatest possible distance to be achieved between the teacher and themselves. Another example of this occurs when students enter a lecture room — the area of the room that gets filled up first tends to be the back row.

Physical characteristics of participants also, to some extent, determine the amount of distance between interactors. Kleck (1969) for example found that persons communicating with physically deformed individuals chose a greater initial distance.

Finally, Mehrabian (1968) noted that personality affected the position of subjects to each other, introverts preferring greater interpersonal distance than extroverts.

Professionals in their everyday working lives should be aware that whatever the position they take up in relation to their clients, it will have an effect on the kind of relationship they are hoping to achieve.

Orientation

This aspect of nonverbal behaviour ought to be considered in relation to the previous component, proximity, since not only do individuals create interpersonal space, but the angle at which one person interacts with another affects the communication pattern. Orientation refers to the position of the body rather than the head and eyes only. It is useful to look at proximity and orientation together since it has been found that there is an inverse relationship between them — that is direct face-to-face orientation is linked to greater distance and sideways orientation linked to closer distance.

Sommer's (1969) studies in North America of seating behaviour, replicated by Cook (1970) in the UK, point to some interesting differences in seating arrangements when individuals are given a choice of where to sit in different situations. Figure 2.1 will help to present some of these findings, the situations clearly indicating that a side-by-side position is considered to be co-operative in nature, while a face-to-face orientation usually conveys intonations of competitiveness. Conversation, however, appears to benefit from individuals taking up a ninety degree angle in relation to each other. At the same time, co-action would be a more conducive situation for studying for different exams, or children required to work independently at a task in the classroom.

Figure 2.1: Seating preferences at a rectangular table

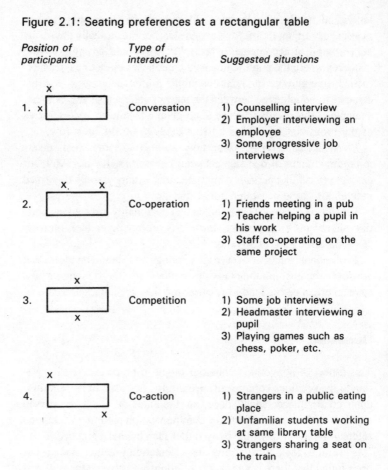

Position of participants	*Type of interaction*	*Suggested situations*
1.	Conversation	1) Counselling interview 2) Employer interviewing an employee 3) Some progressive job interviews
2.	Co-operation	1) Friends meeting in a pub 2) Teacher helping a pupil in his work 3) Staff co-operating on the same project
3.	Competition	1) Some job interviews 2) Headmaster interviewing a pupil 3) Playing games such as chess, poker, etc.
4.	Co-action	1) Strangers in a public eating place 2) Unfamiliar students working at same library table 3) Strangers sharing a seat on the train

PHYSICAL CHARACTERISTICS

Physical characteristics, as a potent aspect of the nonverbal channel, cannot be over-emphasised, particularly in its influence in initiating some form of social contact. Before we even know what a person sounds like or what he has to say we are beginning to make judgements about him or her on the basis of physical appearance (see Chapter 6 for a further discussion on this issue). In our society physical attractiveness is one of the key dimensions of appearance, although we do manipulate our appearance on other occasions to signify a particular occupation, status or personality type. The importance of physical attractiveness is abundantly evident in both the amount and variety of artefacts, such as make-up, jewellery, wigs, false nails, perfume, after-shave, high-heeled shoes, foundation garments, etc. which are readily available in the high street shops. The potency of attractiveness can be shown in an interesting study of trainee teachers by Hore (1971) who found that female student teachers who were considered 'attractive' by their male college tutors received consistently higher grades on teaching practice than those who were considered 'unattractive'. It would, however, have been interesting to find out if Hore would have obtained similar results from a survey of female tutors' grades of male student teachers.

In more recent writings, Berscheid and Walster (1978) found that physically attractive persons are consistently judged more favourable in initial interactions and suggest that the effects of physical attractiveness even outweigh the influence of expressive style. However, Riggio and Friedman (1986), in a study designed to identify those nonverbal and verbal cues which determined likeability, confidence and competence when persons were engaged in public speaking, found that physical attractiveness, although initially important, in the long term was less important than other social skills such as expressive facial behaviours and speaking and gestural fluency. This finding is endorsed by Barnes and Rosenthal (1985), investigating the effects of physical attractiveness and attire in same and mixed-sex dyads. Results indicated that 'when actual people are used instead of photographs, the strong effect of physical attractiveness may become diluted by the amount of other information available' (p. 445).

These findings have implications for a number of professionals. For instance, McHenry (1981) argues that in the selection interview, a candidate may often be selected within the first four minutes of the interview and that interviewers are strongly influenced by physical cues such as 'physical attractiveness, beards, spectacles, height, clothes, etc., which have rather little correlation with the abilities being sought' (p. 19). The same author claims that it is impossible to eliminate biased judgements completely but that by teaching an interviewer what to look for in a candidate, value judgements regarding appearance cues can be minimised. In addition, Mayfield (1972) noted that factors such as physical attractiveness and being liked was related to sales effectiveness, especially when the salespersons had similar characteristics to the customers in terms of background (e.g. education and work history) and appearance (e.g. physique).

Hair, face, body shape and clothes can be manipulated by individuals and continually serve as a communication function. At the present time, length and colour of hair are important to certain groups of males in our society. Some adolescents, for example, favour keeping the hair long while many of their elders regard long hair as representative of a lack of both moral and social standards. More recently, shaving the head or wearing hair extremely short in 'skinhead' fashion or dyeing it in outrageous colours, depicts rebelliousness or a rejection of the present standards of society. Teachers in school, in a bid to get adolescents to conform to the cultural norm, often insist that a boy's hair must be cut when it reaches the shirt collar. Yet some young men find that to have long hair is more appealing to their young male and female counterparts. This is where the dilemma begins.

Facial expressions, as we saw earlier in the chapter, can tell us a great deal about a person but so also can the skin and the way it is decorated or left undecorated. For instance, age can often be determined by the amount of wrinkles which are present on the face. We therefore get clues as to the kind of interaction which would be appropriate for certain age categories of persons. Women, especially, attempt to conceal signs of ageing by using make-up, or more drastically with face-lifts, yet generally men do not. Some interesting studies have found that people who wear spectacles are considered intelligent while girls who wear an abundance of make-up, particularly painted lips, are seen as more frivolous (Argyle and McHenry, 1971).

Not only do we learn a great deal about others from their body shape but we also like to find out what we think of ourselves — our self-image. As we grow we develop a picture of the ideal body type and this results in varying degrees of satisfaction with our own bodies in relation to that ideal type — particularly during adolescence. Generally, females consider that smallness and slimness are states to be attained, while males are more satisfied with their shape when it is tall and muscular. Thus weight watchers groups, health and beauty clubs and dance centres flourish to cater for female whims, while weight training, body building and rugby, football or other sports clubs flourish to satisfy men. Indeed, despite the advent of the women's liberation movement in recent years, there is little evidence to suggest that these sex differential patterns are changing rapidly.

Finally, although clothes basically serve to protect us from the cold, they also provide us with a great deal of information about the wearers. For example, personality characteristics can be reflected in the style of clothes, conservative individuals preferring more muted colours and conventional styles to more extrovert persons who tend to dress in the latest fashion and favour more flamboyant colours. It is interesting to note that persons who are going for a job interview often take great pains over choosing a sober shirt, tie and suit in order to appear conventional and serious, yet may favour 'gear' clothes in their non-work time. Social status, self-awareness and self-evaluation, too, can be inferred from the type of clothes worn (Solomon and Schopler, 1982). Thus schools have often gone to great lengths to impose school uniform on children, in an attempt to 'de-individualise', i.e. make pupils less aware of themselves as individuals. Uniforms, as well as occasionally protecting individuals from harm (e.g. deep sea divers, firemen, grand prix drivers and test pilots), act as a means of identification and are immediately recognisable. Bickman (1974) found, for instance, that compliance with simple requests (i.e. putting a dime in a parking meter for someone else) was greatest when the asker was dressed in a uniform (as opposed to a coat and tie, etc.). These specific features may have a profound influence on resulting behaviour. The danger comes in stereotyping too closely those associated with a distinct physical appearance and dress. Research on impression management has long demonstrated that most people are willing to make inferences about the personal characteristics of others based upon scanty information (Schneider, Hastorf and Ellsworth, 1979). Professional interactors, especially in first encounters with clients, must examine the basis of their initial impressions of another since it will affect subsequent encounters and more importantly the expectations brought to future encounters.

ENVIRONMENTAL FACTORS

Most people will have had the experience of being invited to someone's home and feeling that the atmosphere was friendly and relaxed, the furniture arrangements pleasant and comfortable, and within no time feeling 'at home'. Conversely, most of us on another occasion will have been invited to a home which would not be unsuited to feature on the pages of *Vogue* but which appears stiff, unlived in and cold. We hesitate to sit down or touch anything lest we upset the neat, clean and tidy arrangement in any way. In other words, environmental situations appear to affect the type of interaction which will be obtained.

Interviewers, intent on relaxing their clients in an attempt to get them to converse more freely, should arrange the physical setting to produce this effect. Easy-type chairs set near a window, perhaps, with pot plants on the ledge, and a coffee table placed near the chairs to hold ashtray and coffee cups, is much more conducive to a relaxed conversation-type interview than hard chairs, placed on either side of a desk in a room with metal filing cabinets and notice boards.

Haines (1975) refers to this essential element when identifying crucial communication skills for social workers. He states that 'courtesy, kind words and gestures and attempts to ensure that clients are seated comfortably in an atmosphere that is warm both physically and psychologically are all aspects of reception that go far to create a sound basis for the development of effective communication' (p. 171). Korda (1976), for instance, carried out research into the arrangement of furniture, particularly within offices, and identified two distinct areas; the zone around the desk he calls the 'pressure area'; the semi-social area is the area away from the desk in which there are armchairs and a coffee table. According to Korda the effective businessman will select that area of his office more appropriate to the task he wishes to carry out with a particular client or colleague. Thus variations in the arrangements of environmental factors such as architectural style (modern or classical), interior decor, lighting conditions, colours, sounds, etc., can be extremely influential on the outcome of interpersonal communication (Canter and Wools, 1970; Smith, 1974). (See Chapter 6 on the effects of the environment on initial perceptions.)

PARALANGUAGE

Paralinguistics is commonly referred to as that which is left after subtracting the verbal content from speech. The simple cliché, language is what is said, paralanguage is how it is said, can be misleading because frequently how something is said determines the precise meaning of what is said. This can be exemplified in the following statement: 'Mary's lending me her book'. If we decide to place more vocal emphasis on certain words we can alter the meaning of that statement:

1. MARY's lending me her book.
1a. *Mary* is the one giving the book; no one else.
2. Mary's LENDING me her book.
2a. Mary's *lending*, not giving or selling her book.
3. Mary's lending ME her book.
3a. The receiver is *me* and no one else.
4. Mary's lending me HER book.
4a. The book being lent is *not from another source*.
5. Mary's lending me her BOOK.
5a. Nothing else is being lent, only her *book*.

Mehrabian and Ferris (1967) lend support to the notion that vocal cues assist in the total impact of any given message. In addition, paralinguistic features of speech also convey emotional features. Jaffe *et al.* (1979) note that most persons can identify paralinguistic expressions such as rhythm of speech pattern, stress on individual words, rate of speech, pitch and volume, and define cultural meaning from their enactment. For instance, Scherer (1979) claims that rate can be directly related to anger: 'hot' anger has a notably fast tempo while 'cool' anger is more moderate in pace. In addition, Scherer also noted that 'Extreme pitch variation and up contours produce ratings of highly pleasant active, and potent emotions such as happiness, interest, surprise and also fear. Down contours have similar effects but do not seem to contain elements of surprise or uncertainty' (p. 251). One emotional state which is likely to produce speech errors is apprehension. In the early stages of interaction with others, participants can be beset by 'speech dysfluencies'. However, as the participants become more familiar with the situation, the frequency of speech errors decreases (Scott *et al.*, 1978).

Silence, or pauses in speech pattern, is a common occurrence although the length or duration of pauses ranges considerably. Matarazzo *et al.* (1965), for example, found that when an interviewer did not respond immediately to a statement by an interviewee, almost 60 per cent of the interviewees began to speak again. Newman (1982) contends that when silence occurs in the talk of strangers and acquaintances, and there is no ongoing activity to account for it, silence is associated with discomfort and negative feelings.

Hargie (1980) reports results which indicate that by pausing after asking a question or after a pupil responds, teachers can increase the level of pupil participation in classroom lessons (this is further explored in Chapter 4).

In addition to conveying meaning and emotions, changes in a speaker's vocal pattern can be useful in gaining and maintaining the attention of others. We have all had experience of the guest speaker at 'Speech Days' who speaks in such a dreary monotone that he can make the most interesting material seem boring. Conversely, quite boring material can become interesting if delivered by someone who stimulates interest, by changing the pitch, tone, speed and volume of his vocal pattern. Politicians and good public speakers use these vocal techniques in order to emphasise points, stimulate feelings and generally obtain and sustain the interest of their audiences. (Watzlawick, 1978).

OVERVIEW

As Goffman (1956) has stated, interactors need information about other people's characteristics, attributes, attitudes and values in order to know how to deal with one another. Direct measures of personality, intelligence, values and social status are often hard to obtain from the person himself. Yet we often infer these states from the behavioural cues presented to us. Of course the situation also works in reverse; not only do we gather information about others from the way they present themselves to us, but we ourselves go to great lengths to present others with a certain type of picture of ourselves. This form of self-presentation does not take place all the time, only when an individual is 'being observed' or in the presence of others.

Thus all of the situations which have periodically been referred to throughout this chapter (such as counselling, teaching, selection interviewing, nursing, careers interviewing, health visiting, social work, public speaking, etc.) are the contexts within which people present, and attempt to control certain aspects of, their self-image. The majority of signals used to communicate these self-images are nonverbal in nature and range as we have seen from appearance to posture, from clothes to facial expressions, from paralinguistic features of speech to the environment itself. The potency of the nonverbal aspects of behaviour cannot be underestimated and professionals should be sensitive to the kind of atmosphere they are creating, the scene they are setting, and the parameters they are placing on an interaction before they even begin to speak.

A knowledge of the various facets of nonverbal communication, and of their effects in social interaction, can enable us to improve both our ability to interpret the cues which are emitted by others, and our ability to control the impressions which we are conveying to others. Many of the elements of nonverbal communication which have been discussed in this chapter will recur in the remaining chapters of this book. At the start of this chapter it was emphasised that all social interaction is dependent upon the interplay, sometimes subtly conveyed, between the verbal and nonverbal messages. Therefore, all the remaining skills, from reinforcement outlined in Chapter 3 through to group interaction set out in Chapter 11, will contain some of the nonverbal aspects which have been discussed in this present chapter.

3

Reinforcement

INTRODUCTION

Few would disagree that in our everyday pursuits we tend to engage in activities which are associated with some sort of positively valued outcome for us. We do things which are considered, often from previous experience, to produce results which we desire. Activities which we perform are, of course, enormously varied. The range of objects and outcomes which we seek also constitutes a virtually inexhaustible list. Some of the more obvious examples pertain to our physical wellbeing and include such things as food, water (or other liquids) and a certain amount of heat. Others, such as money and the presence of an attractive companion, are less basic but still important. We also value events which are much less tangible, for example, a friendly smile, a word of praise from someone we respect, or an enthusiastic reaction from an attentive listener. The fact that such things can influence our behaviour is central to the concept of reinforcement.

In order to appreciate fully the significance of this skill in interpersonal interaction, it is necessary to have some knowledge of its theoretical background. Ivan Pavlov, the eminent Russian physiologist, is commonly accredited with having introduced the term 'reinforcement' into Psychology (Pavlov, 1927). It is a concept which has been the subject of much theoretical debate by psychologists, some of whom hold differing views about its nature. This debate has mostly been concerned with why and how reinforcement operates to modify behaviour — the fact that it does is commonly accepted. Since the early years of this century a massive body of empirical material has been accumulated, from studies (involving both animals and humans) designed to investigate the extent to which a range of behaviours could be modified by means of reinforcement techniques. One psychologist who has made a substantial contribution in this area over a number of decades has been B.F. Skinner (Skinner, 1953, 1969, 1978) and it is largely his views which form the basis of reinforcement, conceived as a social skill. While reinforcement as a method of influencing behaviour is well established, its application as a social skill is a more recent development.

OPERANT CONDITIONING

The application of reinforcement procedures in keeping with Skinnerian principles is known as Operant Conditioning. According to Baldwin and Baldwin (1981, p. 36), a central tenet of this process 'is that the consequences that occur after a behaviour, change the probabilities of future performances of that behaviour'. A broad distinction can be made between respondent and operant behaviour. The defining characteristic of the former is that it is 'triggered off' by preceding stimuli encountered in the environment. So, for example, our pupils contract when we are exposed to the stimulus of a bright light, we startle in response to a car backfiring, or we freeze at the sight of a snake (if we happen to have a fear of snakes). Skinner, however, stressed the operant nature of much of human behaviour. We don't wait passively until a stimulus arrives which is capable of eliciting a particular response from us. Rather man is essentially an active agent emitting behaviour spontaneously. The environment modifies and shapes that behaviour, not through the action of eliciting stimuli, but by means of the consequences attendant upon it. Thus a child will learn successfully to ride a bicycle as a result of inappropriate behaviours leading to falling off and possibly pain, while other more appropriate actions serve to maintain balance and move the machine forward. Consequences which increase the probability of the preceding behaviour recurring in the future are called *reinforcers* or *reinforcing stimuli*. A reinforcing stimulus, therefore, acts to increase the likelihood that the piece of behaviour which produced it will be repeated. In order to be termed reinforcers, however, it is important that such stimuli function as consequences, rather than antecedents, of that particular action and be made contingent upon it. This condition has been stressed by Higgins and Morris (1985), who point out that it is often not made explicit in many of the definitions which exist in the literature.

The frequency of occurrence of behaviour can be increased by either positive or negative reinforcers. When a pleasant or positively valued stimulus is made contingent upon some action the more frequent performance of that action which results is due to *positive reinforcement*. A bird pecking the top off a bottle of milk on the doorstep in order to obtain cream is an example. In the case of *negative reinforcement*, the termination of some noxious, or negatively valued stimulus, promotes the behaviour which effects this outcome. Turning the appropriate control on the radio in an anticlockwise direction in order to reduce the volume which has become uncomfortably loud would be a case in point. In his research with pigeons, Skinner demonstrated how they could be induced to increase the rate at which they pecked a button in their cage when doing so resulted in the termination of a mild electric shock. It will be appreciated that negative reinforcement involves the application of an aversive stimulus whenever the organism displays behaviour other than that which was targeted.

Some writers have, however, regarded negative reinforcement as being synonymous with *punishment*. This confusion in terminology has been highlighted by Green (1977) who noted the inconsistent manner in which the term negative reinforcement has been used. According to Rachlin (1970) the fundamental difference between negative reinforcement and punishment is that the former acts to increase the frequency of the behaviour under focus, while punishment has the opposite effect. Thus if the pigeon had received the electric shock (rather than had it terminated as was the case with negative reinforcement) each time it pecked the button then that response would have been punished and would have been less likely to have recurred. When a reinforcing stimulus, which has consistently been applied following a piece of behaviour, is terminated it has been found that the frequency of performance of that behaviour is gradually reduced to its pre-reinforcement level. This process is called *extinction*. Extinction refers to the 'undoing' of the effects of reinforcement. When a response which previously was followed by the receipt of a piece of food, for example, suddenly leads to no significant consequence whether positive or negative, it will be extinguished. While there are important differences between punishment and extinction both have the effect of reducing the rate of performance of a response.

While punishment and negative reinforcement can be used to modify behaviour, the fact that both involve aversive stimuli limits the appropriateness of their application to social interaction. The administration of stimuli which cause physical pain is, of course, particularly restricted and raises important ethical issues. Until relatively recently the use of corporal punishment in schools was not only widely practised but generally accepted. Some parents, of course, still maintain the right to punish their children physically. But certain aversive stimuli are more social in nature and take a much more subtle form. Examples of these include sarcasm, derision, ridicule and scolding. Pupils have indicated that one of the things which they dislike most about a teacher is his use of sarcasm. A number of undesirable side-effects have been associated with punishment, some of which are summarised by Balsam and Bondy (1983). It can produce negative emotional reactions which can generalise, beyond the response being punished, to the teacher, perhaps to the subject which he teaches, and indeed to school itself.

While pupils constitute a relatively captive (if not always captivated) audience the use of abrasive comments in many other situations can result in the premature termination of the interaction. The appropriateness of punishment and negative reinforcement to the type of social interaction typically conducted by teachers, doctors, nurses, health visitors, social workers, etc., during the course of their work, is severely restricted. When we speak, therefore, of reinforcement as a social skill, it is the judicious use of positive reinforcement to which we refer. Indeed, the use of aversive social behaviours could, in many circumstances, be considered to represent a lack of social skill (see Chapter 1).

Primary and secondary reinforcement

Positive reinforcement can take a number of different forms, some of which have a more direct relevance to social interaction than others. Food constitutes a positive reinforcer, gaining its positive value from our biological dependence upon it. For this reason food, together with a number of other stimuli which have this property in common, have been labelled *primary reinforcers*. Additional members of this class include water, air, a certain amount of body heat and sex. While the intrinsic value of these items will be readily acknowledged, their limitation as a means of influencing the complexities of everyday behaviour in present-day society will also be quickly realised. We do not normally attempt to influence another's behaviour by making air, water or even food dependent upon it. Instead, most of what we do is determined by immediate outcomes which are less basic.

Secondary reinforcers refer to reinforcing stimuli which have no intrinsic worth but are valued because of their association with primary reinforcing stimuli. Money is one obvious example of an extremely potent secondary reinforcer, which some people will even risk their lives in order to obtain. The effects of secondary reinforcement have been demonstrated in the laboratory. In one experiment, a chimpanzee learned to put a poker chip into the slot of a vending machine in order to obtain a grape. It was subsequently discovered that the chimp would carry out other tasks in order to receive poker chips. These chips had, therefore, secondary reinforcing properties bestowed upon them. Teachers, especially of young or retarded children, frequently employ secondary reinforcement techniques in the classroom. The conferment of gold stars and such like which, at the end of the day or week can be exchanged for sweets or reduced homework, represent one example. Nevertheless, as with primary reinforcers, the extent to which such techniques can be employed in the wider professional context during social interaction with interviewees is somewhat restricted.

Generalised reinforcement

Of more relevance in this respect, however, is a group of stimuli which Skinner identified and labelled generalised reinforcers. One important example is approval.

> A common generalized conditioned reinforcer is 'approval' . . . It may be little more than a nod or a smile on the part of someone who characteristically supplies a variety of reinforcements. Sometimes . . . it has a verbal form 'Right! or Good!' (Skinner, 1957, p. 53).

A further example is the giving of attention to another during interaction. 'The attention of people is reinforcing because it is a necessary condition for other reinforcements from them. In general, only people who are attending to us reinforce our behaviour' (Skinner, 1953, p. 78).

Few people enjoy being ignored. Children, in particular, actively seek the attention of parents and later of peers and other adults, sometimes resorting to extreme behaviour such as 'showing off' in order to do so. Receiving the attention of those we accept and respect is something which we positively value and, therefore, something which can be used to influence our behaviour. Unlike the other stimuli which have been mentioned which can have reinforcing properties, attention is exclusively social in nature — it demands the direct involvement of another person. For this reason attention has been referred to as social reinforcement. Using a rather broad definition, Raben *et al.* (1974, p. 39) considered, 'a reinforcing stimulus to be social if its reward value is related to another individual or group interacting with the reinforced subject'.

Attending plays a central role in the social skill of reinforcement. How can one tell, however, when attention is or is not being provided by the others with whom we interact? What can we actually do to modify the behaviour of a partner in interaction by means of this skill? Some of the more obvious examples of lack of attention readily spring to mind. A person who is engaged in some other activity unrelated to the ongoing interaction is commonly considered not to be paying attention, as is a person who does not accept his speech turn, or if he does, says something which has no bearing on the existing topic of conversation. Likewise a person who seldom looks at the other, is felt to be less than attentive. As shall be seen in a subsequent section of this chapter, there are also a number of more subtle behaviours which can be used to signal attention and which have been found to have reinforcing effects in the social context. Before considering these, however, the various functions which reinforcement, as a social skill, performs will be examined. (Further information on Operant Conditioning and the various characteristics of reinforcement can be found in such texts as Rachlin, 1970; Honing and Staddon, 1977; and Baldwin and Baldwin, 1981.)

FUNCTIONS OF REINFORCEMENT

In this section, and for the remainder of the chapter, reinforcing stimuli in the form of behaviours displayed during the normal course of interaction, which constitute the skill of reinforcement and which are more relevant to the social context than are some other examples of primary and secondary reinforcers, will be discussed. Some of the more important functions served by reinforcement so defined include:

(1) To promote interaction and maintain relationships.
(2) To increase the involvement of the other.
(3) To influence the contribution of the other to the conversation.
(4) To increase appropriate and decrease inappropriate behaviour.
(5) To demonstrate a genuine interest in the ideas, thoughts or feelings, expressed by the other.

(6) To make interaction enjoyable and rewarding.
(7) To create an impression of warmth and understanding.
(8) To increase the social attractiveness of the source of reinforcement.
(9) To improve the confidence and self-esteem of the other.

During social interaction we not only welcome, but even demand, a certain amount of reinforcement from the other participants. If, for instance, a minimum of attention is not provided we find it rather disconcerting, and may consider it sufficient grounds for terminating the encounter. A persistent lack of such reinforcement over a number of episodes may result in the relationship being abandoned. In a study undertaken by Jones *et al*. (1982), college students who were lonely, when compared with their more gregarious colleagues, were found to be markedly less attentive to their conversational partners. Trower *et al*. (1978) have noted the marked lack of reinforcement evinced by certain groups of mental patients during conversations. It is suggested that their condition may be exacerbated by a lack of social reinforcement, leading to reduced social contacts and relationships which, in turn, results in a further deterioration in their state with fewer opportunities for social interaction, thus creating a debilitating downward spiral. A minimum of reinforcement is, therefore, essential for the other participant to continue to take part in the interaction thereby maintaining the encounter and, at a more general level, the relationship. For professionals and paraprofessionals who spend a substantial proportion of their working day interacting with others, simply maintaining the interactive episode, while necessary, is not sufficient. It is important that the client or interviewee is encouraged to be actively involved, if the goals of the encounter are to be achieved by the interviewer. The costs incurred by the interviewee in terms of time and energy must be offset by rewards provided by the interviewer for this to happen. Reinforcement is, therefore, one method of increasing the level of interviewee participation.

Apart from extending the general level of interviewee involvement, most people have learned to provide a sufficient amount of reinforcement to both maintain encounters and encourage the active participation of the other during them. The planned, systematic and selective use of this technique, however, to induce the interviewee to continue the detailed exploration of certain topics or issues, and to disregard others of lesser relevance, requires much greater skill. Research has shown that reinforcement can be used effectively in this more specific manner, thereby providing a valuable tool to guide selectively the interviewee's verbal explorations. It shouldn't be assumed though that practising interviewers, as a matter of course, optimise the use of this skill. Cannell *et al*. (1977), investigating the performances of survey interviewers, discovered that adequate or appropriate responses received proportionately less positive interviewer reinforcement than did less desirable answers. Refusal to respond, the least desirable response, received proportionately the highest levels of reinforcement.

The potential effects of this technique extend, of course, to more global aspects of functioning. It has been found, for example, that teachers can increase the incidence of appropriate pupil behaviour in the classroom by means of the selective use of reinforcement (Hargie, 1980). By administering reinforcement only when pupils are working quietly, and ignoring (and thereby extinguishing) disruptive behaviour, a gradual increase in desirable, together with a reduction in inappropriate, behaviour can be achieved. Again it would seem that teachers frequently fail to make as much use of this skill in the classroom as they might. Focusing upon teacher praise, Brophy (1981), having reviewed a number of studies, concluded that it 'typically is infrequent, noncontingent, global rather than specific, and determined more by students' personal qualities or teachers' perceptions of students' need for praise than by the quality of student conduct or achievement' (p. 8). The need for more systematic instruction in this respect would seem warranted.

In addition to influencing the behaviour of the interviewee, the interviewer, by using reinforcement, also conveys information about himself in terms of the impression which he creates. People who provide substantial amounts of reinforcement, in comparison to those who don't, are commonly perceived to be taking a keen interest in those they interact with and in what they have to say. They also create an impression of being warm, friendly and understanding. On the other hand those who are regarded as being cold or aloof display little reinforcement, especially in the form of smiles. Boring people, also, provide little reinforcement and often the topic of conversation which they select holds few attractions for the listeners. Interactions with those who display appropriate reinforcing behaviours tend, for the most part, to be more enjoyable and such individuals are usually more socially attractive (the term attraction is used here in a general sense and is not restricted to physical features or notions of romantic attachment). According to Kelly (1982, p. 4), those 'interpersonal skills that facilitate the building of relationships have in common with one another the fact that they increase the social attractive or reinforcement value of the person exhibiting them'.

The topic of *interpersonal attraction* has been subject to a plethora of research and a sizeable literature now exists. While a comprehensive review of this area is decidedly beyond the scope of this chapter, some investigators, including Lott and Lott (1968) and Clore (1977), have made use of the concept of reinforcement in attempting to explain the findings. Briefly stated, they proposed that those responses and pleasurable feelings which are a reaction to receiving reinforcers can become associated with the provider of those rewards, or even with a third party who happens to be consistently present when reinforcers are received. Indeed a number of investigations have determined that, perhaps unsurprisingly, people like to receive praise and compliments and tend to like those who provide them (Aronson, 1984). But such attraction is neither universal nor unconditional depending, as it does, upon how what is taking place is construed by the recipient. The source of the reinforcement is more likely to be found attractive if, for example, the action being praised is regarded by the recipient as praiseworthy; praise from that individual is valued; and if it reflects a change from a more negative disposition by the source towards the recipient (Raven and Rubin, 1983). If, on the other hand, it is thought that the source has ulterior motives for lavishing praise, and flattery or ingratiation are perhaps suspected, liking for the individual will be reduced (Kleinke, 1986). It is also, of course, improbable that such stimuli will, in fact, serve as reinforcers under these circumstances. O'Donnell *et al.* (1983) found that those subjects who reported that they were aware of the experimental manipulation in a verbal conditioning experiment, but who did not produce an expected increase in the targeted response, tended to regard the experiment as an attempt at social influence.

It is likely that there is a positive relationship between these two functions of reinforcement (viz. influencing the behaviour of the other and promoting interpersonal attraction) such that those who are more popular are regarded as being an important source of reward, are more positively valued and, therefore, are in a position to extend greater control over the behaviour of others by means of the regulated dispensation of reinforcements. Having said that, Brokaw and McLemore (1983) have cautioned against social reinforcement invariably being equated with friendly behaviour *per se*. Emphasising the importance of complementarity between the social reinforcer and its target behaviour, they discovered that confederate hostile-submissive responses to subjects' hostile-dominant statements produced a greater likelihood of that type of statement being repeated than did friendly-submissive utterances.

Positive reactions of others produce not only more favourable attitudes towards them (under certain circumstances), but may also result in greater self-esteem. *Self-esteem* refers to the worth which an individual bestows upon him or herself and can range from feelings of love and acceptance to hate and rejection. The process of self-evaluation which gives rise to various degrees of self-worth is based, in part, upon social comparison — how we seem to stand in relation to others. It is also determined by how others react to us. Sullivan (1953) believed that one's concept of self develops out of the reflected appraisals of significant others. Thus positive, rewarding interpersonal experiences with parents and other adults lead to positive views of self while negative reactions including blame, constant reprimands, ridicule, etc., result in feelings of worthlessness. While being subjected to more positive reactions from others can promote self-esteem, it would also seem that it may require to be long-term and persistent in extreme cases of low self-esteem in order to be effective. In the interests of maintaining a consistent and congruent concept of the self, conflicting positive perceptions may be ignored or distorted. There is some evidence to suggest that those with low self-esteem tend to attribute their successes to situational factors rather than to their own abilities. Attributions of causality can be altered, though, by reinforcement procedures which emphasise success (Kennelly *et al.*, 1985). Swann and Read (1981) further proposed that we may actually behave in ways which make others respond in a manner consistent with our beliefs about ourselves. People with a morbidly low self-esteem may therefore make it difficult for others to reinforce them in spite of the views of, for example, Maslow (1970) and Rogers (1951) that a general need exists to be positively valued by others and to feel self-worth.

A further dimension of personality which is of functional relevance to social reinforcement is *locus of control* (Rotter, 1966). This term refers to the extent to which individuals regard themselves as having control over the reinforcement which they receive. Those who believe in internal control have the opinion that reinforcement which they encounter is contingent upon their own performance and a reflection of their relatively enduring characteristics and qualities. At the other end of the continuum, an external locus of control is typified by the idea that although some positive event may have followed an action, it was not contingent upon it and was due to luck, chance, or was determined by some powerful other. Seligman (1975) proposed that a continuing experience of lack of control over the events which impinge upon one can lead to *learned helplessness* — the view that nothing which one can do will make any significant difference to what takes place, with commensurate feelings of apathy and depression. Under these circumstances simply providing indiscriminate reinforcement may be ineffective.

Such characteristics and dispositions of the recipient are obviously an important factor when considering the effectiveness of the skill of reinforcement. Although they have frequently been ignored in the research which has been conducted this has not always been so. Kennelly and Mount (1985), for instance, assessed pupils' locus of control and found that internality together with perceptions of teachers' reinforcement being contingent upon their behaviour was predictive of good academic achievement and ratings of pupil competence, rather than helplessness, by teachers.

BEHAVIOURAL COMPONENTS OF THE SKILL OF REINFORCEMENT

It will be recalled that, theoretically, anything which increases the frequency of a preceding piece of behaviour can be considered a reinforcer. Even if this list is restricted to those elements of interpersonal behaviour which are generally considered to be desirable, the resulting number of potential reinforcers could be extensive. This section will concentrate upon those elements which are widely recognised and, for the most part, the effects of which have been studied by means of experimental inquiry. A broad distinction can be made between those components which are verbal and those which are nonverbal in nature. Further groupings will be made under these two main headings.

Verbal components

The verbal channel of communication constitutes an important source of social reinforcement. Many of the things which we say when interacting can have the effect of validating and strengthening the recipient's feelings of self-esteem and worth and will be positively valued by him, while others may have the opposite effect. Verbal components of reinforcement range in complexity from simple expressions such as 'yes', to more elaborate responses which relate to some aspect of the functioning of the other participant. Reflections (see Chapter 5) are one example of a complex response of this type. It is possible to identify three classes of verbal reinforcer and these will be examined individually.

Acknowledgement/confirmation

This category contains utterances, words and phrases which acknowledge, confirm or agree with what has been said or done. Examples include vocalisations and verbalisations such as 'mm-hmm', 'OK', 'yes', 'right', 'fine', 'I see', 'You are correct', etc. A common feature of many conversations are utterances such as 'mm-hmm', 'yes' and 'right' which are performed by the listener. They are particularly noticeable if one should happen to listen to another conducting a telephone conversation. It seems, in part, that they serve to signal to the speaker that his message has been successfully received and understood, and that the listener is paying close attention. They also appear to indicate that the listener does not wish to take a speech turn at that point but rather prefers the speaker to continue. A rapid sequence, such as 'mm-hmm, mm-hmm', may signal impatience — that the listener has no difficulty following the speaker and that the latter can proceed more quickly.

The reinforcing effects of utterances of this type have been revealed in a number of experimental investigations, one of the most widely reported of which was conducted by Greenspoon (1955). Subjects in this study were simply asked to produce as many individual words as they could think of. Each occasion on which a plural noun was given, the experimenter responded with 'mm-hmm' while all other types of words were largely ignored. It was found that gradually the number of cases of plural nouns increased substantially. A similar experiment, producing a comparable outcome, was carried out by Reece and Whitman (1962).

Other researchers have demonstrated the reinforcing effects of the expression 'mm-hmm', upon subjects' self-referenced statements (Kennedy and Zimmer, 1968; Hoffnung, 1969; Hekmat, 1974) and affect statements (Salzinger and Pisoni, 1960). Positive outcomes have also been reported when the targeted behaviour has been present participles (Donohue and Tryon, 1985); the word 'she' (Carnevale, 1971); and interviewee verbal productivity (Matarazzo and Wiens, 1972; O'Brien and Holborn, 1979). Siegman (1976), however, failed to increase significantly subjects' verbal productivity in this manner. A likely explanation was that these utterances were administered on a non-contingent basis. It emerged, nevertheless, that interviewers who provided 'mm-hmms' were noted by interviewees as warmer and more responsive. They also reported that they felt less anxious when being interviewed by these individuals.

Praise/encouragement/support

Unlike the previous category, reinforcers in the present one go beyond the simple acknowledgement, confirmation or agreement with what has been said or done by expressing praise, encouragement or support. Someone who praises pronounces his appreciation, approval and admiration for the other person and his action. Thus, for example, a health visitor who calls on a young mother who has put on a lot of weight and has been ordered to diet by her doctor, and finds since her visit last week that she has lost five pounds may respond, 'What a marvellous effort Mrs Jackson, you have done exceptionally well'. By so praising Mrs Jackson, the health visitor indicates that she realises the effort involved, and positively values the young mother for making it. She also expresses that she positively values the action. In these respects, therefore, praise does much more than merely acknowledge or confirm what has taken place.

Encouragement and support reveal that the person who provides them is in agreement with what the other person is doing, but they also express a commitment to help (even if only verbally) the other and a desire for the other to act or continue to act in a particular way. A physical education teacher who sees a boy beginning to wilt at the start of his fifteenth press-up and says encouragingly, 'Come on John, you can do it, just one more', suggests that he is on 'John's side', that he believes that John has the capacity to perform the act and that he wants him to carry out this particular piece of behaviour.

Specific examples of verbal reinforcers which belong to this category include words like 'good', 'excellent' (and various other superlatives) and phrases such as, 'what a brilliant idea', 'you almost got it right, try again' and 'I would have done exactly the same thing if I had been in your position', when used in the appropriate contexts. Reinforcers of this type are commonly employed by a wide spectrum of professionals and paraprofessionals when interacting with clients. Teachers are one obvious group who can use praise and encouragement to good effect in the classroom. A number of reviews of reinforcement including praise, in the classroom have been conducted (Kennedy and Willcutt, 1964; Turney *et al.*, 1983; Lysakowski and Walberg, 1981; Brophy, 1981; and Cairns, 1986). It would seem that improvements in pupil achievement, motivation and classroom behaviour can be effected by these means. Kennedy and Willcutt, (1964, p. 331) concluded that, 'Praise has been found generally to have a facilitating effect on the performance of school children while blame has been found generally to have a debilitating effect on the performance of school children'. However, there are some inconsistencies in the research findings and the current general consensus of opinion is somewhat more guarded. Brophy (1981) has been particularly critical of praise, as it is commonly used by teachers, serving as an effective reinforcer in class. Whether or not it does probably depends upon a number of qualifying variables including characteristics of the pupils such as reinforcement history, the type of task, the nature of the praise and the manner in which it is administered, together with characteristics of the source. O'Leary and O'Leary (1977) suggested that its success as a reinforcer can be increased by ensuring that, firstly, it is contingently applied, secondly, it specifies the particular behaviour being reinforced, and thirdly, it is credible, varied according to circumstances and sounds sincere. Brophy (1981) extended this list by advocating that it should be used sparingly and with those pupils who respond favourably to it. Not all do, of course, with some finding it patronising or embarrassing when delivered in the presence of their peers.

The influence of such factors as race, sex, age and socio-economic status on children's susceptibility to reinforcers has been the subject of a number of investigations. The latter variable has attracted the attention of many researchers, leading Russell (1971, p. 39) to conclude that, 'One of the most consistent findings is that there is a social class difference in response to reinforcement'. Less tangible reinforcers such as praise and approval have been regarded as being more successful with middle-class than with lower-class children. However, Schultz and Sherman (1976), based upon a comprehensive review of the area, were quite adamant that this view was ill-founded. They stated that, 'social class differences in reinforcer effectiveness cannot be assumed in spite of our predisposition to do so' (p. 52). This position is supported by Cairns (1986). Relationships between these variables, if they do exist, are likely to be much more complex. Thus Miller and Eller (1985) reported that significant increases in intelligence test scores took place among lower- and middle-class white pupils in response to praise although middle-class white females were more susceptible to this influence than their male counterparts. Praise also improved the performance of lower-class white males but not females. According to Marisi and Helmy (1984), age differences are also likely to play a part, and McGrade (1966) has speculated that the socio-economic status of the reinforcing agent may also be significant.

Other factors which have been found to mediate reinforcement influences include pupils' locus of control (Henry *et al.*, 1979; Kennelly and Mount, 1985); age and status of the person providing the praise (Henry *et al.*, 1979; Stock, 1978) and the nature of the task being performed (Fish and White, 1979). There is also good evidence, at least with older subjects, suggesting that extroverts are more receptive than introverts to the conditioning effects of praise (Boddy *et al.*, 1986).

Social reinforcers also occur in professional contexts other than the classroom, although their impact has been less well researched. Nurses frequently provide encouragement when, for example, performing some task such as taking a blood sample, which may cause the patient some discomfort — 'There, I am almost finished'. Dentists often use praise when a child or perhaps a rather nervous patient shows restraint — 'That's it, you are doing very well'. In addition, social workers commonly find opportunities, when interviewing to praise, encourage and support attitudes and behaviour, on the part of the client, which they wish to promote.

It has been found that such expressions can bring about changes in the behaviour of the other person involved in the interaction. Hildum and Brown (1956) outlined the results of an investigation which involved a number of interviews conducted by telephone using an attitude questionnaire. It transpired that the interviewer's use of the word 'good' following a response had a significant effect upon the favourableness of the attitudes displayed by the respondents. A similar finding was documented by Goldman (1980). This verbal reinforcer has also been found to promote increases in self-referenced statements (Arenson, 1978), thematic responses (Stewart and Patterson, 1973), and present participles (Donohue and Tryon, 1985). The reinforcing potential of similar expressions such as 'right' (Tamase, 1978) and 'wonderful' (Hekmat and Lee, 1970), have also been noted. However, in some cases, especially in the earlier studies, few steps were taken to control for the possible effects of contemporaneous nonverbal behaviour.

Some investigators have compared the relative effectiveness of reinforcers belonging to the present category with those pertaining to the previous one, i.e. acknowledgement/confirmation/agreement. Thus Hekmat and Lee (1970) examined the differential effects of 'mm-hmm', 'good' and 'wonderful' used to reinforce subjects' production of affective self-referenced statements. It emerged that the frequency of such statements was highest when the individuals were reinforced with 'wonderful' and lowest when 'mm-hmm' was used.

Hildum and Brown (1956) also compared the effects of 'mm-hmm' and 'good' and found that the latter acted as a more potent reinforcer.

In sum, it would appear that, under particular circumstances, the provision of praise, support or encouragement can have reinforcing consequences.

Response development

There is, in a sense, a progressive sequence of increasing involvement and acceptance which commences with the mere acknowledgement of a response, continues with the positive evaluation of it by means of praise, for example, and proceeds to the further exploration, development and perhaps use of that response by the interviewer. It has been said that imitation is the highest form of flattery. In a similar vein, the development and use of a response or idea may, perhaps, be regarded as the highest form of praise. It is quite easy for an interviewer to express a few perfunctory words of acknowledgement or praise before changing the topic, but the development of a response indicates, first, that the interviewer must have been carefully attending and, secondly, that the information contained in the response must have been considered worthy of the interviewer's time and effort in order to explore it further. A response can be developed in a number of ways. It can be accomplished by questioning techniques (see Chapter 4) or less directly by means of reflections (see Chapter 5). It is interesting to note that studies which have compared the reinforcing influences of reflections and various forms of praise, encouragement and acknowledgement have invariably found the use of reflections to be more effective. Alternatively, a teacher, for example, may develop a pupil's response by elaborating upon it himself. The potential reinforcing effects for a pupil of having his idea actually form part of the teacher's lesson will readily be appreciated. In a group, members may be asked to contribute their suggestions and be reinforced by having their responses further explored by the group leader (a method which is obviously similar to the use of pupil responses by a teacher).

Research concerning the reinforcing effects of the development of another's response is less prevalent than investigations involving reinforcers included in the previous two categories. In one study, however, Bandura *et al.* (1960) examined the effects of an interviewer's approaching or avoiding client responses which expressed hostility. 'Approach' by the interviewer was defined to include labelling the feeling expressed by the client as hostile and expressing interest in it by exploring it further. When a hostile statement was responded to in this way, rather than being avoided, the probability that the client pursued that theme in his next speech turn was significantly higher. In a comparative study of a group of experienced psychiatric interviewers and a group of inexperienced medical students, the latter were found to be less likely to develop topics introduced by their interviewees (Dudley and Blanchard, 1976). Such behaviour tends to contribute to feelings of being ignored (Geller *et al.*, 1974).

A limited number of studies in the teaching context have been concerned with the relationship between the teachers' use of pupil ideas and pupil achievement. Rosenshine (1971) reviewed a total of nine such investigations and found consistent positive correlations recorded by eight of them, although these results failed to reach an acceptable level of significance. However, this rather disappointing finding could well have been caused by the rather broad definition of the variable, 'use of pupil ideas', used in the majority of these studies. Much more research effort is required to investigate further the effects of the use of pupil ideas by teachers in the classroom. Indeed it would seem that the reinforcing effects of response development, in general, require further exploration since the potential of this form of reinforcement has not yet been fully demonstrated.

Nonverbal components

The administration of reinforcement is not solely dependent upon the verbal channel of communication. It has been established that a number of nonverbal behaviours, such as a warm smile or an enthusiastic nod of the head, can also have reinforcing influences on the behaviour of the other person during interaction. This fact should not surprise us unduly if it is remembered (see Chapter 2) that the nonverbal channel of communication is more important than the verbal channel with regard to the conveyance of information of an emotional or attitudinal nature. Indeed when information of this type resulting from one channel contradicts that carried by means of the other, greater credence is placed on the nonverbal message.It would therefore seem that the nonverbal channel is particularly adept at communicating states and attitudes such as friendliness, interest, warmth, involvement, etc. Since such attitudes are frequently positively valued, behaviours which depict them are likely to have a reinforcing potential.

The selection of criteria to form a basis for the categorisation of nonverbal reinforcers is somewhat arbitrary. In the sections to follow we will consider, separately, gestural and proximity reinforcement.

Gestural reinforcement

In this category will be included relatively small movements of specific parts of the body. 'Gestural' in this sense is broadly defined to encompass not only movements of the hands, arms and head, but also the facial region. Concerning the latter, two of the most frequently identified reinforcers are smiles and eye contact. Some research evidence exists to suggest that smiles can have a reinforcing effect. In one experiment, Showalter (1974) succeeded in conditioning affect statements through the selective use of this behaviour by the interviewer. Many studies have combined smiles with other nonverbal and verbal reinforcers. For example, Verplanck (1955) used a smile together with agreement and a paraphrase to increase the frequency of statements of opinion. Similarly, Krasner (1958) combined smiles with head nods and 'mm-hmm' to increase the use of the word 'mother' by subjects. Pansa (1979) increased the incidence of self-referenced affect statements provided by a group of reactive schizophrenics, using a comparable procedure. Less positive results were obtained by Hill and Gormally (1977), Saigh (1981), and O'Brien and Holborn (1979). The latter researchers suggested that the experimenter's smiles were misinterpreted by the subjects. It should be realised that smiles can convey scorn and contempt as well as warmth and understanding. The specific meaning attributed to this piece of behaviour is probably dependent upon contextual features including accompanying behaviour. The constant use of an isolated smile by an interviewer would undoubtedly seem rather strange and unnatural to an interviewee and, therefore, fail to serve as a reinforcer.

Eye contact is an important element of interpersonal interaction. The establishment of eye contact is usually a preparatory step when initiating interaction. During a conversation continued use of this behaviour may indicate attention, interest and involvement and its selective use can, therefore, have reinforcing consequences. Kleinke *et al.* (1975), in an interview-type experimental situation, instructed interviewers to (1) look at the interviewee constantly, (2) look at the interviewee intermittently, or (3) refrain from looking. It was found that interviewees in the 'no gaze' condition, compared to the other two experimental treatments, made briefer statements and talked less. Interviewers in the 'constant gaze' condition were rated by interviewees as being most attentive, while interviewers who did not look at those they were interviewing were considered to be least attentive.

A positive relationship between interviewer eye contact and subjects' verbal productivity was also documented by, for instance,

Klein *et al.* (1975), Duncan and Fiske (1977), and O'Brien and Holborn (1979). Goldman (1980) also reported that verbal encouragement could be used to more effectively reinforce expressed attitudes when coupled with eye contact. It should be appreciated that in certain situations, however, the over-use of eye contact or gaze can be threatening and therefore cause discomfort or distress. In this sense, eye contact could be punishing rather than reinforcing (although this did not seem to take place in the Kleinke study).

Certain movements of the hands and arms can signal appreciation and approval. Probably the most frequently used gestures of this type in our society are applause and the 'thumbs-up' sign. Both of these have a limited applicability to many of the professional contexts considered in this book. Head-nods, however, are gestures which have a much wider relevance. Their frequent use can be seen during practically any interactive episode, being commonly used to indicate acknowledgement, agreement and understanding. The reinforcing capability of this gesture has been emphasised by Forbes and Jackson (1980), among others. As with smiles, the majority of research studies which have exploited the reinforcing effects of head-nods, have combined them with various other nonverbal and verbal reinforcers. Thus Mock (1957) reported that a combination of head-nods and 'mm-hmm' utterances could be used to increase the number of times the word 'mother' was said when subjects were asked to talk about childhood experiences. Matarazzo and Wiens (1972) found that the use of head-nods by an interviewer had the effect of increasing the average duration of utterance given by an interviewee. Although total verbal output of subjects increased significantly, Scofield (1977) obtained a disproportionately higher number of self-referenced statements following contingent application of interviewer head-nods combined with a paraphrase, restatement or verbal encouragement. Measures of interviewer's use of head-nods have also been discovered to predict successfully ratings of their competence by experienced judges (Dickson, 1981).

In summary, it would appear that a number of nonverbal behaviours, including smiles, eye contact, hand gestures and head-nods, can, when used appropriately, act as reinforcers during normal interaction to increase the frequency of selected behaviours emitted by the other partner.

Proximity reinforcement

Unlike the previous category, the present one includes gross movements of the whole body or substantial parts of it. Proximity reinforcement refers to potential reinforcing effects which can accrue from altering the distance between oneself and another during interaction. A reduction in interpersonal distance usually accompanies a desire for greater intimacy and involvement. It is also more difficult to avoid attending to another when this distance is small and lack of attention is likely to be much more noticeable. However, while someone who adopts a position at some distance from the other participant may be seen as being unreceptive and detached, a person who approaches too closely may be regarded as over-familiar, dominant or even threatening. In a study by Goldman (1980), already referred to, attitudes of subjects were more successfully modified by means of verbal reinforcers when the interviewer stood at a moderate (4–5 feet) rather than a close interpersonal distance (2–3 feet). The optimal distance will depend upon a number of factors including the nature of the relationship, the sex of the participants and the topic of conversation. With these conditions in mind, a purposeful reduction in interpersonal distance, by signalling a willingness to become more involved in the interaction, can be used as a reinforcer (Rierdan and Brooks, 1978).

With participants who are seated, as most professionals often are during encounters, it is obviously much more difficult to effect sizable variations in interpersonal distance. However, this can be accomplished, to a certain extent, by adopting forward or backward leaning postures. Mehrabian (1972) reported that a forward leaning posture was one component of a complex of behaviours which he labelled 'immediacy' and which denotes a positive attitude towards the other person. Similarly, Brammer and Shostrom (1977) stated that this type of posture conveys acceptance and respect when used in counselling. As with some other nonverbal reinforcers, studies which have been conducted in part to establish the reinforcing effects of a forward leaning posture have combined it with several other reinforcers. However, there is some research evidence supporting the reinforcing effects which a forward leaning posture can have (Banks, 1972).

Touch represents a lack of interpersonal distance and, on occasion, can be used to good effect to encourage a partner to continue with a line of conversation. According to Jones and Yarbrough (1985), it can be construed in a number of ways to mean, among other things, affection, appreciation and support. In many situations, however, touch is inappropriate and even socially forbidden (see Chapter 2 for further details). Nevertheless, apart from the ritualistic sequences of behaviour connected with greetings and leave-taking, touching can be used during an interview when the interviewee is, for example, expressing strong emotions, perhaps of joy, but particularly, sadness, distress or anxiety.

Although not as thoroughly researched as gestural reinforcement it would appear that increasing the intimacy and involvement in an encounter by reducing, within limits, interpersonal distance, even if this is simply effected by means of a more forward leaning posture, can serve to reinforce desired behaviours displayed by the other interactor.

GUIDELINES FOR THE USE OF THE SKILL OF REINFORCEMENT

In the preceding sections a number of verbal and nonverbal behaviours, which can be used at the discretion of the interviewer to exercise a certain amount of control over the behaviour (and in particular the verbal behaviour) of the interviewee, were presented. The effectiveness of their application will largely depend upon how they are administered, however. In this section seven points concerning the use of the skill which tend to promote its effectiveness will be outlined.

Appropriate use

Throughout this chapter an attempt has been made to stress the fact that some stimuli which may have reinforcing properties in some situations may not have the same effects in others. It is, therefore, important that one remains sensitive to the characteristics of the situation, including the other person or persons involved, when choosing the type of reinforcement to use. (This also applies to most of the other skills included in this book.) Thus some forms of praise which would be quite appropriate when used with a child may seem extremely patronising if used with another adult. The reinforcement given should also be appropriate to the response being reinforced. For example, if a teacher reinforces a rather mediocre pupil response with extreme praise, e.g. 'What an absolutely ingenious idea', this could be construed as sarcasm. Attention should, in addition, be paid to the reinforcement history of the individual. Not only is it the case that different people may prefer certain reinforcers to others but the same individual, on different occasions, may find the same reinforcer differentially attractive.

Genuineness of reinforcement

It is absolutely imperative that reinforcement given is perceived as genuinely reflecting the esteem of the source. If not, as in the above example, it may come across as sarcasm, veiled criticism or perhaps a bored habit. Complementarity of verbal and nonverbal behaviour is important in this regard.

Contingency of reinforcement

In order for the various social behaviours reviewed in this chapter to function as effective reinforcers it is important that their application be made contingent upon the particular action which it is intended to modify. This does not mean that the random use of such behaviour will fail to produce an effect. It may well serve to create a particular impression, interpret the situation in a particular way, or as Saigh (1981) speculated, put the other person at ease. It is highly improbable, however, that it will selectively reinforce as desired.

Although some differences of opinion exist, there is evidence to suggest that conditioning can take place without the person involved being consciously aware of the association between his behaviour and the social reinforcement provided. In many situations, though, it may be prudent to specify, quite precisely, the focus of attention. Reference has already been made to O'Leary and O'Leary's (1977) recommendation that praise by teachers should specify the particulars of the behaviour being reinforced. If it is seen to be blatantly manipulative, however, and if the source is thought to harbour ulterior motives, the anticipated outcome of such application may not materialise.

Frequency of reinforcement

It is not necessary to reinforce constantly each and every instance of a specific response, for that class of response to be increased. It has been found that following an initial period of continual reinforcement the frequency of reinforcement can be reduced without resulting in a corresponding reduction in target behaviour.

It will be recalled that Brophy (1981) recommended that praise should be used sparingly to maximise its reinforcing efficacy. A total withdrawal of all reinforcement will, however, initiate extinction.

Variety of reinforcement

The continual and inflexible use of a specific reinforcer will quickly lead to that reinforcer losing its reinforcing properties. If an interviewer responds to each interviewee statement with, for example, 'good', this utterance will gradually become devoid of any evaluative connotations, and consequently will rapidly cease to have reinforcing effects. An attempt should therefore be made to employ a variety of reinforcing expressions and behaviours while ensuring that they do not violate the requirement of appropriateness.

Timing of reinforcement

Based on animal studies it has been recommended that the reinforcing stimulus be applied immediately following the target response, since length of delay was found to be inversely related to effectiveness. If reinforcement is delayed there is a danger that other responses may intervene between the one which the reinforcing agent wished to promote and the presentation of the reinforcer. With human subjects, though, it is unlikely that delayed reinforcement will be ineffective provided that the individual appreciates the target of the reinforcer.

Partial reinforcement

In this context partial reinforcement refers to the fact that it is possible to reinforce selectively certain elements of a response without necessarily reinforcing it in total. This can be accomplished during the actual response. Nonverbal reinforcers such as head-nods and verbal reinforcers like 'mm-hmm' are of particular relevance in this respect since they can be used without interrupting the speaker. Partial reinforcement can also be applied following the termination of a response. Thus a teacher may partially reinforce a pupil who has almost produced the correct answer to his question, with, 'Yes, Mary, you are right, Kilimanjaro is a mountain — but is it in the Andes?' By so doing he reinforces that portion of the answer which is accurate while causing the pupil to re-think the element which is not.

4

Questioning

INTRODUCTION

Questioning is perhaps one of the most widely used social skills, and one of the easiest to identify in general terms. Together with the skill of reinforcement, questioning is one of the core skills in social interaction. In most social encounters questions are asked and responses reinforced — this is the method whereby information is gathered and conversation encouraged.

A question can be defined as a request for information, whether factual or otherwise. This request for information can be verbal or nonverbal. For example, a highpitched 'guggle' such as 'hmmm?' after someone has made a statement, will usually indicate to the speaker that he or she is expected to continue speaking. Similarly, a nod of the head, after asking one member of a group a question, can indicate to another group member that his or her participation is desired also and that the question is being redirected to them. Questions, then, may be nonverbal signals urging another person to respond, or indeed they may even be statements uttered in a inquisitive fashion (e.g. 'You are coming to the party?'; 'Tell me more'). Statements which request information are referred to by Woodbury (1984) as 'prosodic questions', and are defined as 'declarative sentences containing question cues that may be intonational, or these utterances are marked as questions by means of a variety of contextual cues' (p. 203).

Although a question can be posed nonverbally, most questions in social interaction are verbal in nature. At the same time, there are certain nonverbal signals which should accompany the verbal message, if a question is to be recognised as such. One of the main nonverbal accompaniments is the raising or lowering of the vocal inflection on the last syllable of the question. Other nonverbal behaviours include:

head movements, rapidly raising or lowering the eyebrows, and direct eye contact at the end of the question accompanied by a pause. The function of these nonverbal behaviours is to emphasise to the other person that a question is being asked and that a response is expected.

The skill of questioning is to be found at every level in social interaction. The young child, exploring a new environment, seems to be naturally inquisitive, always seeking answers to an ever-increasing number of questions. At this stage questions play a crucial role in the learning and development process, as the infant attempts to assimilate information in order to make sense of his surroundings. The importance of the skill of questioning is, therefore, recognised from an early age.

The study of the nature and functions of questions has developed rapidly during the past decade, with texts devoted to this topic in the fields of linguistics (Stenstroem, 1984), logic (Kiefer, 1982), counselling (Long *et al.*, 1981), psychology (Graesser and Black, 1985), survey interviewing (Sudman and Bradburn, 1982), teaching, (Hyman, 1979), law (Kestler, 1982) and journalism (Metzler, 1977). In addition, a large number of papers, articles and book chapters have been written about the use of questions in various professional contexts. Furthermore, a journal entitled *Questioning Exchange* has been introduced, in order to foster a multi-disciplinary approach to the study of questions.

Investigations into the use of questions in various professional contexts have also been carried out. An early study was conducted by Corey (1940) in which she had an expert stenographer make verbatim records of all classroom talk in six classes. It was found that, on average, the teacher asked a question once every 72 seconds. A similar study was conducted by Resnick (1972). Working with teachers and pupils in an infant school (serving five-to-seven year-old children) in south-east London, she found that 36 per cent of all teacher remarks were questions. Furthermore, this figure increased to 59 per cent when only extended interactions were analysed. In a review of such studies, Dillon (1982) reports that 'teachers have been observed to ask an average of two questions per minute and their pupils all together two questions per hour, which yields a projected average of one question per pupil per month' (p. 153). When the teachers were asked about their use of questions, it was found that they actually asked three times as many questions as they estimated they had asked, and received only one-sixth the number of pupil questions estimated. This would indicate that teachers need to develop a greater awareness of the skill of questioning.

A study of the use of questions by doctors has revealed parallel findings. West (1983) found that, out of a total of 773 questions identified in 21 doctor-patient consultations, only 68 (9 per cent) were initiated by patients. Furthermore, the nature and volume of doctor questions meant that patients had little scope to reply, let alone formulate a question. Interestingly, when patients did ask questions it was found that nearly half of these were marked by speech disturbances, indicating patient discomfort at requesting information from the doctor.

These findings suggest that there is a status and control differential in relation to the use of questions. In most contexts it is the person of higher status, or the person in control, who asks the questions (perhaps the ultimate stereotype being the German SS officer in old war films, who shouts 'Ve vill ask ze questions!'). Thus the majority of questions will be asked by; teachers in classrooms, by doctors in surgeries, by nurses on the ward, by lawyers in court, by detectives in interrogation rooms, and so on. Indeed, it is for this reason that some counselling theorists would argue that counsellors should try not to ask any questions at all of clients, to avoid being seen as the controller of the interaction (Rogers, 1951). However, the type of questions asked will be of importance in most settings, and this issue will be discussed later in the chapter.

Another facet of questioning is that the respondent in many instances is experiencing stress when being asked questions. This is certainly true in the above examples where stress and anxiety is often experienced by patients on the ward or in the surgery, by suspects in police stations, by pupils in classrooms, and by defendants in court. Furthermore, in the latter two cases, the person asking the questions already knows the answers, and this makes these situations even more stressful and removed from normal interaction. In everyday conversation, we do not ask questions to which we already know the answers, or if we do we employ elaborate verbalisations to explain our behaviour (I was surprised to discover something . . . Let me see if you can guess . . .). In the courtroom where lawyers are advised to 'ask only questions to which the answers are known' (Kestler, 1982, p. 341), the creation of stress in witnesses is regarded as a legitimate tactic. In the classroom, however, the heightened anxiety of pupils may be dysfunctional, and detrimental both to learning and to pupil-teacher attitudes. Teachers should bear this in mind when asking questions in the classroom.

FUNCTIONS OF QUESTIONS

The use of questions can serve a number of functions, depending upon the context of the interaction. Thus salesmen ask questions to assess customer needs and relate their sales pitch to the satisfaction of these needs (Poppleton, 1981), negotiators ask questions to slow the pace of the interaction and put pressure on their opponents (Rackham and Carlisle, 1978), doctors use questions to facilitate diagnoses (Maguire, 1984), and so on. However, the main general functions of questions are as follows:

(1) to obtain information;
(2) to maintain control of the interaction;
(3) to arouse interest and curiosity concerning a topic;
(4) to diagnose specific difficulties a respondent may have;
(5) to express an interest in the respondent;
(6) to ascertain the attitudes, feelings and opinions of the respondent;
(7) to encourage maximum participation by the respondent;
(8) to assess the extent of the respondent's knowledge;
(9) to encourage critical thought and evaluation;
(10) to communicate, in group discussions, that involvement and overt participation by all group members is expected and valued;
(11) to encourage group members to comment on the responses of other members of the group;
(12) to maintain the attention of group members, by asking questions periodically without advance warning.

These are the chief functions which can be attained by employing the skill of questioning. It should be realised that the type of question asked can determine the extent to which each of these various functions of questions can be fulfilled. Indeed it is the responses made to questions which determine whether or not the objective has been achieved. In this sense, a question is only as good as the answer which it evokes.

TYPES OF QUESTIONS

A number of different classifications of questions have been proposed. Once again, the context is important — whether it be interviewing, teaching, counselling, interrogating or merely engaging in social conversation, and the type of questions used will vary accordingly. Rudyard Kipling put forward an early categorisation of questions in the lines:

> I keep six honest serving men,
> (They taught me all I knew);
> Their names are What and Why and When,
> And How and Where and Who.

As will be seen, these lines reflect, to a fair degree, the different classifications of questions which have been identified.

Recall/process questions

This division of questions refers to the cognitive level at which the questions are pitched. Recall questions are often referred to as lower-order cognitive questions, while process questions are known as higher-order cognitive questions (Hargie, 1980). The distinction between recall and process questions is most commonly made within education, and can be found in classroom interaction research studies.

Recall questions

Recall questions, as the name suggests, involve the simple recall of information. In this sense, they are of a lower-order cognitive nature, since they only test the ability of the respondent to memorise information. Examples of recall questions would include; 'Where were you born?'; 'When was the Battle of Waterloo?'; 'What nationality was El Greco?'; 'Who wrote *Treasure Island*?' All of these questions have a specific answer, which is either correct or incorrect, and the respondent is being asked to recall the answer in each case.

Recall questions serve a number of useful purposes in different settings. A teacher, for example, may employ recall questions at the beginning of a lesson in order to ascertain the extent of pupil knowledge about the lesson topic. Such questions provide information for the teacher and also serve to encourage pupil participation at the outset. Similarly, at the end of a lesson a teacher may use recall questions to determine the extent of pupil learning which has taken place as a result of the lesson, and also to highlight to pupils that this learning has occurred.

In interviewing contexts, recall questions may be employed at the beginning of an interview as a form of 'ice-breaker' to get the interviewee talking. Recall questions also form the basis of questioning by detectives of eye-witnesses at the scenes of crimes. In this instance the detective is either interested in building up a picture of a suspect or suspects, or in establishing the facts about what exactly occurred at the time the offence was committed. In the former case, the detective may ask questions such as 'How many people were in the car?'; 'What height was he?'; 'What colour was his hair?' In the latter case he may ask questions such as 'How fast was the car going approximately?'; 'Who fired the first shot?'; 'How close were you to the accident when it happened?' If a case goes to court, the eye-witness may be in the position of having to answer these questions again, and be asked to defend the answers.

These are but a few of the social contexts in which questions of a recall nature are employed. In medicine, recall questions are also of importance in the diagnosis of an illness. Thus a doctor will use questions such as 'When did the pain first begin?'; 'Have you had any dizzy spells?'; or 'Do you remember what you ate before you were sick?'

Process questions

Process questions are so called because they require the respondent to use some higher mental process in order to answer them. This may involve giving opinions, justifications, judgements or evaluations, making predictions, analysing information, interpreting situations or making generalisations. In other words, the respondent is required to think, at a higher-order level, about the answer. Examples of process questions include: 'What might have happened if Japan had not bombed Pearl Harbor?' 'How do you think you could improve your relationship with your wife?'; 'Why should anyone who is fit and doesn't work receive money from the state?'; 'What do you think are the characteristics of a good manager?' All of these questions require the respondent to go beyond the simple recall of information and frequently there is no correct answer to a process question. Furthermore, process questions usually require longer responses and can seldom be answered in one or two words.

Process questions are employed in situations where someone is being encouraged to think more deeply about a topic. For this reason they are often utilised in order to assess the ability of an individual to handle information at a higher-order level. In executive-type selection interviews, process questions are frequently used in this assessment function (e.g. 'What type of person are you?'; 'What can you offer this company?'; 'How are imminent technological developments likely to affect the labour market?'). In addition, process questions can be usefully employed in teaching, whereby pupils are encouraged to think for themselves about the material which is presented to them. The ability of pupils to do so may then be tested by the use of process questions either in written formal examinations, or in certain cases the pupil may be assessed orally (e.g. in the examination of foreign languages in schools). At universities many degree and higher-degree courses involve a *viva voce* wherein the candidate is examined orally, to test his understanding of the subject matter, and here again process questions will play a central role.

Research in the classroom context has found that teachers tend to ask more recall questions than process questions. In the Corey (1940) study, cited earlier, it was found that 54 per cent of teacher questions required factual answers, which pupils either knew or did not know. Only 21 per cent of the questions asked required thoughtful answers. Gallagher (1965), in a study involving 235 junior and senior high-school pupils placed in ten classes for gifted pupils, also found that some 50 per cent of teacher questions were in the recall category, while under 20 per cent required evaluative answers. Research reviews by Gall (1970) and Hargie (1983) confirm these proportions of classroom questions.

These are somewhat disconcerting findings, since the type of questions asked by teachers will determine the degree of creativity or expressiveness available to pupils and process questions provide more scope for such creativity than do recall questions. In a world where technological advances move at a rapid pace, facts can rapidly become outdated and the ability to evaluate new information is of great importance. There would seem to be a need for teachers to incorporate more thought-provoking questions into their lessons.

Evidence for this need is provided in a study by Pate and Bremer (1967), who report a research study in which 190 elementary-school teachers were asked to respond to the question, 'What are three important purposes of teachers' questions of pupils?' Of the responses, 68 per cent emphasised the importance of checking on teaching effectiveness by measuring pupil learning, 47 per cent emphasised the importance of the pupils' ability to recall facts, 54 per cent said that questions helped to diagnose pupil difficulties, while only 10 per cent stressed the importance of encouraging pupils to use facts, generalise or make inferences. This result is probably indicative of the examination-oriented curriculum in schools, which encourages teachers to emphasise memory skills. Given this situation, Hargie

(1983) concludes that 'more attention should be given to means whereby teachers can increase their use of thought-provoking questions, as opposed to factual or recall questions' (p. 190).

There is firm research evidence to support such a proposal, since Rousseau and Redfield (1980), in reviewing a total of 20 studies, conclude that 'gains in achievement over a control group may be expected for groups of children who participate in programmes where teachers are trained in questioning skills . . . gains are greatest when higher cognitive questions are used during instruction' (p. 52). However, Turney *et al.* (1976) point out that caution should be exercised in attempting to generalise about the use of process as opposed to recall questions. Research evidence tends to suggest that process questions may be more effective in increasing both participation and achievement of individuals of high intellectual ability, whereas recall questions appear to be more effective in these respects with individuals of low intellectual ability (Ryan, 1973). For teachers with mixed-ability classes this general research finding poses some obvious difficulties with regard to questioning skills, in that the consistent use of process questions is likely to stimulate pupils with a high IQ but be inappropriate for, or confuse, pupils with a low IQ.

Closed/open questions

Another widely-used division of questions relates to the degree of freedom, or scope, given to the respondent in answering the question. Some questions place more restrictions on respondents than others. Questions which leave the respondent open to choose any one of a number of ways in which to answer are appropriately referred to as open questions, while questions which require a short response of a specific nature are referred to as closed questions. This distinction between open and closed questions is most commonly employed in a variety of interviewing and counselling contexts.

Closed questions

Closed questions are those questions wherein 'the respondent does not have a choice in his response other than those provided by the questioner' (King, 1972, p. 158). Closed questions usually have a correct answer, or can be answered with a short response selected from a limited number of possible responses. There are three main types of closed question:

(1) The Selection Question. Here the respondent is presented with two or more alternative responses, from which he is expected to choose. As a result, this type of question is also known as a forced-choice question. Examples of this type of question include: 'Do you prefer tea or coffee?'; 'Would you rather have Fyfe, Cameron or Thompson as the next President?'. 'Do you want to travel by sea or by air?'
(2) The Yes-No Question. As the name suggests, this is a question which may be adequately answered by a 'yes' or 'no', or by using some equivalent affirmative or negative. Examples of this type of closed question include: 'Are you Irish?'; 'Did you go to university?'; 'Would you like some coffee?'; 'Has there been any bleeding?'
(3) The Identification Question. This type of question requires the respondent to identify the answer to a factual question and present this as the response. While the answer to an identification question may involve the recall of information (e.g. 'What is your maiden name?'; 'Where were you born?'), it may also be concerned with the identification of present material (e.g. 'What time is it?'; 'Where exactly is the pain occurring now?') or future events (e.g. 'Where are you going in holiday?'; 'When is your baby due?').

Closed questions have a number of applications. Most people will find closed questions easy to answer, and so by employing this type of question it is possible to get someone involved in an interaction at the outset. In fact-finding encounters, closed questions are of particular value and are often used in a variety of research and assessment-type interviews. In the research interview it is the responses of subjects which are of importance, and responses to closed questions are usually more concise and therefore easier to record than responses to open questions; this in turn facilitates comparisons between the responses of different subjects. In many assessment interviews, the interviewer will have to ascertain whether or not the client is suitable for some form of grant or assistance. To do so, the interviewer will have to find out whether the client meets a number of specified requirements (e.g. a social welfare official will have to ask a client about his financial affairs, his family background, etc., before deciding if he is eligible for state allowances).

Closed questions, then, can usually be answered adequately in one or a very few words. They are restricted in nature, imposing limitations on the possible responses which the respondent can give. They give the questioner a high degree of control over the interaction, since a series of closed questions can be prepared in advance in order to structure a given social encounter, and the possible answers which the respondent may give can usually be estimated. Where time is limited and a diagnosis has to be made, or information has to be gathered, closed questions can be gainfully employed.

Open questions

Open questions are questions which can be answered in a number of ways, the response being left open to the respondent. With open questions the respondent is given a higher degree of freedom in deciding which answer to give, than with closed questions. Open questions are broad in nature, and require more than one or two words for an adequate answer. At the same time, however, some open questions will place more restriction upon respondents than others, depending upon the frame of reference subsumed in the question. Consider the following examples of questions asked by a detective of a suspect:

(1) 'Tell me about your spare time activities.'
(2) 'What do you do in the evenings?'
(3) 'What do you do on Saturday evenings?'
(4) 'What did you do on the evening of Saturday, 19 January?'

In these examples, the focus of the questions has gradually narrowed from the initial very open question to the more restricted type of open question. This could then lead into more specific closed questions, such as:

(5) 'Who were you with on the evening of Saturday, 19 January?'
(6) 'Where were you at 7.00 pm that evening?'

This approach, of beginning an interaction with a very open question, and gradually reducing the level of openness, is termed a 'funnel' sequence (Kahn and Cannell, 1957) (see Figure 4.1). Such a structure is common in counselling interviews, wherein the helper does not want to impose any restrictions on the helpee about what is to be discussed, and may begin a session by asking, 'What would you like to talk about?' or 'How have things been since we last met?' Once the helpee begins to talk, the helper may then want to focus in on certain aspects of the responses given.

An alternative approach to this sequencing of questions is to use an 'inverted funnel' sequence (sometimes referred to as a 'pyramid' sequence), whereby an interaction begins with very closed questions and gradually opens out to embrace wider issues. Such an approach

Figure 4.1: Types of questioning sequences

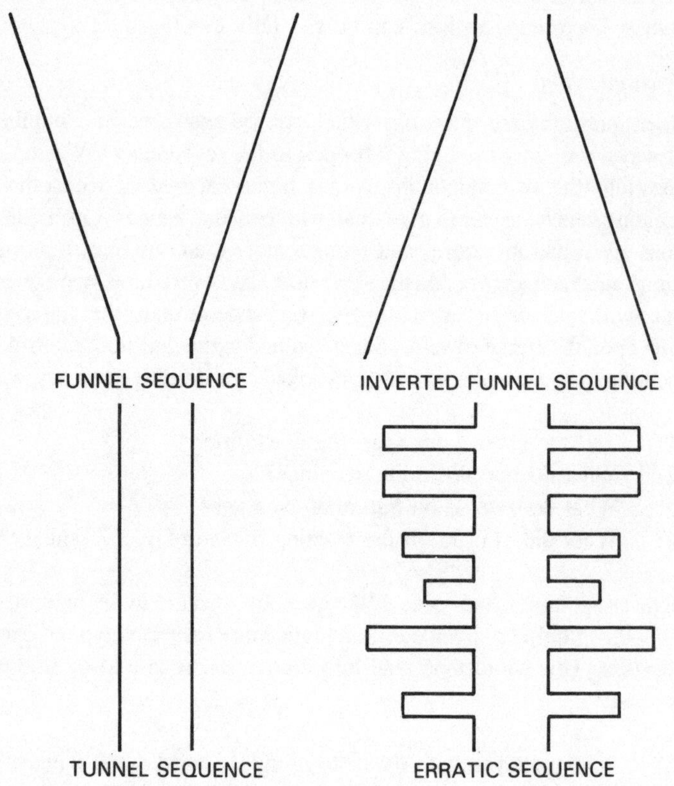

is often adopted in careers guidance interviews in which the interviewer may want to build up a picture of the client (e.g. academic achievements, family background, interests, etc.) before progressing to possible choice of career and the reasons for this choice (e.g. 'Why do you think you would like to be a soldier?', 'What factors would be important to you in choosing a job?'). By using closed questions initially to obtain information about the client, the careers interviewer may then be in a better position to help the client evaluate possible, and feasible, career options.

A third type of questioning sequence is referred to as the 'tunnel' sequence. In this type of sequence, all of the questions employed are at the same level and are usually closed. A series of closed questions may be used in certain types of assessment interview, wherein the objective is to establish a set of factual responses from the respondent.

This type of closed tunnelling for information is often characteristic of 'screening' interviews, where the respondent has to be matched against some pre-set criteria (e.g. eligibility for some form of state welfare benefit or grant).

There is some research evidence to suggest that a consistent sequence of questions facilitates participation and understanding in respondents, whether the sequence be of a tunnel, funnel or inverted funnel nature (see Figure 4.1). Turney *et al.* (1976), for example, highlight the dangers of using an erratic sequence of open and closed questions (or of recall and process questions), as being likely to confuse the respondent and reduce the level of participation. Erratic sequences of questions (also known as rapid variations in the level of cognitive demand) are common in interrogation interviews where the purpose is to confuse the suspect and 'throw him off his guard' since he will not know what type of question to expect next. Indeed, in courtrooms, Kestler (1982) recommends that lawyers should use an erratic sequence, involving 'a quick change of focus designed to catch the witness off-balance, with thoughts out of context' (p. 156).

Open questions are useful in allowing a respondent to express opinions, attitudes, thoughts and feelings. They do not require any prior knowledge on the part of the questioner, who can ask open questions about topics or events with which he is not familiar. For these reasons open questions are useful in exploring a wide range of areas. By using open questions, the respondent is encouraged to talk, thereby leaving the questioner free to listen and observe. This means, of course, that the respondent has a greater degree of control over the interaction and can determine to a greater extent what is to be discussed. It also means that the questioner has to pay attention to what is being said in order to indicate interest and attentiveness to the respondent.

Another advantage of open questions is that the respondent may reveal information which the questioner had not anticipated. Where a respondent has a body of specialised knowledge to relate, the use of open questions can facilitate the transmission of this knowledge. At the same time, however, where time is limited, or with over-talkative clients, open questions may be inappropriate in many instances. Answers to open questions may be time-consuming, and may also contain irrelevant, or less vital, information.

At first sight, there would appear to be little difference between the recall/process and the closed/open categorisations of questions, and indeed many closed questions are of a recall nature, while many process questions, are also open questions. However, it is possible to have closed process questions, and open recall questions. Consider a science teacher who has explained to pupils the chemical qualities of water and limestone, and then asks, 'What reaction will occur when I pour water onto a piece of limestone?' While the question is process, it is also closed. Similarly a question such as 'What did you do during the holidays?' is both open and recall. Thus there are differences inherent in these two classifications of questions and both are useful in varying contexts.

A number of research studies have examined the relative effects of open and closed questions in different situations. Dohrenwend (1965), for example, found that, in research interviews, responses to open questions contained a higher proportion of self-revelation than did responses to closed questions when the subject matter under discussion was objective, and a lower proportion when the subject matter was subjective. This finding suggests that when concerned with self-disclosures, closed questions may be more effective in keeping the respondent to the topic of the question. (For more information on self-disclosure see Chapter 9.) Dohrenwend also found, however, that responses to open questions were about three times longer than responses to closed questions, as measured by amounts of verbalisation. Again, responses to subjective open questions were significantly shorter than responses to objective open questions, whereas length of response to closed questions did not vary with subject matter.

Dohrenwend concludes that 'closed questions offer more definite advantages than open questions in research interviews' (p. 183), because closed questions exert a tighter control over respondents' answers. Open questions, while answered in more detail, tended to result in responses which deviated from the topic of the question, whereas with closed questions the respondent was more likely to answer the question in a direct fashion.

Generalisations about the relative efficacy of open or closed questions can be difficult, since the intellectual capacity of the respondent must be taken into consideration. There is evidence to suggest that open questions may not be so appropriate with respondents of low intellect. Schatzman and Strauss (1956) compared respondents who had not gone beyond the grammar-school level, with respondents who had spent at least one year at college. They found that open questions tended to be more effective with the latter group than with the former group, as judged by the questioning behaviour of experienced interviewers who were given a certain degree of freedom about what type of questions to employ. The interviewers used more open questions with the respondents of higher education, than with those of lower education.

Jesudason (1976) carried out a study on some 1,151 Indian women, the majority of whom were illiterate, in order to compare the relative efficacy of open and closed questions. The study attempted to ascertain those food items regarded by these women as taboo during lactation. Respondents were either asked to name foods that were taboo, if any (open form), or were read a list of twelve food items previously identified as taboo and asked whether they ate each food during lactation (closed form). Approximately 53 per cent of women did not report any food taboos in answer to the open question, but when these same women were then read the list of twelve items, 32 per cent reported that they considered five or more items in the list as taboo. This again indicates the disadvantage of the open question with respondents of low intellect. Jesudason also reports in this study the finding that 8.6 per cent of the women who did not identify any of the initial twelve items as taboo, reported at least one food item not contained in the list as taboo when asked an open question following the closed one. In arguing for the inclusion of both open and closed questions in research interviews Jesudason concludes that 'if the study had used only a closed-ended question, information about additional food items would have been lost' (p. 68).

Research comparing the use of open and closed questions in counselling, has found that open questions are more effective in promoting interviewee self-disclosures, in producing more accurate responses, and increasing perceived counsellor empathy (Hargie, 1984). Thus most texts on counselling recommend that counsellors should concentrate on asking open questions while reducing the number of closed questions asked.

In a different context, Loftus (1982) found that in the questioning of eye-witnesses, open questions produce more accurate information, but less overall detail, than specific closed questions. As a result, she recommends that in the questioning of eye-witnesses, questions should be open initially ('Tell me what happened') to obtain accuracy of information, followed by specific closed questions ('What colour was his hair?') to obtain a fuller picture.

However, more research is needed in this field to chart the relative effects of open and closed questions across situations. Lazarsfield, in 1944, pointed out that, in the absence of research findings, decisions about when to use open or closed questions would have to be based upon the experience of the interviewer. Dohrenwend, in 1965, pointed out that little had happened to change this advice in the interim 20 years. Unfortunately, while some research has been carried out in this area, the current state of knowledge remains much the same as it was in 1944.

Affective questions

Affective questions are questions which relate specifically to the emotions, attitudes, feelings or preferences of the respondent — that is to the *affective* domain. An affective question can be either recall, process, open or closed, depending upon which aspect of the client's feelings is being explored. Where an attempt is being made to ascertain the reactions of the respondent to a past event, a recall question may be employed (e.g. 'Who was your favourite teacher at school?'). On the other hand, when present feelings are being explored, a closed question may be used (e.g. 'Do you feel embarrassed talking about this?').

The utilisation of recall or closed questions, however, places restrictions upon respondents in terms of what they are expected to relate about their feelings. Where it is important that the client be given time and freedom to discuss emotions, open questions may be more advantageous. Open questions can relate to past emotions (e.g. 'How did you feel when your mother died?') or to the present emotional state ('What are your feelings towards your husband now?'). By using open questions it is hoped to ascertain the true feelings of the respondent.

In order to encourage a respondent to think more deeply about feelings, and about the underlying reasons for these feelings, process questions may be more applicable. Rather than merely asking for a report about underlying feelings, process questions require the respondent to evaluate the cause of these feelings (e.g. 'Why did you hate your father so much?', 'Why have your feelings towards your wife changed?'). This type of question encourages the respondent to interpret reasons for feelings and perhaps become more rational in exploring them.

As the examples used in this section illustrate, affective questions are particularly relevant in counselling contexts, where an individual visits a counsellor in order to seek help with some problem. The discussion of feelings is very important in such situations, and a variety of affective questions can encourage a client to verbalise feelings or emotions. In emphasising the importance of affective questions in counselling, Nelson-Jones (1983) points out that since 'many clients are poor at listening to their own feelings, this may give them useful practice at this' (p. 77).

Affective questions are also employed in many other contexts. In the medical profession, doctors and nurses frequently adopt an affective questioning technique with patients (e.g. 'How are you feeling today?', 'Are you worried about this operation?'). In the classroom, teachers also employ affective questions to explore pupil attitudes to various topics. Similarly, careers guidance interviewers utilise affective questions in discussing occupational choice (e.g. 'Would you like a clerical job?', 'How would you feel about working in an office every day?'). In these and many other contexts a variety of affective questions can be employed to discuss respondents' feelings and emotions, and the possible reasons for these feelings and emotions.

Leading questions

Leading questions are questions which, by the way they are worded, lead the respondent towards an expected response. This expected answer to a leading question is implied within the question itself, and may, or may not, be immediately obvious to the respondent, depending upon the phrasing of the question. There are four different types of leading questions.

Conversational leads

As the name suggests, these are leading questions which are used in everyday conversations. A normal conversation between two people contains a number of comments that anticipate a certain type of response. This would include comments such as 'Isn't this a lovely day?'; 'Have you ever seen my mother looking better?'; 'Isn't this meal really delicious?' As Dohrenwend and Richardson (1964) point out, these comments which 'stimulate the flow of conversation in social situations, not only anticipate the response, however, but usually anticipate it correctly' (p. 77).

Thus the conversational lead is intended to suggest the answer which the respondent would have given in any case, and thereby encourages the respondent to participate. This technique would seem to be useful, when applied expertly, in interviewing contexts. Dohrenwend and Richardson (1964) report research findings which indicate that, in interviews, conversational leads convey to respondents the impression of friendliness and strong interest on the part of the interviewer, but only when these leading questions accurately anticipate the respondent's answer. Correct conversational leading questions create the feeling amongst respondents that the interviewer is listening carefully and understanding what is being said. This, in turn, stimulates respondents to continue developing their ideas, feeling confident that the interviewer is paying attention and understanding their responses.

Simple leads

These are questions which are unambiguously intended to lead the respondent to give an answer which the questioner expects to receive. This type of leading question usually exerts a degree of pressure on the respondent to reply in a certain fashion. Unlike the conversational lead, the simple lead anticipates the answer which the questioner expects, as opposed to the answer which the respondent would have given in any case. The simple lead, then, takes less cognisance of the respondent's thoughts and feelings. Examples of this type of leading question include 'You do, of course, go to church, don't you?'; 'Surely you don't support the communists?'; 'Aren't the taxes in this country far too high?'

There is some evidence to suggest that the use of simple leads which are obviously incorrect, may induce respondents to participate fully in an interview in order to correct any misconceptions inherent in the question. Beezer (1956), for example, conducted interviews with East German refugees in which he found that simple leading questions that were clearly incorrect yielded more information from respondents than did questions which were not leading. Thus when respondents were asked, 'I understand you don't have to pay very much for food in the East Zone because it is rationed?', most respondents replied by trying to correct the interviewer's impressions about general conditions in East Germany.

Dohrenwend and Richardson (1964) suggest that the blatantly incorrect simple leading question serves to place the respondent in the position of expert *vis-à-vis* the misinformed interviewer. As a result, the respondent may feel obliged to provide information which will enlighten the interviewer. Some of this information may involve the introduction of new topics not previously mentioned by the interviewer. This may explain the finding reported by Richardson (1960), that leading questions are more likely to elicit volunteered information than are non-leading questions.

While these results tend to suggest that leading questions can be effective in encouraging participation, it is not possible to state how, and in what contexts, simple leading questions can be most gainfully employed. It may be that in certain situations, and with particular types of respondent, the use of simple leading questions could be counter-productive. As Loftus and Zanni (1975) point out, most authors of texts on interviewing have eschewed this form of question as being bad practice. Furthermore, in the courtroom, leading questions are not permitted in the direct examination of a witness by the counsel for the side calling him, although they are allowed during cross-examination of the other side's witnesses. Kestler (1982) positively recommends the use of leading questions by lawyers during cross-examination since they 'permit control of the subject matter and scope of the response. The witness is constrained to answer "yes" or "no" ' (p. 59). In other settings, however, such constraint on the respondent will not be so desirable, and simple leading questions will need to be used with caution, or avoided altogether.

Implication leads

These are questions which lead the respondent to answer in a specific fashion, or accept a negative implication if the answer given is contrary to that anticipated. This type of leading question exerts a much greater degree of pressure on the respondent to reply in the expected manner, than does a simple leading question, and for this reason it is sometimes referred to as a 'complex leading question'. An example of this type of question would be: 'Anyone who cared for his country would not want to see it destroyed in a nuclear attack or invaded by a foreign power, so don't you think any expenditure on an effective defensive deterrent is money well spent?' In this case, a negative answer to this question places the respondent in the position of apparently being unpatriotic.

If a respondent disagrees with the anticipated response to this type of implication lead, some type of justification is usually expected by the questioner. For this reason, implication leads are often used by radio and television interviewers when interviewing political, or controversial, individuals. Similarly in arguments and debates, implication leads are employed in order to put opponents under pressure, and emphasise a certain point of view. Loftus (1982) gives another example of an implication lead, namely 'Did you know that what you were doing was dishonest?' Again, the respondent is put under pressure to either accept the negative implication of dishonesty or respond at length.

Subtle leads

These are questions which may not be instantly recognisable as leading questions, but which nevertheless are worded in such a way as to elicit a certain type of response. An example of how the wording of a question can influence the respondent to answer in a particular way has been reported by Harris (1973). Subjects were informed that they were taking part in 'a study in the accuracy of guessing measurements, and that they should make as intelligent a numerical guess as possible to each question' (p. 399). Subjects were then asked either 'How tall was the basket-ball player?' or 'How short was the basket-ball player?' On average, subjects guessed about 79 inches and 69 inches, respectively, indicating the influence of the words *tall* and *short* in the respective questions. Other questions asked by Harris along the same lines produced similar results — thus the question 'How long was the movie?' resulted in average estimates of 130 minutes, whereas 'How short was the movie?' produced an average of 100 minutes.

Loftus (1975) reports similar findings in a study in which 40 people were interviewed about their headaches and about headache products 'under the belief that they were participating in market research on these products' (p. 561). Subjects were asked either 'Do you get headaches frequently, and if so, how often?' or 'Do you get headaches occasionally, and if so, how often?' The *frequently* subjects reported an average of 2.2 headaches per week, whereas the *occasionally* group reported 0.7 per week. Loftus also asked either 'In terms of the total number of products, how many other products have you tried? 1? 2? 3?' or 'In terms of the total number of products, how many other products have you tried? 1? 5? 10?' Responses to these questions averaged 3.3 and 5.2 other products, respectively. In another study Loftus and Palmer (1974) had subjects view films of car accidents, and then questioned them about what they had seen. The question 'About how fast were the cars going when they smashed into each other?' produced higher estimates of speed than when the verb 'smashed' was replaced by 'hit', 'bumped', 'collided' or 'contacted'. One week later those subjects who had been asked the former question were also more likely to say 'yes' to the question 'Did you see broken glass?', even though no glass was broken in the accident.

In a similar piece of research Loftus and Zanni (1975) compared the effects of questions containing an indefinite article with the same questions containing a definite article. In this study 100 graduate students were told that 'they were participating in an experiment on memory' (p. 87). They were shown a short film of a car accident and then asked questions about this. It was found that questions which contained a definite article (e.g. 'Did you see *the* broken headlight?') produced fewer uncertain or 'I don't know' responses, and more false recognition of events which never in fact occurred, than did questions which contained an indefinite article (e.g. 'Did you see *a* broken headlight?').

This 'false recognition' was also reported in the Loftus (1975) study. She conducted four different experiments, each of which highlighted the way in which the wording of questions, asked immediately after an event, can influence the responses to questions asked considerably later. In one of these experiments 150 students were shown a video-tape of a car accident and asked a number of questions about the accident. Half of the subjects were asked 'How fast was the white sports car going when it passed the barn while travelling along the country road?', while half were asked 'How fast was the white sports car going while travelling along the country road?' Although no barn appeared in the film, 17.3 per cent of those asked the former question responded 'yes' when later asked 'Did you see a barn?', as opposed to only 2.7 per cent of those asked the latter question.

These findings have been confirmed in the sphere of interviewing suspects of crimes. Buckwalter (1983) points out that suspects are more forthcoming when asked to 'tell the truth' rather than 'confess your crime'. Similarly, in cases of murder, motives are given more readily to the question 'Why did you do it?' than to 'Why did you murder him?' Buckwalter advises interviewers to avoid terms such as kill, steal, rape, and replace them with words such as shoot, take, sex.

In reviewing research findings relating to the use of subtle leads, Dillon (1986) concludes: 'It is obvious that the wording of a question affects the answer . . . What is more, the wording of the question can influence people not only to over/under-report but also to give truly answers about non-existent things' (p. 107). The implications of these findings are likely to be of interest to many individuals, particularly those concerned with obtaining accurate recall of facts from others, including nurses, doctors, detectives, insurance investigators, lawyers and assessment interviewers.

Probing questions

Probing questions are questions which are designed to encourage respondents to expand upon initial responses, and, in this sense, they are 'follow-up' questions. Once a respondent has given an initial answer, it can be explored further in a number of ways. Turney *et al.* (1976) have identified a number of different types of probing questions and these are as follows:

Clarification probes

These can be used in order to elicit a clearer, more concisely-phrased response, in situations where the questioner is either confused or uncertain about the content or meaning of the initial responses. Examples of clarification probes would include 'What exactly do you mean?', 'Could you explain that to me again?' or 'Are you saying that you did not do it?'

Justification probes

These require respondents to justify initial responses by giving reasons for what they have said. Questions such as 'Why did you say that?', 'How did you reach that conclusion?' or 'What evidence have you got to support that?' all require the respondent to expand upon the initial response by giving a justification for having made it.

Relevance probes

These are questions which give respondents an opportunity to re-assess the appropriateness of a response, and/or make its relevance to the main topic under consideration more obvious. This type of probing question enables the questioner to ascertain which relationships are being made by the respondent, between objects, people or events and in addition encourages the respondent to reflect on the validity of these relationships. Relevance probes include: 'How does this relate to your home background?', 'Is this relevant to what we discussed earlier?' or 'Why are you telling me this now?'

Exemplification probes

These require respondents to provide concrete or specific instances of what they mean by what may, at first, appear to be a rather vague statement. Asking a respondent to give an example to illustrate a general statement often helps to clarify the statement, by providing a definite insight into the thoughts of the respondent (see Chapter 7 for a discussion on the use of examples). Included here would be questions such as 'Could you give me an example of that?', 'Can you think of a specific instance of this?' or 'Where have you shown leadership qualities in the past?'

Extension probes

These can be used to encourage a respondent to expand upon an initial response by providing further information pertinent to the topic under discussion. An extension question is best employed in situations where it is felt that a respondent should be able to make further responses which will facilitate the development of the discussion. Examples of extension probes include: 'That's interesting, tell me more', 'Is there anything else that you can remember about it?' or 'And then what happened?'

Accuracy probes

These are questions which draw the respondent's attention to a possible error in fact that has been made in a response, and thereby offers the respondent an opportunity to adjust or restructure the response where necessary. Accuracy questions are most useful in situations where either it is absolutely vital that the respondent is certain about the accuracy of responses (e.g. an eye-witness being cross-examined in court), or where the questioner knows the correct answer and wishes to give the respondent a chance to reflect upon an initial response (e.g. a teacher questioning pupils). Accuracy probes include questions such as 'Are you quite sure about that?', 'You are certain that you could identify him?' or 'It definitely happened before 3.00 pm?'

Echo probes

These are so called because they are questions which 'echo' the words used by the respondent in the initial response, by containing these same words in the follow-up question. Echo probes are often employed in interpersonal interaction, but if these are over-used it is likely that they will be counter-productive, since if every answer given by the respondent is echoed, the respondent may soon become very aware of this procedure and, in all probability, will stop responding. Examples of echo probes are included in the following:

A. After the meal he became very romantic, and told me that he loved me.
Q: He told you that he loved you?
A: Yes, and then he took my hand and asked me to marry him.
Q: He asked you to *marry* him?!

Nonverbal probes

These are behaviours which are employed in such a manner as to indicate to the respondent a desire for further information. Included here would be the use of appropriate paralanguage to accompany expressions such as 'Ohh?!', or 'Never?!', together with inquisitive nonverbal behaviours (e.g. raising or lowering of eyebrows, sideways tilt of the head, and eye contact). The use of pauses following an initial response can also serve as a form of probe indicating a desire for further responses. The importance of pausing has been investigated by Rowe (1969). She found that by increasing the average 'wait-time' before and after pupil responses, teachers could thereby increase the length of these responses. Furthermore, by increasing the length of pauses, the teacher tended to ask more process questions and the number of questions asked by pupils also increased. In addition, pupils who did not tend to say much, started talking and produced novel ideas. In one experiment cited by Rowe, twelve teachers each identified their five best and five poorest pupils. After sampling the teachers' wait-times it was found that the teachers waited significantly less time for weaker pupils to reply to questions. When these twelve teachers deliberately increased their wait-times for the poorer pupils, the responses of these pupils increased gradually at first and then rapidly. This research indicates the value of pauses, as a form of probing, in eliciting maximum respondent participation.

Consensus probes

These are questions which give an opportunity for a group to pause in a discussion and for individual respondents to express their agreement or disagreement with an initial response. Asking consensus questions is a useful technique for a group leader to employ in order to gauge the extent of support within the group for any proposed idea or line of action. By asking 'Does everyone agree with that?' or 'Is there anyone not happy with that?' it is usually possible to evaluate the level of group consensus at any given time.

Rhetorical questions

A rhetorical question is a question which does not expect an answer, either because the speaker intends to answer the question, or because the question is equivalent to a statement (as in 'Who would not wish their children well?' to mean 'Everyone wishes their children well').

In the former case, rhetorical questions are often used by public speakers in order to stimulate interest in their presentation by encouraging the audience to 'think things through' with them. The use of rhetorical questions has been found to raise the level of audience attention and increase their retention of information (Bligh, 1971). As Turk (1985) puts it: 'Asking questions is the best way to promote thought . . . We are so conditioned to provide answers to sentences in question form, that our minds are subconsciously aroused towards an answer, even if we remain silent' (p. 75).

With large audiences, questions are usually not appropriate since only a few members of the audience would be given a chance to answer, and the rest of the audience may have difficulty in hearing the responses. For this reason, lecturers, politicians and other individuals, when addressing large groups of people, often employ rhetorical questions (Brown, 1982). An example of the use of such questions is contained in the following extract from a lecture on industrial economics: 'Although productivity agreements have been, and are being, applied quite widely in industry, they have not provided the solution to Britain's low level of productivity compared to other countries. Well, why should this mechanism have failed to provide a solution to Britain's problems? There are a number of reasons . . . '

Multiple questions

A multiple question is a question which is made up of two or more questions phrased as one. While a multiple question may contain a number of questions of the same type, quite often it comprises an open question followed by a closed question which narrows the focus (e.g. 'What did you do during the holidays? Did you go to Spain?'). Multiple questions may be useful where time is limited and it is important to get some answer from a respondent. For this reason multiple questions are often used by radio and television interviewers who have a given (often brief) period of time in which to interview a respondent.

In most situations, however, multiple questions are wasteful — especially where the questions subsumed within the multiple questions are unrelated. Such questions are liable to confuse the respondent, and/or the responses given by the respondent may confuse the questioner who may be unclear exactly which question has been answered. For example:

Q: Have you lived here long? Do you like it? I mean, what about the neighbours?
A: Yes.
Q: Yes, what?

In the classroom context, Wright and Nuthall (1970) carried out a study in which they observed 17 teachers teaching three lessons each to eight-year-old children in schools in Christchurch, New Zealand. They found that the tendency on the part of a teacher to ask one question at a time was positively related to pupil achievement, whereas the tendency to ask more than one question at a time was negatively related to pupil achievement. While it is difficult to generalise from the results of one study, this research does highlight the possible disadvantage of using multiple questions in classroom interaction. Whether similar disadvantages may accrue in other settings has yet to be investigated.

RELATED ASPECTS OF QUESTIONING

In addition to the various types of questions discussed in the previous section and the objectives they serve in interpersonal interaction, there are a number of related aspects of questioning which anyone wishing to use this skill effectively should be aware of. These aspects are concerned with how questions are asked, rather than what questions can be asked, and include the following techniques.

Structuring

In certain social situations where a respondent is likely to be asked a large number of questions, it may be useful to structure the questions in such a way as to indicate to the respondent what questions are likely to be asked, and why it is necessary to ask them (e.g. 'In order to help me advise you about possible future jobs I would like to find out about your qualifications, experience and interests. If I could begin with your qualifications . . . '). By structuring the interaction in this way, the respondent knows why questions are being asked, and also knows what questions to expect. Once the respondent is aware of the immediate goals of the questioner, and recognises these as acceptable goals, it is likely that the interaction will flow more smoothly with the respondent attempting to give adequate answers (see also the skill of set induction in Chapter 6 for a fuller discussion of this type of structuring).

Prompting

Prompting is the technique which can be adopted to encourage a respondent to give an adequate answer, following either an unrelated answer, or no answer at all, to an initial question. Depending upon the hypothesised cause of the respondent's failure, the questioner may prompt in different ways. If it is thought that the respondent did not correctly hear the initial question, the questioner may simply restate the same question. If it is thought that the respondent did not understand the initial phrasing of the question, it may be rephrased either in parallel fashion, or at a simpler level. It may, however, be deemed necessary to prompt the respondent either by reviewing information previously covered (e.g. 'You remember what we talked about last week') or by giving a clue which will help to focus attention in the right direction. An example of this latter type of prompt is included in the following excerpt from a radio 'phone-in' quiz:

Q: With what country would you associate pasta?
A: Spain
Q: No, think of Chianti. (prompt)
A: Oh yes, of course, Italy.

Pausing

The function of pausing as a form of probing question has already been considered in this chapter. However, as well as pausing after receiving a response, it is possible to pause both before, and after, asking a question. By pausing before asking a question, it is often possible to stimulate the attention of the listener and give the question greater impact. By pausing after asking a question, the respondent is given the distinct impression of being expected to give some form of response. The use of pauses after asking a question also reduces the likelihood of the questioner asking multiple questions. Finally, pausing after a respondent gives an initial response can serve to encourage the respondent to continue talking. The consistent and considered use of pauses during questioning may well be a feature of skilled interaction. Indeed, there is evidence to suggest that the inability to slow down the pace of an interaction by using appropriate pauses is a common failure amongst trainee teachers (Turney *et al.*, 1976) and novice counsellors (Ivey, 1971).

Distribution

In group contexts, a group leader may wish to involve as many respondents as possible in the discussion. One method whereby this can be achieved is by distributing questions to all groups members, so that all points of view can be heard. This is a useful technique to employ, especially with individuals who may be reluctant to express their views unless specifically given an opportunity to do so. The redirection of a question from one group member to another may be of particular value in achieving a discreet distribution of questions, without exerting undue pressure, or embarrassing any one individual in the group. In the classroom, the need for greater distribution of questions has been emphasised by Adams (1969) and Delefes and Jackson (1972), who report results which indicate that one-quarter of pupils receive some 54 per cent of the teachers' positive verbalisations, possibly because teachers spend 90 per cent of their lesson time at the front and centre of the classroom.

Responses

Just as there is a wide variation in types of questions which can be asked, so too is there a wide variation in the range of possible responses which can made. Dillon (1986) has identified a large number of possible answers to questions, and these can be summarised as follows:

(1) *Silence*. The respondent may choose to say nothing.
(2) *Overt refusal to answer*, e.g. 'I'd rather not say'.
(3) *Unconnected response*. The respondent may change the topic completely.
(4) *Humour*. For example, to the question 'How old are you?', the respondent may reply 'Not as old as I feel!'
(5) *Lying*. The respondent may simply give a false answer.
(6) *Stalling*. Again, to the question 'How old are you?' the respondent may reply 'How old do you think I am?' Answering a question with a question is a classic stalling technique.

(7) *Selective ambiguity*. Thus to the question about age, the respondent may reply 'Don't worry, I'll finish the marathon OK'. In other words, the respondent pretends to recognise the 'real' question, and answers it.

(8) *Withholding and concealing*. In this instance, respondents will attempt to avoid disclosing information which may be damaging to them or those close to them. This is a problem commonly faced by investigators (criminal, insurance, etc.), but is also applicable to those professionals who have to deal with sensitive or taboo issues such as child abuse, incest, drug abuse and so on.

(9) *Distortion*. Respondents in many instances will give the answers they think the questioner wants, or the answers that they feel are socially desirable, often without consciously realising they are so doing. Thus in survey interviews, respondents tend to overestimate voting, reading books, and giving to charity, and underestimate illnesses, financial status and illegal behaviour (Bradburn and Sudman, 1980).

(10) *Direct honest response*. Finally, in most instances the respondent will give a direct, truthful answer to the majority of questions asked.

In any interaction, the professional will need to evaluate the responses received, and make decisions about how to follow these up with appropriate probing questions.

OVERVIEW

Although, at first sight, questioning would seem to be one of the simplest of all social skills, upon further examination it can be seen that, in fact, the skill is quite complex. As Dillon (1986) points out: 'It is easy to ask questions in everyday situations. And it is easy to ask everyday questions in professional practice. But it takes *great care* to prepare an educative question' (p. 112). There is a large variety of different types of questions which can be asked in any given situation, and the answers received will be markedly affected by both the wording, and the type, of question asked.

There are no hard-and-fast rules about which types of question to use in particular social encounters, since much more situation-specific research is needed in order to investigate the effects of different types of questions, on a variety of respondents, in any given social context. However, the categorisations of questions contained in this chapter should provide a useful starting point for the analysis of the effects of questions in social interaction. Furthermore, the examples given, and the research reviewed, should provide the reader with some insight into the different modes of usage, and the accompanying effects, to which different types of questions can be applied.

5

Reflecting

INTRODUCTION

Consider the following two short fictional interview transcripts. The first involves an excerpt from a survey interview conducted by a student (I) within the Faculty of Social Sciences at the local University of Newtown. The research project in which he is engaged is concerned with population shifts. The interviewee (Ie), Mrs Dillon, has just recently moved to Newtown.

I: How long have you been married?
Ie: It will be two years now, next month.
I: Do you have any family?
Ie: Yes, we have one boy.
I: Uh-huh. Is your husband currently employed?
Ie: Yes, he works down at Smiths . . . that's the shoe factory . . . But there's talk of it closing shortly.
I: What type of work does he do there?
Ie: He's on the machines, I think.
I: Do you have a job of any sort?
Ie: No, I would like to but there isn't much work around here. Then there's the baby . . . I wouldn't want to leave him with anyone else . . . Well I don't really know anyone around here who would look after him.
I: I see. How long have you been living at your present address?
Ie: Oh we only moved in a few months ago . . . just over five months.
I: Where did you live previously?
Ie: We lived with my mother in Smalltown but my husband was laid off and he couldn't find any work there so we had to move.

I: Do you have any relations living in Newtown?

. . . And so it progresses.

The second interview again involves Mrs Dillon. A local health visitor has been informed that a mother with a young baby has just moved into the area and consequently she decides to pay her a visit. We join the interview after the normal preliminaries:

I: Well, Mrs Dillon, how are you settling in?
Ie: Oh things still seem in a mess. Somehow when we lived at my mother's everything seemed so neat and tidy . . . Now I can never find anything when I need it.
I: It's a big upheaval moving house.
Ie: Yes, I never realised that it would mean so much . . . that it would make such a difference. When we lived with my mother we always wanted a place of our own but . . . now we have it . . .
I: You haven't got used to being on your own.
Ie: I don't think I will ever get used to living in a flat . . . in a tower block. I never see anyone from one day to the next. There is nowhere to go . . . At home my mother was there all day . . . and the neighbours.
I: You find it lonely then. At your mother's there was always someone to talk to but here you don't seem to have anyone.
Ie: Yes. I don't even know who lives next door. I never see them. I am never out of the flat except to go shopping . . . there is no place else to go . . . and, of course, with the baby . . .
I: You almost feel like a prisoner.
Ie: That's it, a prisoner in solitary confinement. Sometimes I wish we had never left my mother's.
I: Although you want a home of your own you still miss living at your mother's a lot.
Ie: Yes, but I don't think it would be so bad if we had a proper house, but this flat . . . Then there's the worry of John being laid off again.
I: Is John your husband?
Ie: Yes.
I: Being cooped up on your own like this with the baby is bad enough but the thought of John being laid off makes it even worse.
Ie: Sometimes I just sit here and burst into tears . . .

These two interviews, while involving the same interviewee, differ markedly in the approaches adopted by the interviewers. In the first situation the interviewer sought to obtain information on a number of pre-established topics relating to the interviewee's background circumstances, such as the length of time she was married, her family, her husband's employment, the length of time she had been living in her present abode, etc. The interviewer and the data which he required was very much the dominating feature of the interview with the interviewee merely providing this information. Questioning was the skill used exclusively to direct the interviewee from one topic to the next, and each question was largely independent of the previous response. The interviewee was encouraged to furnish only information which was directly relevant to the needs of the interviewer and when she did begin to go further to explain how she would like a job, but could not get anyone to look after her baby since she did not know anyone in the area, she was expeditiously redirected by means of another question.

The second interview, however, centred very much upon Mrs Dillon and the difficulties which she was experiencing, with the interviewer staying, conversationally, much more in the background. Rather than directly leading the interviewee to areas which the interviewer wished to explore, the health visitor gently guided the interviewee and facilitated Mrs Dillon's discussion of matters which seemed important for her to ventilate. Unlike the first interview, in the second case only two questions were asked by the interviewer with the rest of her utterances taking the form of statements. These statements were reflections. While some inconsistencies have been identified by Dickson (1986) among the definitions which exist in the literature, reflections can be regarded as statements, in the interviewer's own words, which encapsulate and re-present the essence of the interviewee's previous message. Carl Rogers, the founder of Non-directive or Client-centred Counselling (Rogers, 1951, 1961, 1980), is commonly credited with coining the term although the technique can, of course, be used in other than a counselling context. An overview of this, together with contrasting theoretical perspectives on reflecting, is provided by Dickson (1986).

Apart from providing examples of this technique, these contrasting excerpts serve to make two points. Firstly, that interviewing is not necessarily concerned with the asking and answering of questions — although questions are commonly associated with this activity. Secondly, and related to this, the more general point that interviewers can differ markedly in the styles which they adopt.

STYLES OF INTERACTING

Style refers to the characteristic manner in which what is done is done. (A more thoroughgoing examination of the concept is provided by Norton, 1983.) A broad stylistic feature of interaction would seem to be that of directness, and approaches which differ in this respect have been commented upon in the contexts of teaching (Flanders, 1970), social work (Baldock and Prior, 1981), counselling and psychotherapy (Patterson, 1980) as well as interviewing (Stewart and Cash, 1985). Directness involves the degree of explicit influence and control exercised by, for example, the interviewer and, correspondingly, the extent to which the interviewee is constrained in responding. At one extreme of this dimension, the interviewer following a direct style will determine the form, content and pace of the transaction. At the other extreme these features will depend upon the concerns and predilections of the interviewee with the interviewer staying conversationally much more in the background, guiding and facilitating.

According to Benjamin (1981), the former style is typified by the use of interviewer leads, the latter by responses. Although acknowledging the difficulties of producing unambiguous definitions of these two terms, Benjamin (1981, p. 115) comments:

> When I respond, I speak in terms of what the interviewee has expressed. I react to the ideas and feelings he has communicated to me with something of my own. When I lead, I take over. I express ideas and feelings to which I expect the interviewee to react . . . When leading, I make use of my own life space; when responding, I tend more to utilize the life space of the interviewee. Interviewer responses keep the interviewee at the center of things; leads make the interviewer central.

Reflections can be categorised as responses, in this sense, and are contrasted with questions, for instance, which are a method of leading.

The particular style adopted by an interviewer is, in part, dependent upon the type of interview being conducted. A more direct, questioning style is most frequently adopted in circumstances where: the interviewee has accepted the interviewer's role as an interrogator; the information required is, basically, factual in nature; the amount of time which can be devoted to the interview is limited; a long-term relationship need not be established; and where the information is directly for the benefit of the interviewer. A more indirect, responsive style is used to best advantage when: the interviewee is the participant who stands to gain from the encounter; the information exchanged is affective; and, when the information is confused, fragmented and imperspicuous due, perhaps, to the fact that it involves a problem which the interviewee has never fully thought through before. Despite this distinction it would be inappropriate to assume that a more direct style of operating is never used under the latter conditions or that the question does not form part of the range of skills employed. Equally it would be erroneous to conclude that in the former circumstances a reflection statement should never be contemplated. Interviewers tend to vary in terms of the directness of their style depending upon the particular school of thought to which they adhere. Consequently some are likely to be more direct across a range of contexts than others. Nevertheless, as a generality, the above distinction holds.

While questions can be used within the second set of circumstances listed above, a reliance on this skill in a counselling-type interview has been strongly discouraged by Boy and Pine (1963). Questions, they argue, are often unrelated to the client's needs, being derived from the counsellor's frame of reference, and are often posed in a routine, unthinking manner. This view has also been echoed by Mucchielli (1983). Among their disadvantages in such a situation is the suggestion that they socialise the interviewee to speak only in response to a question and to merely reveal information which is directly requested. They also encourage the interviewee to let the interviewer take complete responsibility for the interaction, and for finding a satisfactory solution to the problems or difficulties experienced by the interviewee. A further drawback is that their use is less likely to foster a warm, understanding relationship, conducive to the exploration of important, but perhaps intimate and, for the interviewee, potentially embarrassing details.

Similar comments have been made by Dillon (1981), when challenging the effectiveness of questions as a means of promoting pupil discussion in the classroom. Far from producing the desired outcome, pupils tend to become dependent and passive, reacting only to further teacher questions. The utilisation of the skill of reflecting, as an alternative in such circumstances, has been proposed.

A number of empirical studies have actually compared the outcomes of an indirect, reflective style with a range of alternatives. Most of this research has an interviewing or counselling orientation. In some cases attitudes of both interviewees and external judges to interviewers manifesting contrasting styles have been sought. Silver (1970), for example, found that low-status interviewees felt much more comfortable with interviewers who displayed a reflective rather than a judgemental approach. Ellison and Firestone (1974) reported that subjects observing a reflective rather than an intrusive interviewer who controlled the direction and pace of the interview in a particularly assertive manner, indicated a greater willingness to reveal highly intimate details. This interviewer was also perceived as passive, easy-going and non-assertive. An interrogative approach in which further information was requested and a predictive style which required the interviewer accurately to predict interviewees' reactions in situations yet to be discussed, were the alternatives to reflecting examined by Turkat and Alpher (1984). Although impressions were based upon written transcripts, rather than actual interviews, those interviewers who used reflections were regarded as understanding their clients. Empathic understanding together with positive regard (two of the core conditions for effective counselling according to the client-centred school of thought) were related to the reflective style of interviewing in a study by Zimmer and Anderson (1968) which drew upon the opinions of external judges who viewed a video-taped counselling session.

Other researchers, rather than focusing upon attitudes, have investigated the effects of reflecting upon the actual behaviour of the interviewee. Some form of interviewee self-disclosure has commonly been measured. (For further information on self-disclosure see Chapter 9.) Powell (1968), for instance, carried out a study on the effects of reflections on subjects' positive and negative self-referent statements (i.e. statements about themselves). Approval-supportive and open-disclosure were the comparative experimental conditions. The former included interviewer statements supporting subjects' self-references while the latter referred to the provision of personal detail by the interviewer. Reflections were found to produce a significant increase in the number of negative, but not positive, self-references. Kennedy *et al.* (1971), while failing to make the distinction between positive and negative instances, similarly reported an increase in interviewee self-statements attributable to the use of this technique.

Vondracek (1969) and Beharry (1976) looked at the effects of reflecting not only on the amount of subjects' self-disclosure but on the degree of intimacy provided. More intimate detail was associated with the reflective style of interviewing in both cases. However, the contrasting conditions of interviewer self-disclosure and use of probes were equally effective in this respect. A similar result was reported by Mills (1983) in relation to rates, rather than quality, of self-disclosure. Feigenbaum (1977) produced an interesting finding concerning sex differences of subjects. While females disclosed more, and at more intimate levels, in response to reflections, male subjects scored significantly higher on both counts in response to interviewer self-disclosure.

An investigation which actually featured marital therapists and couples undergoing therapy was conducted by Cline *et al.* (1984). A complex relationship emerged involving not only sex but also social status of subjects. Thus therapist reflectiveness was found to correlate positively with subsequent changes in positive social interaction for middle-class husbands but with negative changes for both lower-class husbands and wives. It also related positively to changes in expression of personal feeling for middle-class husbands and wives. When assessed three months after the termination of therapy, a positive relationship emerged between therapist reflections and outcome measures of marital satisfaction but for lower-class husbands only.

In sum these findings would suggest that attitudes towards interviewers who use a reflective style are largely positive. At a more behavioural level, this technique would also seem capable of producing increases in both the amount and intimacy of information which interviewees reveal about themselves although it would not appear to be significantly more effective than alternative procedures such as interviewer self-disclosures or probes. In the actual therapeutic context there is some evidence linking reflecting with positive outcome measures for certain clients.

FACTUAL AND AFFECTIVE COMMUNICATION

While some have regarded reflecting as a unitary phenomenon, others have conceived of it as an 'umbrella' term encompassing a varying number of related processes. These include reflection of content (Nelson-Jones, 1983), reflecting experience (Brammer, 1973), content responses and affect responses (Danish and Hauer, 1973), and restatement (Auerswald, 1974). Perhaps the most commonly cited distinction is between reflection of feeling and paraphrasing. Although sharing a number of salient characteristics, these two skills have one important difference. In order to appreciate fully this difference some preliminary considerations are necessary. It should, firstly, be realised that many of the messages which we both send and receive provide two types of information. One type is basically factual or cognitive concerning ideas, places, people, objects, happenings, etc. The other is predominantly feeling or affective concerning our emotional states or attitudinal reactions to our environment. More accurately, messages vary along a continuum ranging from those which are factual to those which are affective. An example of the former would be, 'It's four-thirty' in response to a request for the correct time (and providing, of course, that the individual with the accurate timepiece does not suddenly realise that he is late for an appointment!). An example of the latter might be 'Oh no!' uttered by someone who has just been informed that a very close friend has just died suddenly. The utterance is not a denial that the unfortunate event has taken place; it is simply an expression of shocked grief, and is therefore affective. The majority of messages, however, contain elements of both types of information. Consider the following statement: 'I worked in the packing department at Hill's. All I did from nine o'clock until five was put tins into cardboard boxes, day after day after day.' The factual element of this statement is that the speaker worked in the packing department at Hill's each day from nine until five and his job consisted of packing tins into cardboard boxes. The affective element, of course, is that the job was found to be routine and boring.

The affective component of a message can take three basic forms:

(1) Explicit. Here the feeling aspect is explicitly stated in the verbal content. For example, 'I am so happy'.
(2) Implicit. In this case the affective information is implicitly contained in what is said. Thus when a patient who has recently been bereaved says, listlessly, 'Some days I just don't get up . . . yet I am always tired. I don't have the energy to do anything . . . I can't even concentrate to read. I keep thinking that I will never be able to manage on my own. Sometimes I think that it would have been better if I had been taken as well . . .', depression is a very obvious emotional message contained within the facts although no 'feeling words' are used to label it.
(3) Inferred. The affective component of a message can be inferred from the manner in which the verbal content is delivered — from the nonverbal and paralinguistic accompaniment. Research has shown that when the verbal and nonverbal/paralinguistic elements of an emotional or attitudinal message conflict as, for example, when someone says irately, 'I am not angry', we are more inclined to base our judgements on the latter source of information (Collier, 1985). In the case of inferred feelings, unlike the previous two, the verbal content of the message does not play a part.

It is, on occasion, a rather perplexing activity trying to decode accurately the affective content when it has not been explicitly stated and, in these cases, caution is recommended. This would seem to be particularly good advice in the case of some types of nonverbal behaviour. While facial expressions are amenable to intentional manipulation, Heslin and Patterson (1982) suggested that they may be more accurate indicators of emotional state than certain body movements or paralinguistic cues. Nevertheless, reflecting nebulous feelings expressed in these less obvious ways can often be not only more difficult but potentially more beneficial (Egan, 1982).

We thus convey and receive both factual and affective information. Paraphrasing involves mirroring-back, primarily, the factual content of a message while reflection of feeling, as the name suggests, focuses upon the affective element.

FUNCTIONS OF REFLECTING

Reflecting serves a number of functions, the most important of which will now be presented. Some of these have been identified by Ivey and Authier (1978), Brammer and Shostrom (1977) and Pietrofesa *et al*. (1978). They are:

(1) To demonstrate an interest in and involvement with the interviewee.
(2) To indicate close attention by the interviewer to what is being communicated.
(3) To show that the interviewer is trying to understand fully the interviewee and what he is saying.
(4) To check the interviewer's perceptions and ensure that his understanding is accurate.
(5) To facilitate the interviewee's comprehension of the issues involved and clarify his own thoughts on those matters.
(6) To focus attention upon particular aspects and encourage further exploration.
(7) To communicate a deep concern for that which the interviewee considers to be important.
(8) To place the major emphasis upon the interviewee rather than the interviewer in the interview situation.
(9) To indicate that it is acceptable for the interviewee to have and express feelings in this situation and to facilitate their ventilation.
(10) To help the interviewee to 'own' his feelings.
(11) To enable the interviewee to realise that feelings can be an important cause of behaviour.

(12) To help the interviewee to scrutinise underlying reasons and motives.
(13) To demonstrate the interviewer's ability to empathise with the interviewee.

While a number of these functions are common to both paraphrasing and reflection of feeling, some are more obviously relevant to one than the other. These will be discussed in further detail, as they apply more directly to either paraphrasing or reflection of feeling, in the respective sections which follow.

PARAPHRASING

Paraphrasing is sometimes also referred to as 'reflection of content'. It can be defined as the process of mirroring or feeding-back to the interviewee, in the interviewer's own words, the essence of the interviewee's previous statement, the emphasis being upon factual material (e.g. thoughts, ideas, descriptions etc.) rather than upon affect. There are three important elements of the definition.

Firstly, the paraphrase should be couched in the interviewer's own words. It is not simply concerned with repeating what has just been said. It may be recalled (from Chapter 4) that one type of probing technique, echoing, involved the repetition of the interviewee's previous statement, or a part of it. This, however, does not constitute a paraphrase. If, when paraphrasing, the interviewer continually repeats the interviewee's words it can quickly lead to the latter becoming frustrated. Brammer and Shostrom (1977, p. 182), commenting on this point, say that 'perhaps, the most glaring reflection error of the novice counsellor is to express his reflection in words already used by the client'. Instead, the interviewer should respond using his own terms, perhaps using synonyms, while not, of course, violating or misrepresenting the meaning of the interviewee's communication.

Secondly, the paraphrase should contain the essential component of the previous message. This requires the interviewer to identify the core of the statement which is embedded in the verbiage, to ask himself, 'What is this person really saying?' It should, therefore, not be assumed that the paraphrase must encompass everything that has just been said, some of which may well be tangential.

Thirdly, paraphrasing is fundamentally concerned with reflecting the factual information received. It largely ignores feelings which may also have been communicated. The word 'largely' is used purposefully, however, since it is often difficult to eliminate affective aspects entirely.

An excerpt from the transcript of an interview reported by Pietrofesa *et al.* (1978, pp. 269–70) neatly demonstrates how this skill can be used to good effect.

Client: I am not sure that I should try to visit Shelly. She and I had a falling out not too long ago.
Counsellor: You had an argument with her recently.
Client: Well, I wrote to her and she didn't answer.
Counsellor: So it is still unresolved.
Client: I also wrote to Maureen, and she said that Shelly was in one of her moods of not communicating with anyone, even her mother. But I don't know.
Counsellor: Sounds like Shelly has cut off a lot of people including you.
Client: Yes, but . . . I did talk to her on the phone when I got back and she sounded friendly . . . but I still feel uneasy about seeing her, I don't know that she'd really want to see me because we broke apart.
Counsellor: Even though she sounded okay, you still are not convinced she wants to see you.
Client: Yeah, I dated a fellow that she had been going out with, but . . . I thought she was all through with him . . . but she got mad at me and I felt bad about it.
Counsellor: She had stopped seeing him, so you thought it was okay to date him but you were mistaken.

The examples of paraphrasing included in this excerpt manifest 'in action' some of the defining characteristics of the skill mentioned previously. They also help to illustrate some of the functions of paraphrasing.

By demonstrating that he can accurately reproduce the fundamentally important part of the interviewee's statement, the interviewer 'proves' that he has been attending single-mindedly to the interviewee, that he feels it is important to understand fully what the interviewee is trying to relate, and that he has, in fact, achieved this understanding. By so doing, he also makes the interviewee aware of the fact that he is interested in and accepts him and is quite prepared to become involved with him and his problem. From the interviewer's point of view the subsequent reaction of the interviewee to his paraphrase also confirms (assuming that it is accurate) that he is on the proper 'wavelength'. In the classroom, teachers often use paraphrases for this purpose when, in response to a question, a pupil produces a rather involved and, perhaps, disjointed response. By so doing they not only establish that they have fully understood what was said, but they also clarify the information provided for the rest of the class. Again, it is not uncommon to hear someone who has just asked for and received directions of how to get to a particular place, paraphrase back what he has been told, e.g. 'So I go to the end of the road, turn right, second on the left, and then right again'. In this case paraphrasing helps both to check accuracy and promote the memorisation of the data.

By encapsulating and unobtrusively presenting to the interviewee in a clear and unambiguous manner a salient facet of that which the latter has previously communicated, the interviewer also gently guides and encourages him to continue with this theme and to explore it at greater depth. Since the interviewee's thoughts, especially when dealing with an apparently intractable problem, are often inchoate and ambiguous, an accurate paraphrase, by condensing and crystallising what has been said, can often help the interviewee to see more clearly the exigencies of his predicament. Paraphrasing also enables the interviewer to keep the interviewee and his concerns, rather than himself, in the forefront, by responding and guiding rather than leading and directing. It has often been said that a good referee is one who controls the game without appearing to dominate it. In many situations the same holds true for a good interviewer. Paraphrasing is one method of accomplishing this. The emphasis is firmly placed upon the interviewee. Using Benjamin's (1981) terminology, the interviewer uses the interviewee's life space rather than his own. By keeping the focus upon those issues which the interviewee wants to ventilate, the interviewer also says, metaphorically, that he acknowledges their import for the interviewee and his willingness to make them his concern also.

Research relating to paraphrasing

The amount of research studies which have centred upon the skill of reflecting in general, and paraphrasing in particular, is limited. The majority of the suggestions and recommendations concerning the skill have been based upon theoretical dictates and also the experiences of those practitioners who have employed and 'tested' the skill in the field. Some research investigations, however, have been conducted. For the most part these have been experimental in design, have been conducted in the laboratory, and have sought to establish the effects of paraphrasing upon various measures of interviewees' verbal behaviour.

In some cases, though, paraphrases are defined in such a way as to include affective material (e.g. Hoffnung, 1969), while in others affective content is not explicitly excluded (e.g. Kennedy and Zimmer, 1968; Haase and Di Mattia, 1976). These quirks should be kept in mind when interpreting the following findings. Kennedy and Zimmer (1968) reported an increase in subjects' self-referenced statements attributable to paraphrasing, while similar findings featuring self-referenced affective statements were noted by both Hoffnung (1969) and Haase and Di Mattia (1976). According to Citkowitz (1975), on the other hand, this skill had only limited effect in this respect although there was a tendency for the association to be more pronounced when initial levels of self-referenced affect statements were relatively high. The subjects in this experiment were chronic schizophrenic inpatients and the data were collected during clinical-type interviews.

The distinction between the affective and the factual has been more explicitly acknowledged by others who have researched paraphrasing. Waskow (1962), for instance, investigated the outcome of selective interviewer responding on the factual and affective aspects of subjects' communication in a psychotherapy-like interview. It emerged that a significantly higher percentage of factual responses was given by those subjects who had their contributions paraphrased. Auerswald (1974) and Hill and Gormally (1977) produced more disappointing findings. In both cases, however, paraphrasing took place on an essentially random basis. Affective responses by subjects were also selected as the dependent variable.

The few studies which have considered the effects of this technique on attitudes towards the interviewer rather than behavioural changes on the part of the interviewee, have reported largely favourable outcomes. A positive relationship was detailed by Dickson (1981), between the proportion of paraphrases to questions asked by employment advisory personnel and ratings of interviewer competency provided by independent, experienced judges. A comparable outcome emerged when client perceptions of interviewer effectiveness were examined by Nagata *et al.* (1983).

It would therefore seem that when paraphrases are used contingently and focus upon factual aspects of communication, interviewees' verbal performance can be modified accordingly. In addition paraphrasing seems to promote favourable judgements of the interviewer by both interviewees and external judges. Counselling trainees have also indicated that this is one of the skills which they found most useful in their interviews (Spooner, 1976).

REFLECTION OF FEELING

Reflection of feeling can be defined as the process of feeding-back to the interviewee, in the interviewer's own words, the essence of the interviewee's previous statement, the emphasis being upon feelings expressed rather than cognitive content. The similarity between this definition and that of paraphrasing will be noted and many of the features of the latter, outlined in the previous section of the chapter, are applicable. The major difference between the two definitions is, of course, the concern with affective matters peculiar to reflection of feeling. Ivey and Authier (1978, p. 82) regard the most important elements of the skill to be: '(1) the direct labelling of the emotional state of the client and (2) some reference to the client via a name or personal pronoun; these may be supplemented by (3) present tense reflection of here and now states for more powerful experiencing (of course, past or future tense may also be used) . . .'

A necessary prerequisite for the successful use of this skill is the ability to identify accurately and label the feelings being expressed by the interviewee. Unless this initial procedure can be adequately accomplished, the likelihood that the subsequent reflection of those feelings will achieve its desired purpose will be greatly reduced. It has already been mentioned, in an earlier section of the present chapter, that feelings may be explicitly stated, may be implied from what is said or may be inferred from nonverbal and paralinguistic cues. Concerning the latter, Ekman and Friesen (1975) described particular facial expressions associated with each of six basic emotions. These were: (1) happiness; (2) sadness; (3) fear; (4) anger; (5) surprise. (6) disgust. Tomkins (1963), among others, suggested that a further three affective states — interest, contempt and shame — could be identified in a similar way but these have not been as consistently established. Davitz (1964) conducted a number of experiments in which actors read verbally-neutral sentences in such a way as to convey different emotions. Tapes of these were presented to judges for decoding. One finding which emerged was that some emotions were more readily identifiable than others from nonverbal characteristics of speech. Fear and anger were two which were most easily recognisable. Research in this area has revealed that, in general terms, some people are more adept at identifying emotions from nonverbal features than are others. As a group, females tend to be more successful than males (Heslin and Patterson, 1982). It would also seem possible to train individuals to improve their performance.

While the terms 'feelings' and 'emotions' are sometimes used synonymously, feelings often refer to more subtle emotional or attitudinal states. For this reason they are typically more difficult to label accurately. It has been suggested that one cause of this difficulty, especially with the novice interviewer, is an insufficient repertoire of feeling terms which makes fine discrimination and identification problematic. Pietrofesa *et al.* (1978) have, therefore, recommended that interviewers memorise a number of broad categories of feeling words such as happy, sad, strong, weak, angry, confused and afraid. Each of these can be expressed at either a high, medium or a low level of intensity. Thus, for example, strongly-expressed happiness is ecstacy; at a medium level it is excitement; and at a low level it is pleasure. By initially determining the broad category and then the intensity level, subtle feelings can, more easily, be deciphered and hence the process of reflecting them back facilitated.

As previously mentioned, the reflection of those nebulous feelings which are either implied or inferred, is typically more beneficial than those which are more obviously stated. The fact that the former are difficult for the interviewer to grasp, means that they are often equally difficult for the interviewee to comprehend fully. Focusing upon such feelings by means of reflection can, therefore, help the interviewee to obtain a more complete understanding of the feeling states he is experiencing. Owing to the possibilities of misunderstanding, however, it is often prudent for the interviewer to exercise caution in these cases by prefacing the reflection with a phrase such as 'It seems to me that you feel . . . ', rather than baldly stating, 'You feel . . . '

The transcript of part of a counselling session reported by Pietrofesa *et al.* (1978, p. 274) provides some useful examples of the use of the skill of reflection of feeling. A brief excerpt follows:

Client (1): I guess I've always lived in someone else's shadow. New interests were more or less forced upon me. Their hobbies were my hobbies. That type of thing. I don't even know what my hobbies are (heavy laughter) . . . and that to me is really sad.

Counsellor (1): You feel separated from yourself and sad about it.

Client (2): Yeah . . . Their ideas and so forth . . . and now, oh boy, I really feel lost.

Counsellor (2): You seem confused about who Judy is . . .

Client (3): I've wondered about that. It didn't really . . . what I felt and what I thought really didn't seem to matter to the most important people in my life . . . and maybe that's the part that really hurts. Whenever I tried to exert myself, I always got — phew — squashed down.

Counsellor (3): You felt squashed and hurt by people closest to you.

The reader should compare the counsellor responses in this excerpt with the examples of paraphrases provided in the previous section. It will be noted that in the present case the counsellor's primary focus is upon the feelings being conveyed by the client. The intent is to encourage further exploration and understanding of them. Although the above examples were drawn from a counselling session it should, of course, be realised that the use of this skill is not confined to that context. It will be recalled that one type of question used by teachers, doctors, nurses and careers guidance personnel, among others, relates to the affective domain. Reflection of feeling is therefore applicable in all these situations as a means of promoting further examination of feelings, emotions and attitudes.

The skill of reflection of feeling shares a number of functions in common with the skill of paraphrasing. Thus by reflecting feeling the interviewer demonstrates his attention to and interest in the interviewee. The use of the skill helps the interviewee to feel understood, to feel that both he and his concerns are important and respected. It also acts as a means whereby the interviewer can check the accuracy of his understanding. Going beyond these common functions, however, reflection of feeling indicates to the interviewee that it is acceptable for him to have and express his feelings in that situation. This is important, since in many everyday conversations the factual element of communication is stressed to the neglect, and even active avoidance, of the affective dimension. In our society it is normally considered inappropriate to express deep personal feelings to any but very intimate acquaintances.

By reflecting the interviewee's feelings an interviewer acknowledges the other person's right to have such feelings and also confirms the acceptability of expressing them during that particular interaction. When performed accurately the skill further serves to encourage exploration and promote understanding of aspects of the interviewee's affective state. By reflecting back the central feeling element of his previous statement, the interviewee is enabled to think more clearly and objectively about issues which previously were vague and confused.

Another function of reflection of feeling mentioned by Brammer and Shostrom (1977), is to help the interviewee to 'own' his feelings

— to appreciate that ultimately he is the source of, and can take responsibility for them. Various ploys commonly used in order to disown feelings have been outlined by Passons (1975). These include speaking in the third rather than the first person (e.g. 'One gets rather annoyed . . .'). Because reflections frequently take the form of a statement beginning, 'You feel that . . .', interviewees are helped to examine and identify underlying reasons and motives for behaviour which they may not, previously, have been completely aware of. They are also brought to realise that feelings can have an important causal influence upon action. Thus someone who, for example, holds a strong negative attitude towards coloured people is likely to behave uncompromisingly towards them. This effect can also be mediated by perception since such a person is less likely to 'see' examples of laudable actions by coloured people which would negate their prejudiced attitude. Rather, they are more inclined to perceive and believe reports of despicable behaviour which reinforce their negative feelings towards this particular minority group. Again, if ever in the company of a coloured person the effects of such feelings may influence the coloured person to be less than cordial, supporting the feeling held which, in turn, will further affect perception and behaviour. Allowing an individual to examine his feelings by means of reflection can, therefore, enable him to realise how much feelings can influence not only his own, but other people's behaviour.

The use of this skill can also serve to foster a facilitative relationship with the interviewee. It has been found that interviewers who reflect feeling accurately tend to be regarded as being empathic. With such an interviewer the interviewee feels deeply understood, sensing that the interviewer is with him and is able to perceive the world from his, the interviewee's, frame of reference. The interviewee in such a relationship is more likely to be motivated to divulge information which is important and personally meaningful.

Reflection of feeling is, therefore, a very useful skill for any interactor, professional or otherwise, to have in his repertoire. It is, however, one which many novices initially find difficult to master. Brammer and Shostrom (1977) have listed some problems associated with it. Anyone attempting to use the skill should be aware of the dangers of reflecting inaccurately. By reflecting feelings which were not expressed, the difficulties experienced by an interviewee may be compounded and, for example in crisis intervention, this may have serious consequences. Another practice which should be avoided is bringing interviewee feelings to the surface but not assisting the interviewee to examine them in further detail. This can sometimes happen at the end of an interview when the interviewer leaves the interviewee 'in mid-air'. This can be avoided by applying proper closure procedures (see Chapter 6).

There is a tendency among many inexperienced practitioners to begin their reflection consistently with a phrase such as 'You feel . . . ' The monotonous use of some such introduction can appear mechanical and indeed 'unfeeling' and can have an adverse effect on the interviewee. For this reason a greater variety of types of statement should be developed. Other malpractices include an over-reliance upon the words of the interviewee by simply repeating back what he said. At the same time, while using his own words the interviewer should be careful to ensure that the language which he uses is appropriate to the interviewee and the situation. He should also guard against going beyond what was actually communicated by including unwarranted suppositions or speculations in his reflection. Conversely, the reflective statement should not neglect any important aspect of the affective message of the interviewee. Perhaps one of the most difficult features of the skill is trying to match the depth of feeling included in the reflection to that initially expressed. If the level of feeling of the reflection is too shallow the interviewee is less likely to feel fully understood or inclined to examine these issues more profoundly. If it is too deep the interviewee may feel threatened, resulting in denial and alienation. This, together with the other potential pitfalls mentioned above, can only be overcome by careful practice coupled with a critical awareness of one's performance.

Research related to reflection of feeling

As with paraphrasing, the various recommendations concerning the use of reflection of feeling have, for the most part, been based upon theory and practical experience rather than research findings. Again studies which have featured this skill can be divided into two major categories: firstly, experiments, largely laboratory-based, designed to identify effects on subjects' verbal behaviour; secondly, those which have attempted to relate the use of the technique to judgements, by either interviewees or observers, of interviewers in terms of such attributes as empathy, warmth, respect, etc. In many instances both types of dependent variable have featured in the same investigation.

A significant relationship between reflection of feeling and ratings of empathic understanding emerged in a piece of research conducted by Uhlemann *et al.* (1976). These ratings were provided by external judges and were based upon both written responses and audio-recordings of actual interviews. Interviewers who reflected feelings not yet named by the interviewee were regarded by them as being more expert and trustworthy, according to Ehrlich *et al.* (1979). A similar procedure, labelled 'sensing unstated feelings' by Nagata *et al.* (1983), emerged as a significant predictor of counsellor effectiveness when assessed by surrogate clients following a counselling-type interview. However, Highlen and Baccus (1977) failed to reveal any significant differences in clients' perceptions of counselling climate, counsellor comfort or personal satisfaction between clients allocated to a reflection of feeling and to a probe treatment.

The effects of reflections of feeling on interviewees' affective self-reference statements have been explored by Merbaum (1963), Barnabei *et al.* (1974), Highlen and Baccus (1977), and Highlen and Nicholas (1978), among others. With the exception of Barnabei *et al.* (1974), this interviewing skill was found to promote substantial increases in affective self-talk by subjects. Highlen and Nicholas (1978), however, combined reflections of feeling with interviewer self-referenced affect statements in such a way that it is impossible to attribute the outcome solely to the influence of the former. One possible explanation for the failure by Barnabei *et al.* (1974) to produce a positive finding could reside in the fact that reflections of feeling were administered in a random or non-contingent manner. It will be recalled that paraphrases used in this indiscriminate way were equally ineffective in producing increases in self-referenced statements. A fuller review of research on reflecting feeling and paraphrasing is provided by Dickson (1986).

OVERVIEW

The following points, which should be remembered when adopting a reflective style, apply both to the skills of paraphrasing and reflection of feeling. Some of them have already been mentioned but their importance makes it unnecessary to apologise for their repetition. The basic guidelines for reflecting are:

(1) Use your own words. Reflecting is not merely a process of echoing back the words of the interviewee. The interviewer should strive rather to reformulate the message in his own words.
(2) Do not go beyond the information communicated by the interviewee. Remember, reflecting is a process of feeding-back only

information already given by the interviewee. For this reason when using the skill, the interviewer should not include speculations or suppositions which represent the interviewer's attempt to impose his own meaning on what was communicated, and while based upon it, may not be strictly warranted by it. The interviewer, therefore, when reflecting, should not try to psychoanalyse; for example:

Interviewee: I suppose I have never had a successful relationship with men. I never seemed to get on with my father when I was a child . . . I always had problems with the male teachers when I was at school . . .

Interviewer: You saw the male teachers as extensions of your father.

Note — this statement by the interviewer is *not* a reflection. It is an interpretation which goes beyond what was said by the interviewee.

(3) Be concise. The objective is not to include everything which the interviewee has said but to select what appear to be the most salient elements of the message. It is only this core feature, or features, which the interviewer should strive to reflect — the essence of what the interviewee has been trying to communicate. Reflections tend to be short statements rather than long, involved and rambling, although the actual length will obviously vary depending upon the information provided by the interviewee.

(4) Be specific. It will be recalled that one of the functions of reflecting is to promote understanding. Frequently an interviewee, perhaps because he has never previously fully thought through a particular issue, will tend to express himself in a rather vague, confused and abstract manner. It is more beneficial if, when reflecting, the interviewer tries to be as concrete and specific as possible, thereby ensuring that both he, and indeed the interviewee, successfully comprehend what is being said.

(5) Be accurate. If an interviewer is frequently inaccurate in his reflections the interviewee will quickly realise that further prolongation of the interaction is pointless, since the interviewer does not seem able to grasp what he is trying to convey. This does not mean that the occasional inaccuracy is disastrous. In such a case the interviewee, realising the interviewer's determination to grasp what he is trying to relate, will generally be motivated to provide additional information and rectify the misconception. Accuracy depends upon careful listening (see Chapter 8). While the interviewee is talking the interviewer should be listening single-mindedly rather than considering what to say next or engaging in other thoughts less directly relevant to the interview.

(6) Do not over-use reflections. It should not be thought that reflections must necessarily be used in response to every interviewee statement. To attempt to do so may restrict the interviewee rather than help him forward. Reflections can be used in conjunction with the other skills which the interviewer should have at his disposal (e.g. questioning, reinforcing, self-disclosure, etc.). In some instances it is only after rapport has been established that reflection of feeling can be used without the interviewee feeling awkward or threatened.
(7) Reflections of feeling and paraphrases typically reflect what has been contained in the interviewee's immediately preceding statement. It is possible, and indeed desirable on occasion, for reflections to be wider-ranging and to cover a number of interviewee statements. The interviewer may wish, for example, at the end of the interview, to reflect the facts and feelings expressed by the interviewee during it. Reflections such as these, which have a broader perspective, are called summaries of content and summaries of feeling, and are a useful means of identifying themes expressed by the interviewee during the interview, or parts of it.,
(8) It has been stated that reflection contains two component skills — reflection of feeling and paraphrasing. It is, of course, possible to combine both factual and feeling material in a single reflection if the interviewer feels that this is the most appropriate response at that particular time. Carkhuff (1973) suggests that by combining both feelings and facts in a format such as, 'You feel . . . because . . . ', one type of information complements the other and enables the interviewee to perceive the relationship between them.

6

Set Induction and Closure

INTRODUCTION

Beginnings and endings are equally important parameters within which social interaction takes place, in that they are structured, formalised sequences during which interactors have a greater opportunity to make important points or create an effective impact on others. How we greet, and part from, others has long been recognised as crucial to the development and maintenance of relationships (e.g. Roth, 1889).

Although in this chapter set induction and closure will be discussed separately, these are complementary skills within any interaction. This can be exemplified by examining the behaviours identified by Kendon and Ferber (1973) as being associated with the three main phases involved in both greetings and partings between friends:

A. Distant phase. When two friends are at a distance, but within sight, the behaviours displayed include hand waving, eyebrow flashing (raising both eyebrows), smiling, head tossing and direct eye contact.
B. Medium phase. When the friends are at a closer, interim distance, they avoid eye contact, smile and engage in a range of grooming (self-touching) behaviours.
C. Close phase. At this stage the friends will again engage in direct eye contact, smile, make appropriate verbalisations, and may touch one another (shake hands, hug or kiss).

During greetings the sequence is ABC, while during partings the reverse sequence CBA, operates. At the greeting stage the sequence seems to underline the increased availability of the participants for interaction, whereas during parting it emphasises the decreasing accessibility for interaction (Goffman, 1972).

SET INDUCTION

Anyone who is familiar with the world of athletics will be aware of the instructions given by the starter to the competitors before a race — 'On your marks. Get set. Go!' By telling the athletes to get set, the starter is preparing them for his final signal, and allowing them to become both mentally and physically ready for the impending take-off, which they know is about to follow. This simple example is a good introduction to the skill of set induction.

Set induction is the term used by psychologists to describe that which occurs when 'an organism is usually prepared at any moment for the stimuli it is going to receive and the responses it is going to make' (Woodworth and Marquis, 1949, p. 298). In other words, set induction establishes in the individual a state of readiness, involves gaining attention and arousing motivation, as well as providing guidelines about that which is to follow.

Set induction is a skill which is widely used, in various forms, in social interaction. At a simple level it may involve two people discussing local gossip, where, to stimulate the listener's attention, they may use phrases such as: 'Wait until you hear this . . . '; 'You'll never believe what happened today . . . '; 'Have you heard the latest . . . '

At another level, on television and at the cinema, there are usually 'trailers' advertising forthcoming attractions in an exciting and dramatic fashion, and here again the object is to arouse interest in what is to follow. Indeed, television programmes usually contain a fair degree of set induction in themselves, employing appropriate music and accompanying action, to stimulate the viewer to stay with the programme. Other examples of set induction in the media include newspaper headlines, the front cover of magazines indicating what stories appear inside and quotations from press reviews on the back cover of books.

The term 'set' has many applications in our everyday lives. For example, how a table is set will reveal quite a lot about the forthcoming meal — how many people will be eating, how many courses there will be and how formal the behaviour of the diners is likely to be. Other uses of the term set include 'It's a set up', 'Are you all set?' and 'Is the alarm set?' In all of these instances, preparation for some form of activity which is to follow is the central theme, and this is the main thrust of the skill of set induction.

In relation to social interaction, the induction of an appropriate set can be defined as the initial strategy utilised in order to establish a frame of reference, deliberately designed to facilitate the development of a communicative link between the expectations of the participants and the realities of the situation. Set induction can therefore be a long, or a short, process depending upon the context of the interaction. It can involve establishing rapport, arousing motivation, establishing expectations and evaluating these in relation to realistic outcomes, and outlining the nature and purpose of the forthcoming interaction.

FUNCTIONS OF SET INDUCTION

Set induction involves more than simply giving a brief introduction at the beginning of a social encounter. It may involve a large number of different activities, depending upon the context in which set is to be induced. However, the main purposes in employing this skill in interpersonal interaction can be listed as follows:

1. To induce in participants a state of readiness appropriate to the task which is to follow, through establishing rapport, gaining attention and arousing motivation.
2. To ascertain the expectations of the participants and the extent of their knowledge about the topic to be considered.
3. To indicate to participants what might be reasonable objectives for the task to follow.
4. To explain to participants what one's functions are, and what limitations may accompany these functions.
5. To establish links with previous encounters (during follow-up sessions).
6. To ascertain the extent of the participants' knowledge of the topic to be discussed.

These are the main generic functions of the skill of set induction. However, depending upon the nature of the interaction, the functions of set induction will vary, so that different techniques will accordingly be employed in order to achieve them. Thus, for example, a helper will use different behaviours to open a counselling session, from a teacher introducing a classroom lesson. There are several types of set which can be put into operation, and each type will be more relevant in one social situation than another, in inducing an appropriate set. These types of set induction are outlined in the following section.

FACTORS INFLUENCING SET INDUCTION

The process of set induction can take an infinite variety of forms both between, and within, social settings. The set used will be influenced by, amongst other things, the subject matter to be discussed, the time available, the time of day, the location of the encounter and the personality experience and socio-economic background of the interactors. These factors should all be borne in mind when evaluating the main techniques for inducing set.

Motivational set

The skill of set induction can be employed in order to gain attention and arouse motivation at the beginning of an interaction. In many situations, particularly in learning environments, it is very important to gain the attention of participants at the outset, so that the task may proceed as smoothly as possible. Otherwise the main objectives of the interaction may be more difficult to achieve. Garramone (1984), for example, found that the way individuals perceive and assimilate information is affected by their initial motivation to attend. A number of methods can be used to induce motivational set.

The use of novel stimuli

Psychologists have long recognised the potency of a novel, or unusual, stimulus as a method for gaining the attention of individuals. There is well-documented research evidence to indicate that the introduction of novel stimuli is an effective technique for arousing interest. Berlyne (1951), working with students, naval ratings and RAF air crews, found that a recently-changed stimulus was more likely to be responded to than one which had remained unchanged for some time. Smock and Holt (1962) carried out a study with 22 boys and 22 girls aged between six and eight years, all in the first grade of a rural elementary school in Indiana. They found that variation in sensory focus was more successful in gaining attention than was constancy of focus. Similarly Paradowski (1967) found that the introduction of novel stimuli increased the achievement of 52 undergraduate students on tests of recall of information. In the sphere of selling, Busch and Wilson (1976) found that when the salesperson had a product which was new or unique, it was easier to secure a sale.

These findings, with widely differing populations, illustrate the efficacy of a new, or unusual, stimulus, both in gaining attention and in increasing retention of information. The implications of these results for learning are fairly obvious. There are a large number of audio-visual aids which can be used in order to arouse motivation. These may be diagrammatic (such as a picture or drawing), real objects, or audio-visual recordings (such as film-strips, slides or tape recordings). By focusing on any of these aids at the outset, the learning environment should be enriched accordingly. A word of caution is needed here, however, in that the stimulus utilised should be related to the task in hand. As Turney *et al.* (1976, p. 92) point out, 'Gimmickry is to be avoided, for unconnected novelty may secure short-term attending . . . but fail to establish an appropriate set enduring for the task'.

The posing of an intriguing problem

Employed at the beginning of an interaction sequence this can engage the listeners' interest immediately, and hold it for a long time if they are required to solve the problem. For example, a science teacher at the start of a lesson places a container full of water in front of the pupils. He then holds a brick over the container, telling pupils to observe carefully what is about to take place. The brick is slowly immersed in the container, and the displaced water collected in a separate vessel. He then asks pupils to explain what has happened, and why. This then leads to a discussion of Archimedes' Principle.

Studies by Allen (1970) and Peeck (1970) have shown that the use of thought-provoking problems at the beginning of lessons is related to increased pupil achievement. However, this technique can be applied to many settings, and is equally applicable whether the problem posed is a technical or a social one. Furthermore, it does not really matter whether or not the problem has a correct solution. The idea here is to establish immediate involvement and participation at either an overt or covert level. The use of case histories can be particularly relevant in this respect, providing the case outlined is applicable to the audience addressed. Thus, for example, a tutor of trainee counsellors may relate the problems presented to him by a difficult client, and ask the trainees how they would have handled the situation which he has described to them.

Making a controversial or provocative statement

This can also serve quickly to encourage participation. For example: at the beginning of a sociology seminar, incorporating both males and females, the lecturer announces that in his view married women should only be allowed to obtain employment once male unemployment has been eliminated. In any case, he continues, the women's natural place is in the home. This then leads to a discussion of the role of women in society.

Following the lecturer's statement it is very likely that some females will feel motivated to respond immediately, and in this way discussion can be encouraged. However, this method of inducing set must be carefully thought out, since the object of the exercise is to provoke comment, rather than aggression, on the part of the listener. With very sensitive topics. or volatile audiences, great caution should be exercised when using this technique!

The initial behaviour of the interactors

This will influence the set which is induced. The adoption of unexpected, or unusual, behaviour can be a powerful method for gaining attention. For example, a teacher may sit with the class, move about the room without speaking, or act out a short story with conviction and expression, in order to stimulate pupils to attend to his lesson. A similar approach is also used by many comedians at the beginning of their stage show, in order to set the audience for the comedy to follow.

This technique for arousing motivation is most successful where the 'initial behaviour' referred to above departs from the normal pattern. As Berlyne (1960) points out, all humans have a basic cognitive structure, which will strive to accommodate new information of an unexpected nature. It is, therefore, the element of behavioural surprise which is central to the efficacy of this method, since this stimulates the individual's attentiveness, and hence facilitates the process of assimilation.

Indeed all of the methods for inducing motivational set will involve an aspect of curiosity arousal. The novelty of a stimulus will influence its degree of effectiveness in gaining attention. Another factor which will determine the efficacy of a stimulus in gaining attention is its intensity. A strong stimulus is more likely to be noticed than is a weak one. Hence a loud noise, a bright light or a large object will usually stimulate attention much more quickly than a faint noise, a dim light or a small object.

Finally, in relation to motivational set, it should be remembered that to catch attention is one thing, but to hold it for an extended period of time is another. As was mentioned earlier, any technique or device employed to induce motivational set should be appropriate for the task in hand. Gimmickry will quickly lose appeal, if it is unrelated to any underlying and enduring theme which will be of interest to those in whom set has been induced. Thus the follow-up to motivational set should be carefully planned to capitalise on the initial attentiveness of participants.

Social set

In order to establish a good rapport with another person, before proceeding with the main business of the interaction, it is usually desirable to employ a number of 'social' techniques. Such techniques serve to introduce a 'human' element into the encounter, and often facilitate the achievement of the main objectives involved. The induction of an appropriate social set is, therefore, often an important preliminary to the more substantive issues which are to be discussed later, in that it serves to establish a good, amicable, working relationship between the participants at the beginning of the interaction. The main techniques which can be employed in order to induce a good social set are as follows:

The initial approach of an individual

This will induce a certain type of set in the other participants, depending upon what this approach is. The use of social reinforcement, in a friendly manner, will serve to make the other person feel more at ease in most situations. Social reinforcement techniques include a handshake, smile, welcoming remarks, tone of voice and eye contact. Kendon and Ferber (1973) point out that 'In the manner in which the greeting ritual is performed, the greeters signal to each other their respective social status, their degree of familiarity, their degree of liking for one another, and also, very often, what roles they will play in the encounter that is about to begin' (pp. 592–3).

Thus the manner in which professionals greet their clients is of considerable importance. Krivonos and Knapp (1975) found that the use of appropriate greeting behaviour has a considerable influence on the success of the ensuing interaction. An important aspect here is the use of the client's name, which leads to a more favourable evaluation of the interviewer by the client (Dell and Schmidt, 1976; Rackham and Morgan, 1977). There is some evidence from the medical field that professionals could improve their greeting behaviour. Studies of health visiting have shown that patients often did not know the name of their health visitor (Robinson, 1982), and that patients complained about the lack of welcome given by health visitors during visits to clinics (Field *et al.*, 1982). Likewise, Maguire and Rutter (1976) found that doctors frequently failed to introduce themselves at the beginning of an encounter with a patient.

It is difficult to be prescriptive about the greeting ritual, however, since this is influenced by factors such as the acquaintance of the people involved, their respective roles, the function of the interaction, the location, and the sex of the interactors. For example, Greenbaum and Rosenfeld (1980) conducted an observational study of 152 greeting dyads at Kansas City International Airport and identified that bodily contact was observed in 126 (83 per cent) of the greetings. The types of contact observed were (a) mutual-lip-kiss, (b) face-kiss, (c) mutual face contact, excluding kiss, (d) handshake, (e) handholding, (f) hand to upper body (touching the face, neck, arm, shoulder, or back), and (g) embrace. Female greeting behaviour was very similar with both males and females, whereas males used markedly different greetings with females as opposed to males. Male same-sex dyads had a significantly higher frequency of handshaking, whereas dyads containing a female had significantly more mutual-lip-kisses and embraces.

The use of non-task comments

Following the initial greeting, this is also a common technique which is employed in order to 'break the ice' in social encounters. This process of 'ice-breaking' is usually a preliminary to the exchange of information at a more substantive level. Statements relating to the weather or non-controversial current affairs are quite common general opening remarks, coupled with comments relating to the specific situation (e.g. the price of a drink in a bar).

Kleinke (1986) reports the results of studies he conducted to determine the least, and most, preferred opening lines for men meeting women, or women meeting men, in situations such as a bar, supermarket, restaurant, laundromat, beach, or general situations. He found that the use of 'innocuous' openings (e.g. 'I feel a little embarrassed about this, but I'd like to meet you') was preferred to smart or 'flippant' openings (e.g. 'Didn't we meet in a previous life?') by both males and females. This is important, since the success of the opening comment can determine whether further interaction will take place.

Shuy (1983) recommends the use of non-task comments by doctors, pointing out that:

> The medical interview can be cold and frightening to a patient. If the goal of the physician is to make the patient comfortable, a bit of personal but interested and relevant chitchat, whatever the

> cost in precious time, is advisable. The patients are familiar with normal conversational openings that stress such chitchat. The medical interview would do well to try to move closer to a conversational framework (p. 200).

The use of non-task comments is useful in a range of situations. Salesmen are usually trained to employ such comments before attempting to secure a sale. An insurance salesman, for example, should avoid entering a house and immediately proceeding to discuss the benefits of particular policies. Rather, insurance salesmen are usually trained to use non-task comments, and to relate these to some possession of the householder (e.g. 'That's a lovely piece of stereo equipment you have') before progressing gradually towards the sale. However, a note of caution is sounded by Sullivan (1954) who warns against the use of non-task comments (which he refers to as 'social hokum') in the psychiatric interview. In this setting, Sullivan emphasises the importance of 'getting started' on substantive issues as soon as possible. Thus, as Saunders (1986) points out, 'in a professional context, establishing rapport by the use of non-task comments needs to be carefully considered and genuinely delivered' (p.179).

The provision of 'creature comforts'

This is another aspect of social set. Creature comforts refer to those items which can be employed in order to make someone feel comfortable in any given situation. This would include: a soft or 'easy' chair on which to sit; an offer of a drink, whether alcoholic or a cup of tea or coffee, which gives the person something to focus upon and also creates further non-task comments (e.g. 'Do you take sugar?'); an offer of a cigarette or cigar; and reasonable lighting and temperature in the room.

All of these creature comforts can be designed to establish a good social set. This is clearly demonstrated by the fact that they are often taken away in situations where an individual is being subjected to stress. A suspect being interrogated by detectives is usually seated on a hard chair and may have a bright light shining into his eyes. These 'tough guy' tactics may, however, be alternated with 'nice guy' tactics where one detective gives the suspect a cigarette, coffee and sympathy, so that he may see him as a friend in whom he can confide. At a lesser extreme a candidate at a difficult selection interview may well be seated in such a way that he is facing the window, and may also be given a chair which is difficult to settle into (e.g. an easy-chair without arms).

In some settings, however, the professional may have little control over the environment. As Nelson-Jones (1983, p. 34) points out, quite often: 'counselling interviews are conducted in less than ideal conditions through no fault of the counsellor, who is then faced with minimizing the impact of adverse working conditions'. In other words, the setting for an interaction should be as conducive as possible, but the behaviour of the professional can help to overcome the lack of certain creature comforts.

These are the main methods which are used to induce social set, and thereby establish a good relationship at the start of social encounters. They include the ritualised, non-verbal indicators of greeting, such as eye contact and raised eybrows, a nod of the head, smile and handshake. Verbally, the use of non-task comments serves to break the ice and establish friendly communication sequences, thereby creating the impression of personal interest, as opposed to more formal interest in the main function of the transaction. The provision of creature comforts also helps to underline a consideration for the other person as a fellow human, and facilitates the development of rapport. If these techniques are used to good effect, they should result in the induction of an appropriate social set.

Perceptual set

The initial perceptions which are received in social situations will influence the expectations of participants. How someone 'sees' a situation will depend upon a number of factors relating to his immediate surroundings. Although it is often true that first impressions can be deceptive, most people, to a greater or lesser degree, will make some judgement about a book, based upon its cover. It has been found that important decisions, such as whether or not to offer someone a job, are indeed affected by the first impressions of the candidate gleaned by the interviewer (Arvey and Campion, 1984). Perceptual set will be influenced both by the environment, and the participants.

The nature of the environment

When an individual enters a room for the first time, he will receive information concerning the layout of tables, chairs and other furnishings. Depending upon the nature of these perceptions, he will in turn translate them into a set of expectancies about the format for the interaction which is to follow. For example, a table and upright chairs will usually convey an impression of a business-like environment, whereas a coffee-table and easy-chairs will suggest a more social or conversational type of interaction. Thus an individual attending a selection interview may be somewhat taken aback if confronted with the latter type of setting, since this will be contrary to his expectations.

Situations which are not relished by most people in general, however, are visits to the doctor or dentist. Such visits are not made any more comforting by the nature of the waiting rooms in most surgeries. Inevitably these tend to be comprised of rather bleak furnishings, with an uncomfortable layout of hard-backed chairs — usually around the walls — which makes conversation rather awkward. Yet a very different perceptual set could be induced in patients, by providing easy-chairs laid out in small groups to encourage social interchange, coupled with appropriate lighting and soft music. While such a change may not completely allay the fears of patients, it would certainly make the period of waiting much more acceptable and less stressful. It would also help to humanise the process of receiving treatment.

Many professionals spend their working lives interacting with clients in situations which are removed from the real world (e.g. hospitals, prisons, schools), and this has a marked effect on interpersonal communication. Burton (1985) describes hospitals as 'strange places where strange things happen to people . . . the strangeness of the hospital setting is so immense that it almost defies analysis' (p. 86). He argues that attempts should be made to restructure the hospital environment to allow the patient more dignity, privacy, respect, autonomy and choice. There is evidence that the restructuring of the furniture and fittings of an old people's home (Blackman *et al.*, 1976) and a psychiatric hospital (Holahan, 1979) resulted in greater interaction between the individuals within these settings. These findings would indicate that professionals should, whenever possible, arrange the environment in which they will interact with clients in such a way as to encourage maximum participation.

The personal attributes of the participants

This will also have an influence upon the expectations of the perceiver. The age, sex, dress and general appearance of the other person will all affect the initial perceptual set which is induced. Generally, older, more mature professionals are often viewed as being more experienced and competent than newly qualified professionals, who may therefore find it more difficult to inspire confidence in clients. However, this is dependent upon the professional context, and the age of the client.

For example, Foxman *et al.* (1982) found that young mothers were less happy with older health visitors, and a similar finding was reported by Simms and Smith (1984) in a study of teenage mothers. In these instances the young mothers would find it difficult to identify with the older health visitors, and as Foxman *et al.* point out may have felt 'threatened' by their own lack of experience in comparison to the health visitor. Thus the ages of both the professional and the client are important considerations which can affect expectations and behaviour.

During social interaction we also tend to respond differently to, and hold differing expectations of, the behaviour of individuals depending upon their gender (Mayo and Henley, 1981). Females tend to be touched more, smile more frequently, require less interpersonal space, use more head nods and engage in more eye contact. Males are likely to be more positively evaluated if they are regarded as being competent, assertive and rational, whereas females are viewed more positively if they portray traits such as gentleness, warmth and tact. Presumably these expectations influence the career choices of females and males, so that in professions such as nursing there is a high preponderance of females.

Another important factor is the attractiveness of the participants (see Chapter 2). Individuals are judged on level of attractiveness from a very early age, since it has been shown that nursery school children exhibit an aversion to chubby individuals, and a greater liking for physically attractive peers (Stewart *et al.*, 1979). In examining the relevance of attractiveness in interpersonal interactions, Altman (1977) points out that persons rated as being highly attractive tend to receive more eye contact, more smiles, closer bodily proximity and body accessibility (openness of arms and legs) than individuals rated as being unattractive.

Cook (1977, p. 323), in reviewing a number of facets of interpersonal attraction, particularly during initial social encounters, and in emphasising the importance of first impressions, points out that:

> The first impression takes in a number of things. In most but not all relationships people look for someone who is attracted to them . . . Some preliminary assessments of personality, outlook, social background — an attempt to 'place' the other — will be made . . . A relatively unattractive or unpopular person who tries to make friends with — or a sexual partner of — someone much more attractive or popular is likely to suffer a rebuff.

In terms of the physical attractiveness of an individual, it would therefore seem that this is an important aspect of perceptual set. It is likely that someone regarded as being very attractive will also be seen as being popular, friendly and interesting to talk to. This, in turn, will influence the way in which the attractive individual is approached by another person, thereby probably creating a self-fulfilling prophecy (Duck, 1977). It will be recalled from Chapter 3, however, that interpersonal attractiveness is usually more than mere physical make-up, since factors which are relevant here include cleanliness, dress, rewardingness, personality and competence. In first meetings with another person the former two variables will obviously be more accessible to evaluation than the latter two. Personality judgements can only be made following an encounter with the other person, while judgements about competency are situation-specific (Rosenblatt, 1977). These findings would suggest that a physically unattractive professional may be successful and popular with clients by ensuring that he has a good interactive style and a professional approach.

People are frequently evaluated on the basis of their mode of dress. The reason for this is that the style of dress which one adopts is often a sign of the group with which one identifies. Thus certain professions have become associated with a particular style of dress, with the deliberate intention of conveying a definite public image. This is exemplified by the adoption of uniforms by members of many institutions and organisations, who may want to present a consistent image, or be immediately identified in their job function. Policemen, soldiers, nurses, hospital doctors, priests and traffic wardens all immediately induce a certain type of set in the obsever. At another level, however, business executives, civil servants, salesmen, solicitors and estate agents have a less formal type of 'uniform' — namely, a suit, shirt and tie. A number of research studies have been conducted into determining the effects of dress, and physical attractiveness, upon evaluations of counsellors. In summarising the findings from these studies, Kleinke (1986) concludes that counsellors who dress formally enough to portray an impression of competence and whose dress is in style rather than old-fashioned, are preferred to those who dress very formally and are consequently seen as 'stuffy' or unapproachable. Likewise, physically attractive counsellors are preferred to unattractive counsellors.

These are the main facets of perceptual set linked to personal attributes. However, judgements about individuals may also be influenced by other features such as height, overall body shape, the use of cosmetics and perfumes, whether or not glasses are worn, and whether a male has a moustache or a beard. Some of these aspects can be manipulated in order to induce a certain type of set in another person. Similarly, the nature of the environment can be manipulated, so that the furnishings of a room can be organised in either a formal or an informal fashion depending upon the purpose of the interaction.

There is, however, some evidence to suggest that the initial effects of appearance upon interpersonal judgements may only be transitory. Argyle and McHenry (1971) found that, while a person wearing spectacles is judged to have an IQ of 13-15 points higher than when he is not wearing spectacles, observing the person talking for five minutes is enough to eliminate the effects of wearing spectacles on judgements about intelligence. This would suggest that the follow-up behaviour is a crucial factor in establishing a lasting set which will endure for the period of the interaction. Whilst first impressions will influence the type of set which is induced, in terms of the personal attributes of the other person, these must then correlate with the behaviour displayed, if the set is to be maintained.

Cognitive set

The main purpose of many social encounters is concerned with substantive issues of fact. Before proceeding to these issues, however, it is important to ensure that the terms of reference are clearly understood at the outset. In order to achieve this objective, it is often necessary to draw up a 'social contract' with the individuals involved so that all parties are in clear agreement as to the nature and objectives of the ensuing interaction. In other words, it is important to induce an appropriate cognitive set in the participants, so that they are mentally prepared in terms of the background to, and likely progression of, the main business to follow, which should as a result flow more smoothly. There are a number of factors which are pertinent to the induction of an appropriate cognitive set, and these are as follows:

Prior instructions

It has long been known that prior instructions, such as techniques to use in solving a problem or special items to be aware of, have been found to improve performance. Reid *et al.* (1960) found that serial learning was speeded up by providing instructions to subjects about how to approach the learning task. Similarly, Kittell (1957) found that pupils improved their performance on discovery learning of principles, when given guidelines about the nature of principle learning. Furthermore, Bruner *et al.* (1956) found that informing subjects of the objectives of an experiment also helped to increase performance on the experimental task.

In reviewing research into prior instructions, Turk (1985) concludes that telling individuals what they will hear actually biases them to 'hear' what they have been encouraged to expect, regardless of what message they actually receive. As Turk puts it 'Telling people what they are about to perceive will radically affect what they do perceive' (p. 76). The effect of prior instructions was also borne out in a study by Simonson (1973), who found that subjects told to expect a 'warm' counsellor actually disclosed more than those who were told they would be seeing a 'cold' counsellor, regardless of the actual behaviour of the counsellor.

Reviewing previous information

This is also very useful in preparing individuals for the activity which is to follow. Aubertine (1968), for example, found that teachers who introduced new material by linking it with knowledge already familiar to pupils, were rated by pupils as being more effective. This process, of linking that which is known with the unknown material to follow, has also been shown to be an effective teaching procedure, in facilitating the understanding and retention by pupils of new information (Novak *et al.*, 1971).

It is also important to ascertain the extent of knowledge which participants may have regarding the subject to be discussed. This information, when gathered at an early stage, enables decisions to be made about an appropriate level for any ensuing explanations and whether or not to encourage contributions. These points are pertinent when addressing a person or persons on a new topic for the first time.

In many interpersonal transactions, one encounter will be influenced by decisions made and commitments undertaken in the previous meeting. Again, it is important to establish that all parties are in agreement as to the main points arising from prior interactions and the implications of these for the present discussion. If there is disagreement, or confusion, at this stage it is unlikely that the ensuing encounter will be fruitful.

This problem is formally overcome in many business settings, where minutes of meetings are taken. The minutes from a previous meeting will be focused upon, and will have to be agreed at the outset, before the main agenda items for the current meeting can be discussed. This procedure ensures that all participants are in agreement about what has gone before, and have therefore a common frame of reference for the forthcoming meeting. In addition, agenda items are usually circulated prior to the meeting, and this in itself is a form of cognitive set, allowing individuals to prepare themselves for the main areas to be discussed.

Ascertaining the expectations of individuals

This is a useful technique to employ at the beginning of an interaction. Each individual will approach a social encounter with certain expectations, which he will expect to have fulfilled. If these expectations are unrealistic, or misplaced, it is important to make this clear at a very early stage. One common problem facing social workers, for instance, is that clients often expect the social worker to be able to offer instant financial, or other material, aid. In most cases the social worker is unable to fulfil these expectations and will have to ensure that the client is aware of this.

If the expectations of individuals are not clearly ascertained initially, the conversation may proceed for quite some time before these become explicit. In some instances this can cause frustration, embarrassment or even anger, where people feel their time has been wasted. It can also result in the discussion proceeding at dual purposes, and even terminating, with both parties reading the situation along different lines. By ascertaining the immediate goals of the other interactors, such problems can often be overcome. This can be achieved simply by asking the other person what he expects from the present encounter. Once his goals are clarified, it is probable that his behaviour will be more easily understood.

Outlining functions

This is another important facet of cognitive set. It may involve the outlining of professional job functions. If someone holds false expectations, as was discussed in the previous section, it is vital to make this clear, and to point out what can and cannot be done within the limitation of professional functions. Thus the social worker faced with a client expecting an immediate 'hand-out', may have to explain why this is not possible, by outlining the functions of the social worker as applied to this specific situation. At the same time, the social worker could also explain how he might be able to help the client obtain financial assistance. Part of this explanation may involve outlining the functions of other related helping agencies and their relationships with the social work service.

Thus, the expectations of the client should be related to the functions of the professional. Once this has been achieved the interaction should flow more smoothly, with both participants aware of their respective roles. As Pope (1979, p. 515) observes

> Another task of the beginning segment of the interview is the mutual adjustment of role expectations that each participant has of the other. If such expectations are not in synchrony with each other, it is not possible to move ahead to the second or main segment of the interview. Unless these expectations complement each other the dyad lacks stability and communication remains inhibited.

Nelson-Jones (1983) uses the term 'structuring' to refer to the process by which counsellors make their clients aware of their respective roles in the counselling interview, and argues that the most important juncture for outlining functions is at the contracting stage of the initial session. At this stage the counsellor has to answer the implicit or explicit client question 'How are you going to help me?' Nelson-Jones points out that counsellors will answer this question in different ways, depending upon their theoretical perspectives, but suggests one exemplar response as: 'I see my role as more to support and help people as they make sense out of their own lives rather than to come up with ready-made solutions' (p. 85).

Outlining the goals of the forthcoming interaction

This is a useful method for structuring a social encounter. It is not possible in many contexts, notably during client-controlled counselling sessions where the client is allowed to structure the interaction and decide what should be discussed (Rogers, 1977). However, in those situations where it is possible, it is helpful to state clearly the goals for the present interaction, and the stages which are likely to be involved in pursuit of these goals.

Indeed the ability of the teacher to structure lesson material in a logical, coherent fashion would appear to be a feature of effective teaching. In his comprehensive review of research into the relationship between teacher behaviour and pupil achievement, Rosenshine (1971) found a positive correlation between the ability of the teacher to structure the introduction of new material, and increases in pupil achievement. This is exemplified in a study by Schuck (1969), who found that student teachers when given training in the skill of set induction received significantly higher ratings from pupils, and effected significantly greater gains in pupil achievement, than a comparable group of student teachers who received no such training. Schuck concludes fron this study that set induction 'is a powerful variable in determining the kinds of learning that will occur in the classroom' (p. 785).

There are many other situations where it is desirable to structure interaction by providing guidelines about that which is to be discussed and the stages through which the discussion will proceed. A careers officer interviewing a young person for the first time will usually indicate what he hopes to achieve by the end of the interview, and state what areas he is going to ask questions about, and why (e.g. school subjects, interests and hobbies, work experience). Similarly a survey interviewer, as well as explaining the purpose of the survey being conducted, should tell subjects the particular areas he will be focusing upon during the interview. In behaviour therapy, better relationships have been found between therapist and client when the therapist clarified his functions and outlined the goals of the interaction at the outset (Goldfried and Davison, 1976).

This technique, of providing guidelines about the probable content of a forthcoming interaction, allows participants to set themselves fully. They will therefore be mentally prepared for the topics to be discussed, and will be thinking about possible contributions they may be able to make. It also means that the individual often feels more secure in the situation, knowing in advance what the purpose of the interaction is, what the main themes are likely to be, how the sequence of discussion should proceed and the anticipated duration of the interaction.

The purpose of cognitive set is therefore to prepare someone for the main substantive, factual part of an encounter. This may involve giving instructions about the nature of a task and how best to approach it. It may also involve reviewing previous information, or highlighting previous encounters, in order to remind the person of what has gone before. Where appropriate, the expectations of the participants should also be ascertained so that these may be taken into account, and related to the realities of the situation. Finally, it involves outlining the goals of the interaction, and how these are to be achieved. These functions of cognitive set can partly be summarised as the process of informing participants where they have been, what stage they are now at, and where they are going.

OVERVIEW OF SET INDUCTION

Set induction is, therefore, a very important process in interpersonal interaction. It is of particular importance during initial social encounters

— hence the expressions 'well begun is half done' and 'start off as you intend to go on'. Where individuals have been interacting with one another over a period of time, certain expectations about behaviour will be built up. Thus different people may be classified as talkative, quiet, nasty, warm, cold, humorous, and so on. Having been allocated a label, people are then expected to behave as categorised. If someone behaves 'out of character' this will usually be noticed and commented upon (e.g. 'You are very quiet tonight').

However, the expectations of other people will change over time, if the new style of behaviour is adopted over a prolonged interval, and the descriptive label will change (e.g. 'He used to be very shy before he joined the army'). In this way, people can be encouraged to change their set for any particular individual.

In the case of first encounters, set induction will vary in length, form and elaborateness depending on the context of the interaction. Motivational set involves the gaining of attention and the arousal of curiosity in order to encourage people to 'sit up and take notice'. Social set involves (verbally and nonverbally) welcoming people, providing creature comforts and generally making them feel settled. Perceptual set refers to the effects of the initial impession formed by people based upon the nature of the environment and the personal attributes of the other interactors. Cognitive set involves establishing expectations and outlining goals for the interaction.

Schuck (1969) neatly summarises the skill of set induction as consisting of four main processes, namely:

(1) Orientation. This involves welcoming people, settling them down, and gaining attention.
(2) Transition. Links with previous encounters should be made. The expectations of the people involved should be ascertained and the functions of the participants should be clarified.
(3) Evaluation. Following the process of transition, an evaluation should be made of the relationship between the expectations of the participants and the realities of the present situation, so that a smooth interaction can follow. If discrepancies arise, between expectations and reality, then these must be clarified. Similarly if disagreement or uncertainty exists about previous encounters, past decisions, or material already covered, this must be clarified as well.
(4) Operation. Only when the processes of transition and evaluation have been satisfactorily completed should the operational stage be implemented. This involves informing people of the goals for the immediate interaction (or deciding jointly upon goals where appro-

priate), explaining why these are the goals which have been decided upon, and pointing out the likely nature, content and duration of the forthcoming interaction.

CLOSURE

Closure is in many ways complementary to the skill of set induction in that while there are social norms for opening an interaction sequence there are also common interaction rituals for closing an encounter. However, there are some differences between the two social skills. Firstly, at a social level, while a person may contemplate and plan the best way to greet someone, particularly when that person is a stranger or a comparative stranger, he will seldom think about the appropriate way to say goodbye to that person. In general social terms, therefore, closure can be seen more as an impromptu action than a planned one. However, it will be argued in this chapter that unplanned closures are the least effective way to achieve formal closure since, as Bakken (1977) observes, goodbyes or parting rituals may serve to regulate and maintain relationship. In other words, how we take our leave of another person will to a great extent determine our motivation for meeting that person again.

A second major difference, suggested by Goffman (1972), is that 'greetings mark a transition to increased access and farewells to a state of decreased access' (p. 79). Perhaps this anticipation of lack of access is one of the factors that contributes to some of the difficulty that many of us have experienced in leave-taking. For instance, many people prolong an interactive sequence simply to avoid being the first to indicate closure markers for fear of seeming to end a relationship. These periods of 'decreased access' signal a change in the amount of access interactants will have with one another. If the probability of future access is very high then phrases such as 'See you soon', 'Bye for now', may well be employed. On the other hand, if the departure is of a more permanent duration, something more dramatic is likely to be said, such as, 'Goodbye' or 'Bon voyage'. The parting terms appropriate in the former situation would be totally inappropriate in the latter and vice versa.

Simply to stop talking is not always an effective method of closing an interpersonal encounter, and in fact any attempt to close in this way could often be interpreted as 'anger', 'brusqueness' or 'pique'. Instead, closure can be defined more appropriately as the ability to 'organise the simultaneous arrival of the conversationalist at a point where one speaker's completion will not occasion another speaker's talk, and that will not be heard as some speaker's silence' (Schegloff and Sacks, 1973, p. 295). In other words, closure can be seen as drawing attention to the satisfactory completion of an interaction sequence.

At a simple, conversational level, short terminal exchanges such as 'Cheerio', 'All the best' or 'So long' will suffice. At a more complex level, where a great deal of information and ideas have been exchanged, it is usually necessary to provide a more structured closure, perhaps in the form of a summary immediately preceding the final social exchange.

Alternatively, leave-taking can have an important supportiveness function often taking the form of an expressed desire to continue the interaction at a later date. After all, as Knapp *et al.* (1973) put it, 'What could be more supportive than doing it all again?' (p. 185).

Drawing upon these findings, closure, in relation to social interaction, can be defined as directing attention to the termination of social exchange by summarising the main issues which have been discussed, drawing attention to what will happen in the future and, finally, breaking interpersonal contact without making participants feel rejected or shunned.

FUNCTIONS OF CLOSURE

The main functions in employing this skill in a wide ranger of interactive sequences can be listed as follows:

(1) To indicate to participants that a topic has been completed, at least for the moment.
(2) To focus the participants' attention on the essential features of the material covered.
(3) To assist in consolidating for participants the facts, skills, concepts or arguments covered in previous episodes.
(4) To give participants a sense of achievement (if a successful conclusion has been arrived at).
(5) To indicate to participants the possibilities of future courses of action.
(6) To assess the effectiveness of the interaction, particularly in relation to participants' knowledge.
(7) To establish a conducive relationship so that participants look forward to a future encounter.

Although these are the main general functions of the skill of closure they are not all appropriate in every interactive situation. Some are more important than others depending upon the social context in which the skill of closure is being employed. For instance, those employed in the 'helping' professions (such as nurses, therapists, social workers, student counsellors, etc.) may lay more stress on establishing a conducive relationship in their closure than in consolidating facts and information which are sometimes at a minimum in this type of encounter. On the other hand, where the interactors are concerned with exchanging facts and information (such as teachers, judges, barristers, television presenters, salesmen, and public speakers, etc.) there may be greater emphasis on summarising and consolidating information for the benefit of their less informed clients.

In addition, the skill of closing, as with opening, can manifest itself in a number of ways depending upon, for example, the number of participants involved, the purpose of the encounter, location, and time of day as well as personal characteristics of participants such as personality, intellect, experience and socio-economic background. Therefore, it is crucial, when assessing the effectiveness of the skill of closing, to consider those factors which directly influence any evaluation thereof.

The remainder of the chapter will focus upon four main types of closure which can be commonly executed, namely, factual, motivational, social and perceptual. The following section will set out in more detail the different types of closure which can be applied and illustrate how each type may be more appropriate in one social context than another.

FACTUAL CLOSURE

Factual closure may be used a number of times within social interaction, following the presentation of facts, information, skills, ideas, opinions, feelings or problems. Thus while factual closure is important at the end of an encounter, it can be used intermittently throughout, particularly if the interaction is of a lengthy duration. In this way the essential features of any sequence can be highlighted in a brief, coherent fashion in order to crystallise for individuals what has been discussed, as well as encouraging them to relate this material to more general, conceptual issues. In addition, it is essential that any new facts or information that have been assimilated should be related both to previous knowledge, and to similar examples and cases covering new situations where possible. In other words, participants should be commended to use the knowledge they have gained to plan and execute future courses of action.

Factual closure can be achieved in a variety of ways depending upon the social context. Among the techniques which are available can be included the following:

Summary

Writing about some of the main functions of speech conclusions, Aristotle, many centuries ago, claimed that recapitulation of the main points of an argument or speech helped to dramatise or draw attention to the speaker's case. Many centuries later, our thinking does not appear to be radically different.

Reynolds and Glaser (1964), for instance, in research into biology teaching found that regular summaries, or 'spaced reviews' as they called them increased pupils' knowledge of the subject area, the implication being that regular and progressive summing up at various intervals facilitates the retention of knowledge. Wright and Nuthall (1970) confirmed this finding when they found from their research that concluding remarks by the teachers were positively correlated with pupil achievement. Although teachers find this a worthwhile skill to achieve in the classroom, other professional interactors should attempt to incorporate it into their repertoire of skills, particularly when a range of ideas and information is being discussed. Testimony to this is the study carried out by Rackham and Morgan (1977) to assess the skills of chairpersons. They noted that group members felt that meetings lacked clarity and structure when the chairperson did not summarise at the end. Thus careers officers, who may be giving pupils information on a range of job opportunities, can usefully employ a summary. Nurses and health visitors, too, when, for instance, they are advising patients about the most suitable way to dress a wound, feed a baby, administer an injection, etc., can quickly and effectively recap the main points of the process to ensure the patient's understanding. However, it must be stressed that brevity is the order of the day. By repeating in a more concise form the essential elements involved, it helps to cement them in the listener's memory.

Marshall *et al.* (1982) identify the 'influencing' summarisation skill in a counselling context. They contend that 'the summarization skill of influencing has the additional component of informing the client of the helper's expectations, whether they be merely the scheduling of the next visit or the completion of some homework assignment' (p. 98). However, in addition they also point out that the influencing summary can serve as a perception check, as well as a means of consolidating and redirecting.

Another function of making an explicit summation, either at the end of an interview or at the termination of a particular topic, is put forward by Benjamin (1974) who feels that it gives both the interviewer and interviewee the chance to check if each has understood the other. Thus, for example, a social worker could end with the words, 'Before you go, I just want to make sure I understand your position . . . Have I left anything out or does that appear to be the right position?' Munro *et al.* (1983) agree that this is a useful technique for counsellors to use but, as an alternative, claim that it is also effective to have the client summarise what has taken place or been discussed in order that the counsellor gets a better understanding of the client's view of things as well as helping the client to assess what progress has been made.

In conclusion it would appear that the summary is a useful technique to employ when achieving closure, although Knapp *et al.* (1973) warn that it can be overlooked in practice. In a study designed to identify functions and elements of leave-taking in an information-seeking interview situation, they found the act of summarising was not evident. However, they speculate that this could have been the limited time available to the subjects in the experimental interviews. It would appear, therefore, that sufficient time ought to be left available for a concise summary to be made where the interviewer considers it to be an important part of the interview process.

Initiating or inviting questions

Drawing again from research into teaching it has been found that the use of oral feedback questions to assess understanding of material previously presented is positively related to pupil learning (Wright and Nuthall, 1970; Rothkopf, 1972; and McKeown, 1977). This could be termed the evaluating aspect of factual closure. Evaluating is an essential part of closure where the focus is on what has been learned. Specific questions can be asked, designed to check for accuracy of facts or understanding, assimilate the logical sequence of ideas, or evaluate the comprehensiveness of a range of arguments. The responses can then serve as a basis for future courses of action such as to supply accurate information, consolidate ideas or provide omissions where they occur.

While initiated questions are useful check-aids for teachers, lecturers, job trainers, coaches and demonstrators, they can be used at various times throughout a dyadic interview type situation as an alternative to the summary. Nelson-Jones (1983) notes this alternative strategy in a counselling context and feels that this process helps the client to consolidate learning. For instance, when the client says that the sessions with the helper have been invaluable in helping to solve a set of problems, the helper should on occasions respond, 'What exactly have you learned that will help you to sort out your problems?' This conveys to the helper exactly what the client has gained from the interactive sessions. Alternatively, the interviewer can ask a candidate at the end of a selection interview, 'Is there anything you would like to ask me now?'

Future links

Along with summarising and checking for accuracy of mutual understanding, closure may also draw attention to the work which will continue after the termination of the interview. At a simple level this may include making future organisational arrangements such as where and when to meet. At another level, it may involve mapping out, albeit loosely, the agenda for a future meeting. In other words, the summary states the position arrived at while the future link focuses on prospective tasks or decisions to be made. For instance, the chairperson of a committee meeting will usually recap the main points of the day's discussion but will also finish with a brief statement of what still has to be discussed at a future meeting. This has the express function of bringing together into a meaningful whole what may seem diverse elements simply because they have occurred over a period of time.

Identifying areas of future concern is considered by Schulman (1979) to be an important function of the counsellor's role. He states that the helper's task is 'to create an agenda for future work, and to use their experience together to determine how the client can continue to work on these concerns' (p. 100). Knapp *et al.* (1973) refer to this aspect of leave-taking as a strategy of 'futurism', that is an expressed desire on the part of the interviewer to continue the interaction at a later date. These authors claim this element has a strong supportive function and as such it will be dealt with more fully under social closure.

MOTIVATIONAL CLOSURE

Although it has been stated previously in this chapter that one of the main functions of the skill of closure is to focus on both the completion and consolidation of the main facets covered during interaction, there are times when to do so would be inappropriate. Instead, it would be more useful to motivate persons to explore and consider further some of the issues which have been revealed during the previous interactive sequence. Not all transactions can be accomplished in any one session and indeed it may be more expedient to employ a motivational type of closure when a series of sessions is required. By employing this type of closure, individuals can be directed to reflect more carefully, consider in greater depth, and relate any new insights gained from the present encounter to more general issues in a wider context. Schulman (1979) notes the need for a motivational closure in some counselling situations when he states, 'The worker's task is to help the client to inventory these [concerns], to create an agenda for future work, and to use their experience together to determine how the client can continue to work on these concerns' (p. 100). In essence, three principal methods can effectively be employed to bring about a motivational closure, the choice of any one being heavily dependent upon the social situation in which it is to be used.

Explicitly motivating statements

These are perhaps the most basic and obvious means of encouraging persons to relate experiences and insights gained to some future event. For instance, final statements such as, 'Give it everything you've got', 'Let's show them what we can do', 'Go get 'em', are frequently used by sales promotion managers, sports coaches, entertainment promoters to name but a few in order to encourage greater effort following the 'pep' talk.

However, this type of statement is not only confined to the business of selling, the sports field or the entertainment business, it can also be used successfully by those in the helping professions, whereby clients can be motivated to put into practice some of the decisions that have been reached during the interview. Concluding statements such as 'You must try these out for yourself . . . ', 'It's up to you to come to some agreement . . . ', 'Only you can make the final decision . . . ', are explicitly employed to facilitate future action.

Thought-provoking comments

The use of thought-provoking comments as well as being a useful device to encourage participation at the beginning of encounters can equally effectively be used at the end with the specific purpose of sending an individual or group away to consider the matter further. Teachers or lecturers often use this technique at the end of lessons in order to motivate their students to study further in their own time. By providing students with a problematic situation to finish, the teacher can effectively encourage his students to explore the situation further so that there is a link between the present and the future lesson.

Some television and radio programmes also flourish using this technique. Thus when a producer makes a television drama series he frequently closes one programme with a number of intriguing questions such as 'What will happen to Mary Jane?', 'Who is the man in the dark suit?', or 'Will John escape from his captors?' Short filmed sequences of the following week's production usually accompany the thought-provoking questions. This is done with the express purpose of encouraging viewers to watch each episode from one week to the next.

Future orientation comments

The use of future orientation comments also allows individuals to give further consideration to issues long after the interaction sequence has ended. In addition, individuals are also given the opportunity to relate any new experience they have gained from the immediate encounter to a similar one in a wider environment or to relate knowledge gained in one context to another outside the present encounter.

Thus, for example, teachers invite their pupils to relate knowledge gained in the classroom context to familiar situations they meet every-day outside the school environment. For instance, a class teacher of eight to nine year olds, helping children to grasp the concept of points on a compass, north, south, east and west, can finish her concept teach by asking the children, when they go home, to find out which room gets the sun first thing in the morning and which room gets the sun before it disappears for the night. Alternatively, teachers often set children homework at the end of the lesson, specifically designed to consider an issue more deeply. Following a lesson which has concentrated on posing questions constructed to illuminate racial prejudice, pupils could be directed to ask the same questions of their parents, grandparents, brothers, sisters and friends to give them greater insights into attitude formation and attitude change.

These future orientation statements or questions are not the sole prerogative of those involved in the teaching profession. Trower *et al.* (1978) stress the need for patients in a clinical context to be given 'between-session homework assignments' in social situations they have found difficult to master during practical skills training sessions. In addition, Ellis and Whittington (1981) suggest that the trainee, engaged in a variety of SST programmes, should be 'asked to obtain feedback from real-life "others" for discussion when he returns to the [training] unit' (p. 74).

Apart from training situations, other professionals can use future orientation comments or questions. For instance, a nurse can motivate her patient to try new and more up-to-date techniques, even when she is not present, with a concluding statement such as 'The next time you need to inject you can use the method I've shown you this morning, can't you?' Similarly counsellors can encourage their clients to examine their problems with new insights gained during the interview session.

In essence, therefore, in a situation where it is neither apt nor fitting to leave a person with a sense of finality or completion, it is more appropriate to use a type of motivational closure; which particular one to employ will depend upon the interactive situation, the nature of the task and the relationship between the interactors.

SOCIAL CLOSURE

In order to ensure that not only has an interaction been a fruitful one in the sense that substantive issues have been dealt with, but also that it has been an enjoyable experience for all parties, it is useful to employ a type of social closure. Support for the importance of this final leave-taking stage of the encounter also comes from Benjamin (1974) when he says, 'Closing is especially important because what occurs during this last state is likely to determine the interviewee's impression of the interview as a whole' (p. 34).

It is important to note, however, that this acknowledgement of 'pleasantries' should follow the factual closure with its emphasis on content, whereas in set, establishing a relationship precedes the factual or cognitive set. The main techniques which can be used in order to provide an effective social closure are as follows:

Task-related supportive statements

Administered immediately following the cognitive closure, these help to give participants a sense of satisfaction by drawing attention to that which has been achieved as a result of the encounter. Statements such as, 'That's good. You've helped me get things in perspective', 'Well done. We're beginning to get somewhere now', 'That's great. You've explained that to me so clearly I've now got the picture', which follow a recap or summary of facts or ideas, convey to participants that the meeting has been worthwhile in that some kind of further understanding has been brought about.

Chairpersons, teachers and lecturers who are engaged in small group discussions or seminars, often employ this technique at the end of the discussion when they thank group members for their individual contributions to the overall discussion. Bales (1950), in his series of studies on group behaviour, noted that group leaders are more effective if they administer rewarding comments both to particular individuals who put forward interesting ideas or pertinent information, and to the group as a whole.

Although these statements are often made towards the end of an encounter it is also appropriate to use them at various points in any interaction where tasks have been partially completed. Thus it is often quite common for two people who have been collaborating on the same task to say, 'I think we'll take a break now', or 'I think we've earned a rest because we are really getting somewhere.' This type of supportive comment provides participants with a feeling that something has been achieved and that even more can be accomplished in the future. Pope (1986) makes the distinction between providing clients with subjective as opposed to objective feedback in a therapist/client interview situation. He claims that subjective feedback can be given by the therapist without aiming to be scientific. On the other hand objective feedback is provided by the therapist being prepared to back up concluding statements (such as 'Well done! You are moving really well now') with supporting reasons. Comparing these two types of responses, Pope comes to the conclusion that objective feedback 'is a stronger form of feedback than the subjective type, but is not necessarily more effective [since] the therapist has to be especially careful that he does not project his own opinions using this technique' (p. 174).

Non-task-related statements

Non-task-related statements are also frequently used when the main business of the interaction has been concluded satisfactorily. Knapp *et al.* (1973) refer to these statements as personal or welfare aspects of leave-taking. In other words, when decisions have been reached, solutions to the problems found or the general business has been concluded, participants recognise the 'human' aspect of leave-taking and invariably proceed to make statements or ask questions designed to show a warm, friendly disposition. Phrases such as, 'When are you going on holiday?', 'Now take it easy', 'I hope the weather stays fine until the weekend', can be used by a range of professionals.

Acknowledgement statements will often follow both task and non-task-related supportive comments and are principally employed to indicate an appreciation of the opportunity to meet. Irrespective of the context, most professionals have the occasion, in a face-to-face situation, to say to their clients, 'It's been nice talking to you. I hope we'll meet again'. Alternatively, at the end of a telephone conversation, it is appropriate to conclude with the words, 'Thank you for talking to me. I look forward to our meeting next Tuesday', for instance. All of these statements help to 'round off' the conversation and signal to the client that his presence has been appreciated. (See Chapter 3 for a fuller discussion on reinforcement.)

In addition, Shuy (1983) notes that non-task-related statements have a useful role to play when transferring from one topic to another. For example, if the dialogue has been serious and intense, there is often a recognised need to offer more light, social chit-chat as a transition to the next serious topic. Even in a medical interview, according to Shuy,

> the interview can become rather heavy unless there is some light talk occasionally. This is not to say that all medical interviews should be light and gay. But, if one goal of the interview is to make the patient comfortable . . . then some heed could be paid to learning how to create and use transitions between topics effectively as a means of putting the patient at ease (p. 201).

PERCEPTUAL CLOSURE

In order to effectively terminate a discussion, conversation, talk or interview, it is important to use specific closure markers, and so avoid embarrassing those who are not quite sure whether to carry on talking or rise and take leave. Goffman (1961) recognises the significance of 'terminal exchanges' by pinpointing a series of physical manoeuvres and positionings related to leave-taking. Schegloff and Sacks (1973) note that what is perceived as the final closing acts can be achieved by verbal means alone (such as 'bye', 'see you', etc.) but that they are usually accompanied by specific nonverbal behaviours (such as posture shifts, extended eye gaze, an increase in interpersonal distance, edging towards an exit, etc.). Knapp *et al*, (1973) found that leave-taking differed between formal and less formal situations. Whilst both types began the parting sequence with social reinforcers, the formal pairs followed up with rationalisations for the leave-taking ('I have an appointment with the dentist', 'The car is parked at a parking meter'), whereas the less formal pairs were making statements concerned with each other's welfare ('Take care now', 'Look after yourself'). Whichever strategy is used to terminate interaction, it is important that closure be accomplished between participants as sensitively and effectively as possible. The two main techniques available to achieve perceptual closure are verbal closure markers and nonverbal closure markers sometimes occurring separately but more often in tandem.

Verbal closure markers

Verbal closure markers are such an integral part of our everyday communication network that to list them might almost seem superfluous. Such terms as 'good-bye', 'cheerio', 'bye-bye', 'cheers', 'goodnight', 'see you', or 'all the best', are used interchangeably in a variety of social settings, yet even how we use them indicates our relationship with others. For instance when we use the term 'good-bye' it often suggests either a more formal departure or that we may not see the other person again for at least some time. A variety of interviews (such as selection, helping, or survey) often terminate with a formal verbal closure remark. Television programmes, including news programmes and chat shows, leave the viewers usually with a 'goodnight' closure. On the other hand, expressions such as 'see you', or 'all the best', have a more informal or casual flavour being used by close friends or work colleagues, and tend to indicate that the interactors will be meeting again in the near future. According to Berne (1964), 'an informal ritual, such as leave-taking may be subject to considerable local variations in details, but the basic form remains the same' (p. 36).

Laver (1981), on the other hand, has devised a flowchart for what he calls 'formalaic parting and greeting routines' based upon the relationship between the participants. The more formal parting ritual, according to Laver, is used between adults, with those who are not kin, with those of higher rank than the other and with those who are considerably older than the other. Thus the speaker's first task is to determine the status (adult versus child for instance) of the interactor, which allows him to make the appropriate verbal closure remark.

Although these departure expressions which have been outlined are important in breaking any interactive sequence and so avoiding offending or snubbing another individual, there are other expressions perhaps more subtly employed which also indicate that some part of the interaction is coming to a close. Words such as 'OK', 'we-ell', 'right', 'now' by themselves do not denote a closing feature, but when accompanied by a downward intonation of the voice and appearing at a possible pre-closing stage of the discussion they effectively become verbal closure markers. It usually signals to participants that this is as far as the topic is to be explored and indeed to introduce new material at this stage would be unwelcome.

It is important to bear all of these aspects in mind when selecting the appropriate closure word or phrase since failure to do so could result in altering, albeit implicitly, the relationship previously set up in the encounter. Knapp *et al.* (1973) neatly encapsulate this when they state, 'Though minute and seemingful irrelevant on the surface, leave-taking behaviours do appear to be powerful interpersonal forces . . . [and] . . . the initiation and reception of leave-taking cues provides an offhand view of general interpersonal sensitivity' (p. 198).

Nonverbal closure markers

Nonverbal closure markers, which can be used to complement the verbal messages, are of two main types. First the kind which has almost universal meaning, such as the handshake, a wave or a kiss which signifies the departure of one person from another. Second are more subtle cues which also signify that the interaction is drawing to a close. These are: a major change in body posture, hand leveraging (on the knees, legs or on the chair itself), breaking eye contact, explosive hand contacts (either on a part of the body such as the thighs, or an object such as a desk, files or books), movement towards an exit or looking at a watch or clock. These more subtle nonverbal cues have the distinct advantage of communicating closure to another person, thus avoiding the use of explicit, less effective verbal markers such as 'You may go now', or 'I've finished with you now'.

Bearing in mind that we are mostly concerned with terminating our interactions on the 'right note', that is on a note of mutual regard, it is important to combine these nonverbal behaviours with supportive verbal ones. According to Zaidel and Mehrabian (1969), verbal and nonverbal behaviours can be at variance with each other, in which case more credence is apt to be placed on what we see rather than what we hear, although they also point out that this varies with age, children and young adolescents paying more attention to visual components than older adolescents and adults. This point is also borne out by Bugental *et al* (1970). Since the support function is such a critical element in leave-taking, it is important to control the use of these nonverbal elements of leave-taking so that misinterpretations do not arise. For example, it is often difficult to break eye contact in situations where one wants to communicate support, but also wants to leave. The use of appropriate supportive verbal statements can help to reduce any potential ambiguity which may arise as to the nature of the relationship. Busy professionals, such as doctors, social workers, college tutors and business executives, who all work to a heavily burdened time schedule, should be aware of the importance of verbal and nonverbal leave-taking behaviours in bringing social encounters to a congenial and satisfactory conclusion.

OVERVIEW OF CLOSURE

Although closure can be technically defined as directing attention to the completion of a task it can be analysed at four distinct levels: factual, motivational, social and perceptual.

Factual closure occurs not only at the end of the interaction but can also be used throughout, particularly when a 'topic shift' occurs. In an interview-type situation, for example, these segments are easily identifiable because they are separated by breaks in the smooth flow of communication where the participants are considering what to discuss next. One of the most common forms of factual closure is the summary. Summaries can include aspects of both feelings which have been expressed during interaction as well as information of a factual nature. In this respect a summarisation can draw diverse facts and feelings together to form some sort of meaningful whole. The final summary of any interaction, however, be it a class lesson, an interview, a sales promotion drive or a consultancy visit, will, of course, range over the entire spectrum and will conclude with the most important features, such as essential information covered, range of feelings expressed both positive and negative, problems explored or decisions reached.

When it is not appropriate to finalise or come to some conclusions about a problem, topic or event, a *motivational closure* can be employed in order to encourage participants to consider issues further long after the face-to-face discussion has taken place. This is an especially useful technique for teachers, lecturers and job trainers to use but can equally effectively be used by any professional helper whose main aim is to give clients the opportunity to help themselves.

A *social closure*, on the other hand, essentially is concerned with leaving participants feeling glad of the social interchange and at the same time feeling disposed to meet again when and if the situation arises. This serves to overcome any possible resentment which may arise if a client feels that he is being pushed out the door, just one of a number on a communication assembly line, or that he has imposed on the interviewer and his time. Such feelings may result in the client being less likely, firstly to implement any decisions which the interviewer has helped him arrive at, and, secondly, to return again at a future date.

Finally a *perceptual closure* is instrumental in terminating any interaction be it formal, informal or conducted in a dyadic, small or large group context. Specific verbal closures varying from a single 'Goodbye' to phrases such as 'I must go now John or I'll be late for my next meeting' effectively terminate any interaction. These verbal markers are in most cases accompanied by nonverbal closures such as showing someone to the door, shaking hands, etc., and help to emphasise that the 'final exchange' has been reached.

These techniques can be operationalised singly or in combination depending upon the social context in which they are being employed. However, whichever techniques are used it is important to recognise that the 'closure' is that last point of contact between interactors and therefore is the one they are most likely to remember. Therefore, not enough emphasis can be put on employing the 'right' closure techniques on any given occasion in interpersonal interaction.

While no claim is made to suggest that this is an exhaustive analysis of the two skills of opening and closing, it is an attempt to add to the range of techniques currently available from which to choose. If our knowledge of these skills is to increase at all, more research is needed into the normative and specialised functions and strategies of these communicative acts. To gain insights into those relatively unexplored aspects of opening and closing, those little-noticed, seemingly irrelevant on the surface, verbal and nonverbal opening and closing behaviours, is to discover crucial information about the nature of social interaction itself.

7

Explanation

INTRODUCTION

It is important at the outset to recognise that the term 'explain' has acquired a number of meanings in everyday usage. On the one hand, explaining can be used synonymously with describing, telling or instructing, where the explainer is mainly concerned with providing information of either a descriptive or prescriptive nature. On the other hand, 'to explain' goes beyond mere description to give reasons or reveal causes for the facts or events under discussion. In other words the key word 'why' is an implicit or explicit feature of this explanatory procedure.

In addition, the term 'explain' has two further meanings. As Turney *et al.* (1983), in their review of the literature on explaining, point out, the verb 'to explain' has 'a meaning which emphasizes the *intention* of the explainer, and a meaning which emphasizes the *success* of the explanation' (p. 14). Thus it makes sense to say 'I explained it to him and it is not my fault if he did not understand it'. In professional usage, however, it has been pointed out that this sense of the verb 'to explain' is frequently not acceptable (Thyne, 1966; Martin, 1970). Rather, when it is said that something has been explained, we assume that it has been understood. Using this frame of reference, to explain is to give understanding to another. As a result, the skill of explaining contains, as an integral component, the use of feedback techniques to check the efficacy of the explanation. If the reader were to listen to a person's conversations during one single day it would usually be found that for much of the time that person was engaged in explaining; that is giving facts, information, directions, reasons, views or opinions. It would also be detected, upon listening to a number of different conversations, that some people are more effective at explaining than others. Gage *et al.* (1968) noted this difference in teachers' explanations when they pointed out that:

> Some people explain aptly, getting to the heart of the matter with just the right terminology, examples and organization of ideas. Other explainers, on the contrary, get us and themselves all mixed up, use terms beyond our level of comprehension, draw inept analogies and even employ concepts and principles that cannot be understood without an understanding of the very thing being explained (p. 3).

The skill of explaining is one of the most important and widely used of the social skills and yet it is one of the most difficult to legislate for. This is because the perceived adequacy of an explanation is directly related to the recipient's age, background knowledge and mental ability. Therefore, the onus is on the explainer to ascertain at what level he should pitch his explanation in order to achieve a balance between being too complicated on the one hand and too patronising on the other. Gleason and Perlmann (1985), analysing the speech patterns and content of adults speaking to young children, note that adults simplify their speech in terms of pronunciation, grammar and vocabulary, as well as exaggerated intonations. Teachers, social workers, clergymen and doctors, etc., should be aware when explaining to children and young adolescents that their cognitive development proceeds in a stage-like sequence from concrete to concept thinking (Bruner *et al.*, 1956). Concepts such as honesty, love, loyalty and fair play may need little explanation when dealing with adults, but with younger children they need to be spelled out in more detail and related where possible to everyday occurrences within the child's experience.

FUNCTIONS OF EXPLANATION

The main functions in utilising the skill of explaining in social encounters can be listed as follows:

(1) To provide others with information which they may otherwise not have access to.
(2) To share information with others in order to reach some common understanding.
(3) To simplify for others more complex phenomena.

(4) To clarify any uncertainties which have been revealed during social interaction.
(5) To express opinions regarding a particular attitude, fact or value.
(6) To illustrate the essential features of particular phenomena.
(7) To demonstrate how to execute a specific skill or technique.

Although these are the principal general purposes of the skill of explaining, it is important to note that some purposes are more important than others, depending upon the context of the interaction. While a teacher may start off her lesson by explaining briefly what the lesson is about and what she hopes to achieve, this technique would be anathema to a non-directive counsellor who will usually only seek to direct a client towards a solution to his problem after first hearing the client's needs and ideas. In addition, participants in a one-to-one interview situation are more likely to share information with each other in order to find an appropriate solution to a problem. While Ley (1983) contends that patients positively value the presentation of information about their illness from their doctor or consultant, in an interesting study carried out by Wallen, Waitzkin and Stoeckle (1979) it was found that less than 1 per cent of total time in information exchange between doctor and patient was spent on doctor explanations to patients. Further studies have shown that giving adequate and relevant information and explanation before operations or investigations can result in tangible benefits to patients in terms of reduced pain and discomfort, reduced anxiety and reduced stress (Wilson-Barnett, 1981; Boore, 1979). Although this evidence is apparent in medical contexts there is every reason to suppose that persons faced with other unknown situations, such as appearing in court as a witness or taking out a mortgage, would equally benefit from effective explanations.

TYPES OF EXPLANATION

Whilst there has been a proliferation of typologies of explanations from the 1960s onwards (Ennis, 1969; Hyman, 1974), one of the most pragmatic and robust set of categories has been provided by Brown and Armstrong (1984), the categories being named as the descriptive, the interpretive and the reason-giving. Descriptive explanations are provided in order to set out in detail specific procedures, structures or processes. Examples are: a midwife describing to a young mother how to bath her new baby, a careers officer outlining the function and format of a curriculum vitae to a school leaver, or a pharmacist instructing a customer on how to use an inhaler. Interpretive explanations define or clarify issues, procedures or statements. Thus, for example, doctors may interpret for particular patients the results of an X-ray taken previously or inform others about the effects of a particular pill or treatment. Alternatively, TV presenters assist their audience's understanding of current affairs by, for instance, clarifying the effects of high inflation rates on job opportunities, or the effects of nuclear waste on the environment. Reason-giving explanations, according to Brown (1986), are produced in relation to questions beginning, 'Why?' Why is coronary thrombosis more prevalent in Western society? Why are some persons more susceptible to advertising than others? Why do birds migrate? Whilst a particular explanation may involve all three types of explanation, when to provide it is heavily dependent upon whether it is planned or unplanned. The latter is frequently used in response to a specific question or problem posed by an individual seeking further clarification. The first two are prepared prior to the actual explaining episode and are the ones which we are concerned with in this text.

Features of explaining

According to Brown and Hatton (1982), planning and presenting are the two essential broad features of explanation, although it must be noted that the two do not necessarily go hand-in-hand. In other words, it cannot be assumed that a well prepared and structured explanation inevitably results in an effectively presented one. Burns summed up this sentiment in the words, 'The best laid plans of mice and men gang aft aglay'. However, studies have shown that training in methods of planning and preparation is linked to clarity of explanations (Hiller, 1971; Brown and Armstrong, 1984).

PLANNING SKILLS

There are four specific components that are important to consider when planning an explanation. They are concerned with:

(i) Identifying the issue requiring explanation.
(ii) Selecting the key elements in the problem, event or procedure, etc., that is being explained.
(iii) Determining the nature of the relationship between these key

elements.

(iv) Structuring and linking the explanation to the background knowledge and mental capacity of the recipient in order to promote maximum understanding.

There is ample evidence from research into teaching to suggest that the teacher's ability to prepare, structure, organise and sequence facts and ideas with the maximum of logical coherence is positively related to pupil achievement (Gage *et al.*, 1968; Nuthall, 1968; Wright and Nuthall, 1970; Hargie, 1980). Ivey and Gluckstern (1976) stress the importance in interviewing of structuring explanations before presenting them to clients. More specifically in planning an interview, the interviewer should have a clear idea of the particular elements involved in the explanation and their relationship with each other. He should also consider the length of time he intends to spend on the explanation, since this will determine the amount of material he can cover in the time available. In addition, it is useful for the interviewer to consider at this stage what exactly he expects the client to know at the end of the explanation. Finally, as has been previously stated, when selecting, linking and structuring terms and ideas, the interviewer should take into account the age, sex, background, experience and mental ability of his client.

Although it is essential to pre-plan an explanation, it needs to be presented before its effectiveness can be judged. The remainder of this chapter, therefore, will look specifically at a number of skills which can be employed in order to present an explanation clearly and coherently.

PRESENTATION SKILLS

Prior to examining the essential presentation features of the skill of explaining it is important to note that there are three main techniques which can be identified and utilised within the overall skill of explanation. These are:

(1) *Verbal explanation*. This usually takes place when no aids are available to facilitate explanation. Radio programmes, newspapers and books often rely solely on this type of explanation.

(2) *Illustration*. Where audio-visual aids are available, such as charts, diagrams, films or hand-outs, these can be used to underline the more important aspects of the explanation, and so aid understanding.

(3) *Demonstration*. This often occurs when a complex technique or skill is being explained and includes the demonstration by another person (or model) of the actual procedures involved in carrying out a practical task.

The effectiveness of an explanation is the result of including one or all of the above techniques into the flow of the discourse in order to enhance the overall clarity of the explanation. Each will be discussed more fully later in the chapter in the category relating to aids to explanation. Whilst few studies have been concerned with the identification of effective planning and structuring skills of explanation, a great deal of research attention has been focused on the subject of presentation skills (Rosenshine and Furst, 1973; Turney *et al.*, 1983; Land, 1985). An examination of these research findings has revealed a number of features and these are discussed and analysed in the remainder of this chapter.

Brevity

Brevity is essential so that listeners can easily recall and therefore understand the explanation given. Verner and Dickinson (1967) found, from a comprehensive review of literature on purely verbal explanation, that recipients' 'learning begins to diminish seriously after fifteen minutes' (p. 90). Support for this finding has been noted by Stewart (1977), who states that one of the barriers to effective listening is the long speech. Ley (1983), reviewing a number of studies related to patients' understanding and recall of information or instructions provided by the doctor, noted that 'Forgetting is associated with the amount of information presented . . .' (p. 94). In other words, the doctor frequently tells the patient more than he can possibly hope to remember.

Fluency

Verbal presentation should be as fluent as possible. It is not only annoying to listen to 'ums' and 'ers' or garbled, rambling sentences, but this annoyance can very quickly lead to inattention. Hiller *et al.* (1969) noted that verbal fluency, as measured by length of sentences, and hesitations such as 'uh', 'um', etc., differentiated between teachers who explained effectively to pupils and those who did not.

One of the causes of punctuating speech with sounds such as 'eh' or 'mm' is trying to put too many ideas or facts across in one sentence. It is better to use reasonably short crisp sentences, with pauses in between them, than long rambling ones full of subordinate clauses. This will generally tend to eliminate speech hesitances. French (1983) asserts that 'Most of us do not notice the frequency with which we and others have these speech habits, until we focus on them' (p. 80). However, he advises that such habits should be minimised when they interfere unduly with the information being communicated so that comprehension of the listener is impaired. Another cause of disfluency in speech is lack of adequate planning. The importnce of the planning stage has already been outlined.

It is also fair to say that a speaker's lack of fluency in speech may be interpreted by his audience as a lack of knowledge. Hiller (1971), in a piece of classroom research, found that a teacher's knowledge of a subject area was directly linked to the amount of vague terms used in his explanation; the more knowledgeable the teacher was in his subject the less faltering his speech pattern. Unfortunately the results could not determine whether the lack of knowledge itself caused difficulty in finding precise definitions or whether the lack of knowledge produced stress in the teacher which resulted in vague and halting speech. Nevertheless, the results clearly indicate that knowledge of the topic to be explained is an important prerequisite to actually delivering the explanation.

Pausing

Pausing for a moment to collect and organise thought processes before embarking on the explanation can also lead to fluency in speech patterns. Added to that, pausing can also help to increase the understanding of the recipient of the explanation. Rosenshine (1968), in a research review of those behaviours which were related to teacher effectiveness, found that those teachers who used pauses following an explanation increased pupils' knowledge by ensuring that not too much material was covered too quickly.

Further support for use of pausing when presenting lengthy explanations is provided by Brown and Bakhtar (1983) in their study of lecturing styles. One of the five most common weaknesses reported by lecturers was 'saying too much too quickly'.

Appropriate language

Any explanation must contain language which is appropriate to the intellectual capacity of the listener. Professionals inevitably use technical terms (i.e. 'jargon') when they are conversing with other professionals in their field of work. A quick scan of the papers to be presented at an annual conference such as British Psychological Society, British Educational Research Association and British Medical Association will surely leave the non-specialised reader nonplussed and bewildered. Yet these same professionals, in their everyday lives, communicate with persons who do not have access to this specialised language. It is therefore important that 'jargon' or 'specialised' terms be translated into everyday terms so that clients are not mystified or confused in their understanding of facts and events. Of course, it is sometimes difficult for professionals to eliminate completely all technical terms, and to do so may gravely jeopardise the clients' full understanding of issues. To illustrate this, consider a careers officer, whose job is to convey accurate job descriptions to prospective employees. Often the actual title of the job is not an adequate description of what one actually does (for instance an Appraisal Adviser, Systems Analyst, or Geophysicist) and needs a further, more comprehensive, explanation of what is involved in the job before understanding comes about. Thus careers officers spend a good deal of their time translating complex job specifications into simple everyday language for young job applicants. After the candidate has had a full explanation of the job the careers officer can on future occasions refer only to the title of the job and indeed can cross refer from one situation to another where jobs are comparable.

Shuy (1983) notes that the use of jargon or specialised vocabulary is one of three types of interference to an effective exchange of information in the medical interview. In particular he observes that, 'The language code used with one group [medical personnel], though perfectly appropriate there, becomes inappropriate for another group [non-medical personnel] either in understandability or through creating social distance' (p. 190). Nevertheless, sometimes words or phrases are used by a speaker which best describe one aspect of an explanation, yet are unfamiliar to particular audiences. Where this is the case it is very easy to give a brief definition of the new term used. However, it is important to emphasise the word brief. It is important to construct the verbal content of an explanation in such a way that specialised terms or words used in an unfamiliar or unique way are always accompanied by brief, precise definitions or terms.

Language also reflects the culture of the people who use it. In the USA, Canada, Australia and Britain, although we all speak the English language, there are very definite cultural differences in the way language is used to express ideas and opinions (Becker, 1963; Barnes *et al.*, 1971; Bernstein, 1971, 1972). Listening to the language a middle-class mother uses with her child on the one hand, and a working-class mother on the other, reveals graphically that the middle-class child is usually provided with a greater range of vocabulary than his working-class counterpart. As these children grow into adulthood so the gap increases.

There is evidence from work carried out by Pendleton and Bochner (1980) that many doctors volunteer fewer explanations to lower social class patients believing that they require and understand less. It is important, therefore, for all those involved in the business of communicating valid and relevant information to be sensitive to the amount and kind of words and phrases they use with people from different social class backgrounds in order to weaken any status differences there may be between them.

Reducing vagueness

An explanation which contains a number of vague indeterminate words and expressions is not as clear as one which employs specific information. Research by Hiller *et al.* (1969) into teachers' explanations found that 'the greater the number of words and phrases expressing haziness, qualification and ambiguity ("some", "things", "a couple", "not necessarily", "kind of") the less clear the communication' (p. 674).

Land (1984) was interested to study the effect that teacher clarity, in particular vagueness of terms, had on student achievement and student perception. From a cohort of 84 undergraduate student lessons, he found that students could accurately distinguish teacher clarity on the basis of presence or absence of vague terms. In particular he noted that high clarity lessons were significantly related to high student ratings on achievement tests along with high student ratings of perception of clarity.

Further evidence on the incidence of vagueness in explaining is provided by Gage *et al.* (1968) and Miltz (1972), who have categorised some of these inexact expressions as follows:

(a) Ambiguous designation — 'type of thing', 'all of this', 'stuff'.

(b) Negative intensifiers — 'was not too', 'was not hardly', 'was not quite', 'not infrequently'.
(c) Approximation — 'about as much as', 'almost every', 'kind of like', 'nearly'.
(d) Bluffing and recovery — 'they say that', 'and so on', 'to make a long story short', 'somehow'.
(e) Indeterminate numbers — 'a couple of ', ' bunch', 'some'.
(f) Groups of items — 'kinds', 'aspects', 'factors', 'things'.
(g) Possibility and probability — 'are not necessarily', 'sometimes', 'often', 'it could be that', 'probably'.

It is fairly obvious that all imprecise expressions cannot be totally eliminated from verbal explanations. Most people will have experienced a situation when they have groped to find the exact term, and, failing to find it, have uttered a less precise, more general term. It is when these vague expressions become habitual rather than occasional that interference with clarity occurs. Ivey and Gluckstern (1976) also stress the importance of concrete, as opposed to vague, explanations in situations where a helper is giving directions to his client. They suggest that if directions are to be effective they must be specific and clear to the client. Consider the counsellor who gives his client the direction that he wants him to relax so that he can concentrate more fully on his problems. The counsellor could give the direction, 'Just relax', yet it is so general and vague that the client does not know what to do in order to bring about a state of relaxation in himself. However, if the counsellor enlarges upon his initial statement with further concrete directions, he could say 'Relax. Sit back in your chair. Let your arms and hands go limp. Feel heavy in your chair and breathe deeply and evenly.' The client now has been given the kind of information to enable him to begin to induce relaxation.

Emphasis

Another important feature which requires consideration when attempting to explain effectively is the need to provide emphasis. By providing points of emphasis the speaker can direct the listener's attention to the most important or essential information in the presentation, while 'playing down' the inessential information. In order to allow the listener to benefit from an explanation it is important that the speaker indicates those elements which are directly relevant to the problem or topic being explained.

Emphasis can be grouped into two categories, nonverbal and verbal. In the first, nonverbal, category, the speaker uses aspects of his nonverbal behaviour (such as head-nodding, finger-pointing, loudness of voice), to indicate the salient features of an explanation. The second verbal category includes those aspects of language which the presenter uses to draw attention to important detailed information.

Nonverbal emphasis

Rosenshine (1971), reviewing research into variations in teacher manner, found that a 'dynamic' presentation was more effective than a 'static' one. In particular, he noted that nonverbal emphasis (voice variation, gestures and movement) resulted in gaining pupils' attention and in addition aided their recall of lesson material. Public speakers, politicians and television presenters, all versed in the skills of oratory, use purposeful variation in their voice to alert their audiences' attention to key issues.

As well as the voice, effective speakers also employ appropriate focused gestures and movements to underline key features of their explanations. In particular, varied movements of the eyes, head, face, fingers, hands and whole body should be used purposefully and in a focused manner to suit the information that is being stressed.

Verbal emphasis

As well as using nonverbal behaviour to accentuate the essential parts of an explanation, the speaker can employ specific verbal techniques to achieve similar results. One technique which is very potent in highlighting specific aspects and also commonly used by a range of interactors is the technique known as verbal cueing.

Verbal cueing

This occurs when an individual employs specific verbal 'markers' which precede that part of the message that is being stressed as important to note or remember. Brown (1982) identified four structuring moves from an analysis of transcripts provided by lecturers on a training programme. One of the skills he identified which was related to clarity of explanation was that of 'foci'. These were statements which emphasised and highlighted the key points of an explanation. These verbal markers could be individual words such as 'first', 'second', 'third', 'important', 'finally', 'major', 'fundamental', or they could be phrases or clauses such as 'listen carefully', 'the important point to remember is', 'take time before you answer this question'. Verbal cueing plays a significant part in helping many interpersonal professionals communicate to their clients what the essential features of any explanation are. It helps to differentiate between the relevant and the irrelevant, the more important and the less important and the specific detail from the general background information.

Mnemonics

Perhaps not so common as verbal cueing but in a sense equally effective in acting as an *aide-mémoire* to the listener is the use of a type of mnemonic. An example of a mnemonic might be that the key words essential to the explanation all begin with the same letter of the alphabet, therefore it is easy to recall them when needed. An education lecturer, giving a lecture on practical teaching to first-year student teachers, may use the mnemonic '3Ps' '*P*lanning, *P*erformance, *P*erception'. This would draw students' attention to the fact that there are three basic facets involved in teaching a lesson. They must *plan* what they intend to present to pupils, they must *perform* or implement the lesson in the classroom, and they must *perceive* the results of their teaching in order to diagnose anylearning difficulties that may have been experienced by individual pupils. This simple device can be effective in helping the listener to classify the information he or she is receiving.

Planned repetition

A third technique to employ is that of planned repetition of selected points during the presentation. This is especially useful if a great deal of new or unfamiliar material is being explained. Pinney (1969) found that periodic revision of material by the teacher throughout a lesson is positively related to the acquisition and retention of knowledge. Thus a careers officer may use this form of emphasis when he is giving a fourth-year pupil information regarding the subjects needed to pursue an advanced academic course on leaving school. He would supply a few pieces of information only and follow this with a short summary which reinforces in the pupil's mind the essential information.

More recently, Ley (1983), from a research review of patient compliance with doctors' prescriptions, has suggested that one major way a doctor can increase patient compliance is to repeat the important points of the instructions. However, Maguire (1985), in an attempt to identify deficiencies in key interpersonal skills for nurses, warns that overuse of repetition can be wasteful and give insufficient time to assess patients properly. Nevertheless, structured summaries occurring at various points throughout a lengthy explanation appear to be beneficial to the recipient of information. (See Chapter 6 for a fuller discussion on summarisation.)

Aids to explanation

Where possible, the speaker should plan to include some kind of aid to facilitate the efficiency of his explanation. Such aids may be simple (such as examples, sketches, diagrams, charts, booklets and maps), or more elaborate (such as film, live demonstrations, excursions or placement visits). The use of a variety of different types of audio, visual, and audio-visual material in teaching contexts has been widely researched and indeed in many modern classrooms a variety of aids can be found including books, wall charts, working models, animal cages, fish tanks and television monitors. Harris (1960), in his comprehensive review of research on the use of these audio-visual materials, found that the advantages of such aids in teaching were that they supplied students with a concrete basis for conceptual thinking, created interest, made learning more permanent, developed continuity of thought, and provided a variety of learning experiences.

Although these results have been obtained from a teaching context there is no reason to suppose that similar results would not be obtained if research were to be carried out in other situations where information and understanding were being transmitted by means of verbal explanation. Very few listeners of any age can master new material without the aid of examples. However, it is important to note that although the relationship between use of appropriate aids and understanding is a positive one, indiscriminate overuse of such aids for emphasis should be avoided since they often lead to confusion and eventually inattention (Rosenshine, 1968). It is advisable, therefore, to consider very carefully whether or not the illustrative material really does what it is designed to do: that is provides concrete examples to illuminate understanding.

Verbal examples

The most simple aid to use in an explanation is the verbal example, analogy or case study. In devising examples it is advisable to use concrete everyday situations whenever possible to make the subject 'come alive' for the listener. Rosenshine (1971) claimed that explanations were more effective if the opening statement was followed by an example or examples and then followed by a related statement. Thus a concept should be introduced as follows:

Statement ⟶ Examples ⟶ Statement

Let us illustrate this by taking the case of a sociology lecturer introducing the concept of 'role' to first-year sociology undergraduates. The lecturer may start by giving the definition (statement) that role is a pattern of behaviour associated with a position in society. He could either give or ask for *examples* of the roles persons perform (e.g. the role of student, teacher, father, mother, sister, brother, friend, etc.). Since a number of these roles may be common to one or other of the students in his lecture the examples are within the students' experience. The *statement* following the examples could be, 'you will note that individuals have many roles, thus a student may simultaneously play the "roles" of son, brother, friend and captain of the rugby team'.

However, Brown and Armstrong (1984), in an analysis of 48 video-recorded and transcribed lessons, found that the rule/example/rule model is more appropriate to an interpretive type of explanation on an unfamiliar topic than for other types of explanations aiming to restructure pupils' ideas. This suggests that the pattern of examples should be related both to the type of explanation given and to the listeners' previous knowledge.

Expressiveness

Listeners will pay more attention and learn more if they are highly motivated. Unfortunately, research is less than specific about how an audience's interest may be stimulated. Studies of expressiveness (Rosenshine, 1972) show that purposeful variations in voice, gesture, manner and use of teaching aids all contribute to the interest in an explanation. Brown (1986), in less specific terms, claims that, 'Expressiveness, which includes enthusiasm, friendliness, humour, dynamism, and even charisma, have long been regarded as essential ingredients of lecturing and explaining' (p. 211). However, research by Abrami, Leenthal and Perry (1982) suggests that expressiveness is more likely to affect students' judgement of the lecturer and attitude to the subject, than to produce significant increases in achievement. Perhaps, in the long term though, favourable changes in attitude to subject matter may be the basis for further interest and eventual study of the subject in hand.

Not only is effective expressive behaviour advocated in a teaching context but there is evidence to suggest it is also highly valued in a consultative context. Friedman (1979), examining the nonverbal behaviour between medical practitioners and patients, noted that expressions of care and concern were related to patient satisfaction with the consultation.

Finally, Knapper (1981) recommends the introduction of humour, if appropriate, into an explanation, including humour at the speaker's own expense but warns that 'too much hilarity may pre-empt learning' (p. 168).

Feedback

It cannot be assumed that an explanation has been adequately understood by the listeners. Therefore, it is essential to find out if understanding has come about as a result of the explanation. There are a number of ways to check the efficacy of an explanation. An initial, and perhaps one of the simplest forms of check, is to note the nonverbal behaviour of the listener or listeners, since this is a rich source of evidence. Experienced and successful teachers and lecturers constantly scan the faces and movements of their audience, both during and after the explanation, to detect signs of puzzlement, confusion or disinterest. Established interviewers, too, are quick to note frowns, blushes, raised eyebrows or 'blank looks' when they are covering material which may be difficult for clients to comprehend. However, since persons vary in the amount and kind of personal behaviour they overtly display it is not always easy, or even possible, to deduce the efficacy of explanations by nonverbal means alone.

Another method of obtaining knowledge of comprehension is to ask a series of general questions. Shutes (1969) found that teachers who asked recall questions at the conclusion of their lessons promoted higher pupil gains of achievement than teachers who did not question. Although this can be a direct measure of comprehension, there may, however, be areas of misunderstanding within the listener's mind which specific recall questions may overlook. For example, some minor detail may be troubling an interviewee which cannot be clarified by a series of global general questions posed by the interviewer.

In order to overcome this problem, another method of obtaining feedback is to invite the listener to ask questions on any aspect of an explanation which he feels requires further clarification. This would appear to be more valid in terms of 'real' problems encountered by listeners, yet there is a real danger that they may not respond for fear of seeming slow or stupid. In many situations, therefore, it is important to continually look out for nonverbal signs of discomfort or lack of confidence in a client in an attempt to detect underlying problems of miscomprehension.

It is also possible to ask the listener to summarise the explanation. Teachers can ask their pupils to summarise the lesson, and interviewers can ask their clients to sum up what they think the interview has achieved. Although this is often an effective technique with pupils in school it can sometimes be less effective in an interview situation, especially when the interview has been inititated by the client. The client may get the impression that he is being 'tested' and may therefore be anxious about articulating his understanding of what took place during the interview. If an interviewee does fail to sum up accurately it is better that the interviewer takes the blame for failing to explain clearly. This can be achieved quite simply and effectively by stating something like, 'I'm not sure I have explained that very well, could you tell me what you gathered from the discussion'. Ivey and Authier (1978), in their interpretation of the skill of 'direction', refer to the 'check-out' as being an important dimension of effective direction-giving for counsellors. They state that, 'If a direction is to be effective, the helpee must be asked explicitly or implicitly if the direction was heard. "Could you repeat what I just said?" or "How does that come across to you?" are ways to check out the clarity of the direction' (p. 100).

Demonstrations

An actual demonstration is another method of aiding an explanation, particularly when the type of information being conveyed is of a practical nature — such as the explanation of how to execute a new skill or technique. It would be unimaginable to listen to a golf expert explaining the rudiments of playing a tee shot to the beginner without actually seeing him demonstrate the swing itself. In addition, manufacturers of sophisticated machines such as dishwashers, rotary-irons, washing-machines, sewing-machines and new car models, usually arrange for first-time buyers to have a demonstration of the new models by an expert. These manufacturers are fully aware that such demonstrations can enthuse prospective buyers to purchase their machines, and at the same time give them confidence to operate the machine for themselves. Basically, the main aims of accompanying an explanation with a live demonstration are to reveal the main features of the skill, to arouse and maintain the onlooker's interest, to learn about the techniques inherent in the skill and to inspire confidence in the viewer to try it out for himself following the demonstration. If an explanation does require a demonstration there are a number of points which should be borne in mind in order to achieve effective results. They can be examined under three main headings: planning, presenting and obtaining feedback.

Planning

Firstly, before proceeding with the demonstration, it is important to check that all items of equipment needed for the demonstration are prepared and available for use. In addition, the chief steps involved in the demonstration should be listed in the sequence in which they are to be presented.

Presenting

Having devised the procedures to be used in the demonstration the next step is to present it in action. Initially, the observer must be alerted to the purpose of the demonstration and what he will be expected to accomplish once the demonstration has been completed. Once the viewers are prepared for the demonstration they should be guided step by step through the action with accompanying verbal descriptions of the essential features at each stage of the demonstration (e.g. 'the first point to remember is keep your feet shoulder-width apart . . . '). In addition, the linkage between one step and the next should be clearly illustrated so that observers can see how each step fits into the overall action.

Depending upon the complexity of the demonstration, it can be worked through completely, followed by a repeat demonstration emphasising the vital features at each stage. If, however, the skill or technique being explained is more complicated, the complete action can be broken down into coherent segments which the observer can practise in parts. Whichever format is adopted will be dependent upon both the task in hand and the knowledge and experience of the observer.

Obtaining feedback

Finally, it is important to assess whether or not the demonstration has been enacted effectively. Feedback can be obtained by a number of methods:

(1) By having the observer or observers repeat the demonstration.
(2) By repeating the demonstration slowly but requesting the onlookers to give the appropriate directions at each stage.
(3) By requesting viewers to verbalise the salient features of the demonstration following the initial enactment.

Whichever method is used to assess the effectiveness of the demonstration will depend again upon the experience of the observers and the complexity of the task.

In summary, research has shown that, in relation to the presentation of explanation, variations in the speaker's voice, gestures and movement, verbal cueing and an assortment of audio-visual aids (ranging from a simple verbal example to a complex demonstration linked to the explanation at appropriate points) can at a simple level attract attention, at another level can help to convey meaning and, finally, can serve to emphasise the salient features in order to aid the acquisition and retention of information.

OVERVIEW

This chapter has explored the nature, functions and some of the techniques of explaining in a variety of professional and social contexts. It is purported that explaining is an attempt to give understanding to others, thus going beyond the mere reporting of facts to reveal causes, reasons, justification and motives underlying the problem or event being analysed. Whilst the bulk of research into the skill of explaining has its roots in educational settings it is by no means the sole prerogative of that profession. Indeed other professions, both on a group or one-to-one basis, are also involved in providing relevant and interesting explanations for their patients or clients.

Research has uncovered that well planned or structured explanations result in greater understanding, that clear, unambiguous explanations are highly valued by listeners and that summaries or feedback checks are effective in aiding retention. Remember, the success of an explanation is indicated by the degree of understanding demonstrated by the listener. This is encapsulated in the maxim 'a little remembered is better than a lot forgotten!'

8

Listening

INTRODUCTION

In interpersonal interaction the process of listening is of crucial importance. For communication to occur between individuals, there must be both the sending (encoding) and the receiving (decoding) of signals from one person to another. In order to respond appropriately to others, it is necessary to pay attention to the messages which they are sending and relate future responses to these messages.

The importance of listening is increasingly being recognised. Most texts on professional interaction devote at least a chapter to this skill, and several books have been written specifically on this topic (Burley-Allen, 1982; Wolvin and Coakley, 1982; Wolff *et al.*, 1983; Floyd, 1985). A number of studies into the percentage of time spent in different forms of communication have found listening to be the predominant communicative activity for most people. As Smith (1986) points out, in terms of different forms of communication, on average 45 per cent of communication time is spent listening, 30 per cent speaking, 16 per cent reading and 9 per cent writing. Paradoxically, however, the skill of listening is still largely ignored in the school curriculum, with the emphasis being upon reading, writing and, to a lesser extent, speaking. Interestingly, Wolvin and Coakley (1982) discovered that: 'As a result of the schools' slight emphasis on the development of adequate listening skills, many leading corporations are recognizing the need to provide listening training for their employees so that costly communication barriers resulting from poor listening will be minimized' (p. 12).

Thus the importance of effective listening has been recognised in the business sphere. However, for professionals in most fields this will also be a core skill, and knowledge and expertise in listening techniques will be central to success in interactions with clients and other professionals. Indeed, for those professionals who play a counselling role, 'the capacity to be a good and understanding listener is perhaps the most fundamental skill of all' (Nelson-Jones, 1983, p. 17). At the same time, as Porritt (1984), in her discussion on nurse-patient communication, points out: 'Most life events, including admission to hospital, do not require highly skilled counselling but do require skilled listening' (p. 80).

Listening is an important skill at the earliest stage of development. The infant begins to respond to a new world by hearing and listening. The child has to learn to listen before learning to speak, learns to speak before learning to read, and learns to read before learning to write. In this sense, listening is a fundamental skill and the foundation for other communication skills. However, there is a lack of consensus in the literature with regard to the actual meaning of the term itself. Thus some theorists regard listening as a purely auditory activity, as a process that takes place 'when a human organism receives data aurally' (Weaver, 1972, p. 5). In terms of interpersonal interaction, the emphasis here is upon 'the process by which spoken language is converted to meaning in the mind' (Lundsteen, 1971, p. 1). Such definitions make an important distinction between hearing and listening, in that hearing is regarded as a physical activity while listening is a mental process. Just as we see with our eyes but read with our brains, so we hear with our ears but listen with our brains. We do not need to learn to see but we need to learn to read. Similarly, we do not have to learn how to hear, but we have to learn how to listen. In this sense, listening is not something that happens physically in the ears, but rather happens mentally between the ears!

Aural definitions of listening ignore the nonverbal cues omitted by the speaker during social interaction. Yet such cues can have an important effect on the actual meaning of the communication being conveyed (see Chapter 2). As a result, listening is often conceived as encompassing both verbal and nonverbal messages. Wolff *et al.* (1983) define listening as the 'process of hearing and selecting, assimilating and organizing, and retaining and covertly responding to aural and nonverbal stimuli' (p. 8). This is the perspective on listening which will be emphasised in this chapter, where listening will be regarded as the process whereby one person pays careful attention to, and attempts to understand, the verbal and nonverbal signals being emitted by another.

FUNCTIONS OF LISTENING

The skill of listening serves a number of purposes in social interaction. While these functions will vary depending upon the context, the main general functions are:

1. To focus specifically upon the messages being communicated by another person.
2. To gain a full, accurate understanding of the other person's communication.
3. To convey interest, concern and attention.
4. To encourage full, open and honest expression.
5. To develop a client-centred approach during interaction.

ACTIVE AND PASSIVE LISTENING

The term 'listening' has two main meanings in social encounters. The first sense in which this term is used emphasises the *overt* nature of listening, and is referred to as 'active listening'. Active listening occurs when an individual displays certain behaviours which indicate that he is overtly paying attention to another person. The second sense of listening emphasises the cognitive process of assimilating information. This second sense of the term 'listening' does not imply anything about the overt behaviour of the individual, but rather is concerned with the *covert* aspects. An individual may be listening covertly without displaying outward signs that he is so doing, and where this occurs the individual is said to be listening passively. Passive listening, therefore, occurs when an individual assimilates information without displaying behaviours to indicate to the other person that he is doing so. In terms of social skills, it is the former meaning of the term listening which is utilised, namely active listening, and it is therefore important to identify those verbal and nonverbal aspects of behaviour which convey the impression of listening.

At the same time, it is recognised that the processes of feedback, perception and cognition are important in relation to the utilisation of the skill of listening. These processes are central to social action, wherein the individual receives responses from others, assimilates these responses and in turn responds to others. For an individual to demonstrate that he has been listening, he will have to pay attention to the responses of others and relate his future responses to those received.

In interpersonal interaction a constant stream of feedback impinges upon the individual, both from the stimuli received from other people involved in an interaction and from the physical environment. Not all of this feedback will be consciously perceived by the individual, since there is simply too much information for the organism to cope with adequately. As a result, only a certain amount of information is perceived and the individual will usually actively select information to filter into his consciousness. Thus a *selective perception filter* (see Figure 8.1) is operative within the individual, and its main function is to filter only a limited amount of information into conscious, while some of the remainder may be stored at a subconscious level (evidence that such subconscious storage does occur can be found in the field of hypnotism, wherein information which a person is not consciously aware of may be obtained from that person when he is under hypnosis).

Figure 8.1: Selective perception process

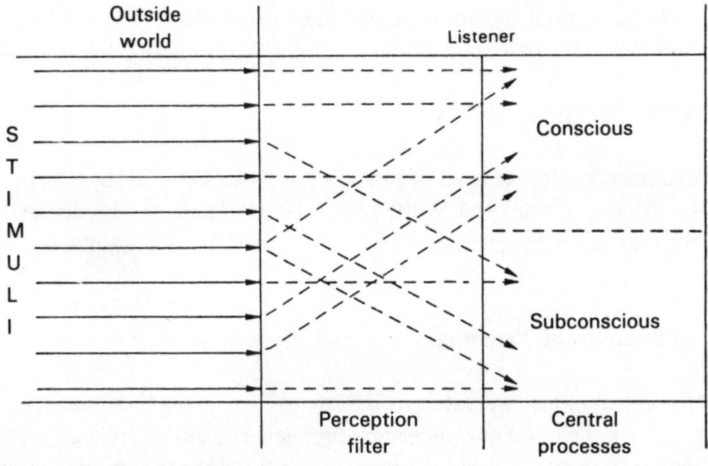

As Figure 8.1 illustrates, from the large number of stimuli existing in the environment, a certain amount of such stimuli will be presented as feedback to the individual. These stimuli are represented by the arrows on the extreme left of the diagram. A proportion of this feedback will either not be perceived at all by the individual, or will be filtered out at a very early stage. Of the remainder, a portion will be filtered into the individual's level of consciousness, while the rest will be filtered out of the conscious and stored in the subconscious.

Within the physical environment, the ticking of clocks, the hum of central-heating systems, the pressure of one's body on the chair, etc., are usually filtered into the subconscious during social encounters, if these encounters are interesting. If, however, one is bored during an encounter (e.g. sitting through a boring lecture) then these items may be consciously perceived, and the social 'noises' filtered into the subconscious! Unfortunately, in interpersonal interaction, vital information from another person may be filtered out, in that it is possible to be insensitive to the social cues emitted by others. Where this occurs, effective listening skills will not be displayed.

In social interaction, in order to listen effectively, it is necessary to be sensitive to the social cues emitted during interpersonal interaction, and to select the most relevant of these cues to focus upon. The cues received can be verbal or nonverbal, and both channels will convey vital information. By observing closely the actions and reactions of others, it is possible to improve one's ability to demonstrate concerted and accurate listening to another, by responding to the central theme of the message being conveyed.

TYPES OF LISTENING

A number of different types of listening have been identified by Wolvin and Coakley (1982) and Wolff *et al.* (1983). These can be divided into four main categories:

Comprehension listening

This occurs when we listen to informative or instructive messages in order to increase our understanding, enhance our experience and acquire data that will be of future use to us. We may practise this type of listening while attending lectures, while conducting fact-finding interviews or while watching radio or TV documentary or news programmes. The emphasis here is upon listening for central facts, main ideas and critical themes in order to fully comprehend the messages being received.

Evaluative listening

Evaluative listening takes place when a speaker is trying to persuade us, by attempting to influence our attitudes, beliefs or actions. We listen evaluatively in order to enable us to make appropriate judgements concerning such persuasive messages. We may practise this type of listening when dealing with sales people, negotiating at meetings, listening to party political speeches, watching TV adverts, or even when deciding with friends which pub to go to for the evening! In all of these instances we have to listen to the available evidence and the supporting arguments, weigh these up and evaluate them, before making a decision. The emphasis here is therefore upon listening for the central propositions being made by the speaker, and being able to determine the strengths and weaknesses of each.

Appreciative listening

We listen appreciatively when we seek out certain signals or messages in order to gain pleasure from their reception. We may listen appreciatively to relax and unwind, to enjoy ourselves, to gain inner peace, to increase emotional or cultural understanding, or to obtain spiritual satisfaction. This type of listening occurs when we play music which appeals to us, when we decide to attend a church service, when sitting in a park or walking in the country while assimilating the sounds of nature, and when we attend a public meeting in order to hear a particular speaker.

Empathic listening

Empathic listening occurs when we listen to someone who has a need to talk, and be understood by another person. Here the listener demonstrates a willingness to attend to and attempt to understand the thoughts, beliefs and feelings of the speaker. While the first three types of listening are intrinsic in that they are for the benefit of the listener, empathic listening is extrinsic in that the listener is seeking to help the speaker. This type of listening is common between close friends, spouses and in formal helping situations. As a result, many professionals will need to develop effective empathic listening skills.

Depending upon the context, however, a knowledge of listening skills may be important for professionals in comprehension, evaluative and empathic situations. Indeed, many of the techniques covered in this chapter will be applicable to all three types of listening.

PROCESS OF LISTENING

As Rackham and Morgan (1977) illustrate, at first sight listening may be regarded as a simple process (Figure 8.2) in that each person takes turns to respond and listen, but in fact this perspective needs to be extended to take full account of the processes involved in listening (Figure 8.3). As we listen to others we evaluate them and what they are saying, we plan our response, rehearse this response and then respond. While the processes of evaluation, planning and rehearsal usually occur subconsciously, they are important because they can interfere with the pure listening activity. Thus we may have decided what we are going to say before the other person has actually stopped speaking, and as a result we may not really be listening effectively. It is, therefore, important when listening to ensure that those activities which mediate between listening and speaking do not actually interfere with the listening process itself.

Figure 8.2: Basic model of listening

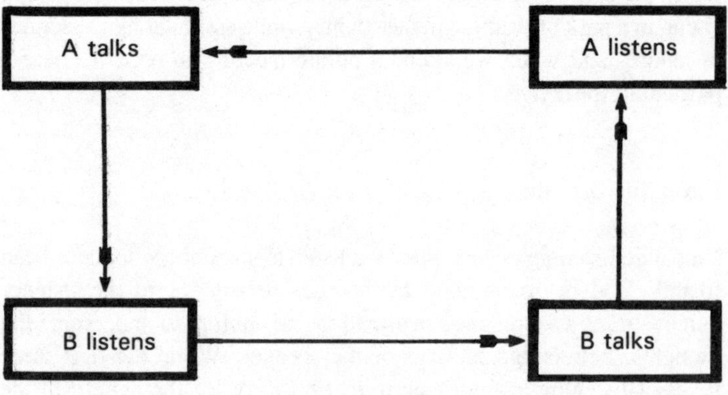

In terms of the verbal message being received, the assimilation of information is influenced by three main factors:

Figure 8.3: Extended model of listening

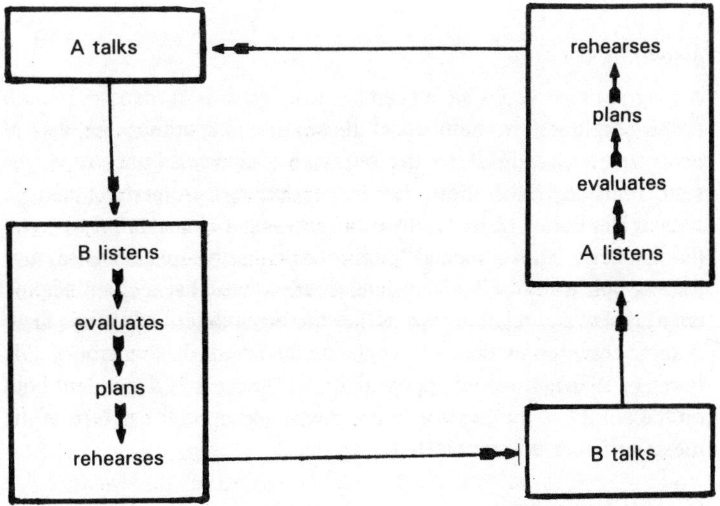

Reductionism

Since we can only retain a limited amount of verbal information at any particular time, if we are presented with a large amount of detail we must contract this in order to cope with it. Thus the message being received will be reduced, sometimes at the expense of vital information. For this reason it is important for the listener to attempt to ensure that the central information being conveyed is remembered. Several techniques have been put forward to facilitate the retention of information. These include:

Recording

Obviously, where it is possible to audio-record the interaction this will provide verbatim recall. However, this is not always feasible.

Note-taking

Retention can be facilitated by noting the main points emanating from the interaction. Watson and Barker (1984) report that note-taking interchanged, rather than concurrent, with listening is more effective in terms of remembering what has been said. It is also socially more appropriate if note-taking does not dominate the interaction, but is rather something which occurs sporadically, and is explained to the speaker ('Can I just note down some details before I forget them?').

Memory devices

A range of techniques have been proposed as aids to memory. Smith (1986) highlights a number of these aids, including: the use of *acronyms*, such as PAIL for the four types of skin cuts Puncture, Abrasion, Incision, Laceration; the use of *rhymes* to remember names, such as Big Bobby Miles hardly ever smiles; and *visualisation* whereby the listener creates a mental 'picture' of what the speaker is saying, for example a counsellor may actually try to visualise a client's home environment and relationships as they are being described. While there is some research evidence to vindicate the use of these memory aids (Gregg, 1986), it would appear that their success is dependent both on the ability of the listener to use them, and upon the nature of the message being communicated.

Organising material

Material should be organised into main themes, ideas and categories, and into a chronological sequence where possible. Such organisation must not, of course, interfere with the act of listening, but where time is available during interaction (as is usually the case), then this type of 'conceptual filing' can facilitate later recall.

Rationalisation

As we listen, we assimilate information in such a way as to make it fit with our own situation and experience. If it does not fit immediately we may rationalise what we hear in order to make it more acceptable. This can occur in a number of ways. Firstly, we may attribute different causes to those presented. Thus a patient may attribute a troublesome cough to the weather, or argue that it 'runs in the family', rather than accept a doctor's explanation that it is due to heavy smoking. Secondly, transformation of language is a common form of rationalisation. This is often due to what Gregg (1986) refers to as *acoustic confusions*, caused by close similarity in the sounds of certain words. For example, in the medical field products with similar-sounding names can be mixed up by doctors, nurses and pharmacists, with potentially serious consequences (e.g. Benorylate/Diorylate, Zyloric/Suluric, Alrheumat/Aldomeat). Thirdly, and perhaps paradoxically given the aforementioned reductionism, there may be the addition of material. A classical instance of this occurs in everyday gossip, whereby a basic story is enlarged and embroidered upon during each retelling, until it eventually becomes a sensational story! Care needs to be taken in professional situations to avoid 'reading too much into' what the client has said.

Change in the order of events

This is a common occurrence in the assimilation of information, whereby data becomes jumbled and remembered in the wrong order. Thus 'take two tablets three times daily after meals' is remembered as 'take three tablets twice daily before meals'; or 'he lost his job and then started to drink heavily' becomes 'he started to drink heavily and then lost his job as a result'. Such mistakes can be avoided by careful conceptual organising of material being received.

FACETS OF LISTENING

There are four main facets which need to be taken into consideration in relation to the process of listening. These are the characteristics associated with the listener, the speaker, the message and the environment.

The listener

A number of positive correlations have been found between characteristics of the listener and ability to listen effectively. These include:

Linguistic aptitude

Those with a wider vocabulary are better listeners, since they can more readily understand and assimilate a greater range of concepts. Academic achievement has also been shown to be associated with listening ability (although as might be expected academic achievement is also usually highly correlated with linguistic aptitude).

Motivation

If the listener is highly motivated she will remember more of the information presented. Such motivation can be caused by a variety of factors, ranging from a school pupil's fear of retribution from a harsh teacher, to the desire of a caring professional to help a particular client.

Organisational ability

As mentioned earlier, the ability to organise incoming information into appropriate categories facilitates learning. Good listeners can identify the key elements of the messages received, and can store these in appropriate conceptual compartments.

Use of special concentration techniques

There are several such techniques employed by effective listeners. One of these is the use of intrapersonal dialogue related to listening, wherein the listener covertly talks to herself to heighten receptivity. This may involve asking covert questions ('Why is he telling me this now?'), the use of covert coaching ('I'm not paying enough attention. I need to listen more carefully'), or self-reinforcement ('I'm listening well and understanding what he is saying'). Another approach is for the listener to attempt to put herself in the speaker's position and try to see the world through his eyes. Finally, the listener can employ some of the memory aids mentioned previously.

Gender

There is some evidence that males score higher than females on oral tests of listening comprehension (Brimer, 1971), while females are more perceptive in recognising nonverbal cues relating to feelings (Haviland and Malatesta, 1981). These findings would suggest that males may be superior at assimilating factual information presented orally, while females may be superior at interpreting feeling information. Much more research is required, however, in order to chart the precise extent of gender influence on listening ability.

Physical condition

Physical condition is important, in that listening ability deteriorates as fatigue increases. Thus someone who is extremely tired will not be capable of displaying prolonged listening. Professionals with a heavy case-load need to attempt to ensure that they do not have to handle their most demanding cases at the end of a tiring day.

Disposition

Introverts are usually better listeners than extroverts, since they are content to sit back and let the other person be the centre of attention. Furthermore, highly anxious individuals do not make good listeners, since they are usually too worried about factors apart from the speaker to listen carefully to what is being said. Also, people who are more susceptible to distractions do not make good listeners, an extreme example being the hyperactive child. Those who can ignore, and remain calm during, minor extraneous noises and interruptions are better listeners.

The speaker

There are a number of aspects pertaining to the speaker which influence the listening process, including:

Speech rate

While the average rate of speech is between 125–175 words per minute, the average 'thought rate' at which information is cognitively processed is between 400–800 words per minute. The differential between speech rate and thought rate gives the listener an opportunity to assimilate, organise, retain and covertly respond to the speaker. However, this differential may also encourage the listener to fill up the spare time with other unrelated mental processes (such as day-dreaming). Listening can be improved by using this spare thought-time positively, by, for example, asking covert questions such as: 'What are the main points being made?', 'What reasons are being given?', 'In what frame of reference should this be viewed?', and 'What further information is necessary?'

Where a speaker drops below the 125 words/minute rate, or far exceeds 300 words/minute, listening can become much more difficult. In the former case, it becomes very difficult to listen to a very slow speaker. Professionals who have to deal with depressed clients will be aware of the problems involved in maintaining concentration with someone who says very little. At the other extreme, it can also be difficult to listen effectively to a very rapid speaker, since we cannot handle the volume of information being received. Wolff *et al.* (1983), in reviewing the literature on speech rate, however, point out that listeners: 'prefer to listen, can comprehend better, and are more likely to believe a message that is presented at the rate of 190 words or more per minute . . . They demonstrate marked efficiency when listening to a speaker talking at 280 words per minute — twice the rate of normal speech' (p. 155). Interestingly, as a result of such findings, television advertisers speeded up the rate of verbal presentation in their adverts, with positive results in terms of viewer comprehension and recall. These findings would also suggest that most professionals will have problems paying attention for lengthy periods to clients who talk at, or below, the normal rate of speech.

However, the topic of conversation and its degree of difficulty need to be taken into consideration in relation to speech rate. A slow speech rate may be appropriate with a complex issue whereas with more basic material a faster rate is usually the norm. As Dabbs (1985) observes: 'Long pauses are accepted by the participants in intellectual conversation as a normal result of trying to ''figure things out'', while long pauses in social conversation indicate things are not going well and will tend to be avoided' (p. 191).

Similarly, in various professional settings long pauses and a slow speech rate by the client may be displayed, and will necessitate concentrated listening by the professional.

Speech delivery

The clarity, fluency and audibility of the speaker all have an influence on listening comprehension. Thus it is difficult to listen to, and comprehend, someone who speaks English with a pronounced foreign accent, or who has a strong regional dialect unfamiliar to the listener. It is also difficult to listen to someone with a severe speech stammer, or other marked speech dysfluency, both because the message being delivered is disjointed, and because the listener is preoccupied thinking about how to respond to the dysfluency. Finally, it is difficult to pay attention to an individual who speaks in a dull monotone (as most students will testify!), or who mumbles and does not have good voice projection.

Emotionality

If the speaker displays high levels of emotion, the listener may be distracted by this and cease to listen accurately to the verbal message. In situations where individuals are in extreme emotional states, their communication is inevitably highly charged with this message emotion. It is often necessary to sustain an interaction in these circumstances. Sustaining can be defined as the process whereby someone experiencing an extreme emotional state is encouraged to ventilate, talk about, and understand, their emotions.

When faced with someone who is experiencing extreme emotions (e.g. of depression or aggression) it is often not advisable either to reinforce positively or to rebuke him for his behaviour, since such reactions may well be counter-productive. For example, by rebuking an individual who is displaying aggressive behaviour, it is likely that this will only serve to heighten the aggression (Owens, 1986). A more reasoned response is to react in a calm fashion, demonstrating an interest in the emotional person without overtly reinforcing him, but also showing a willingness to listen and to attempt to understand what exactly has caused the emotional state to occur.

Only when strong emotional feelings begin to decrease can a more rational discussion take place. If someone is 'too emotional about something', it is likely that he will be 'too worked up about it' to listen to reasoned arguments. When listening to an individual who is displaying high levels of emotion, it may be necessary to be prepared to wait for a considerable period of time before the emotion is ventilated. During this period the anxiety of the listener may interfere with his ability to listen carefully, and this can become a serious obstacle to effective listening. The listener may pay too much attention to the emotional message being conveyed by the speaker, and as a result may not assimilate important information of a more factual nature (Montgomery, 1981). Conversely, the listener may concentrate only on the factual content and attempt to ignore the emotional message. In both of these cases, message distortion will occur, in that the listener is not perceiving the total message being conveyed by the speaker.

Status

If the speaker is regarded as an important person, listening comprehension is increased. Thus if the speaker is a recognised authority then more credence will be attached to what she has to say. Also, more attention will be given if the speaker is in a position of superiority over the listener. Listening is therefore facilitated if the listener has admiration and respect for the speaker, and if the speaker has high credibility in terms of the topic.

The message

The nature of the message itself can influence the process of listening, in terms of:

Structure

If the message is unclear and lacking in any coherent structure it will be more difficult to listen to and comprehend. Quite often the speaker may be consciously or unconsciously distracting or misleading. He might not be saying anything important, could be emphasising the trivial, being deliberately vague and evasive or speaking for a long time without a break. Thus it is sometimes the goal of the speaker to confuse the listener by distorting the message being conveyed (many politicians are quite adept in this field!), or the speaker may be incapable of expressing himself clearly. In both of these cases, it is often necessary to interrupt the speaker at times, by asking questions in an attempt to understand what is being said.

Significance

If the message is of particular interest, or of special significance to the listener, comprehension and recall are heightened. For example, a social worker who suspects a parent of child abuse will pay careful attention to both the parent and the child when they are discussing parent-child relationships.

Values

When the message conveys similar values, attitudes or viewpoints to those held by the listener, listening is facilitated. In this sense, most people like to have their beliefs and expectations confirmed. Paradoxically, however, it has also been found that if a message contains a disconfirmation of listener expectations, listening is also heightened since presumably the listener is motivated to evaluate the unexpected message.

Complexity

The difficulty of the material being delivered by the speaker will also affect listening. As discussed in relation to speech rate, the listener can cope more effectively with basic material delivered at a fast rate, but with complex information a slower rate of speech is required in order to allow the listener time to assimilate such information fully.

The environment

The final facet of listening which needs to be considered is the environment in which the interaction is taking place. In particular, three elements of the environment are important:

Ventilation and temperature

Listening is impaired if the environment is either unpleasantly warm or cold, and optimum listening occurs when the room temperature is at a comfortable level. Likewise, ventilation is important, especially where individuals are smoking cigarettes in the room, since it has been found that such smoke adversely affects the performance of non-smokers.

Noise

Listening comprehension deteriorates when there is intrusive noise entering the room (such as a pneumatic drill outside the window). However, background noise does not have an adverse effect on listening. Indeed most pubs, restaurants and hotel lounges will play some form of background music to encourage conversation. Thus the level of noise is important, since background noise can easily be filtered out whereas intrusive noise cannot (see Figure 8.1). However, the nature of the interaction is also important, so that a lecturer would not encourage even background noise, since he wants total concentration from students. Dentists, on the other hand, often play background music to encourage patients to relax while in the surgery.

Seating

It is important for the listener to have a comfortable chair if he has to listen for a prolonged period. Yet most schools provide hard, uncomfortable chairs for pupils and expect sustained, concerted attention from them throughout the school day! In group contexts, a compact seating arrangement is more effective than a scattered one. People pay more attention and recall more when they are brought close together physically, as opposed to when they are spread out around the room.

OBSTACLES TO EFFECTIVE LISTENING

In addition to some of the above factors, there are a number of other factors which may be operative within a social encounter, which militate against effective listening, and have therefore to be overcome by the listener. As Egan (1977) points out 'the good listener is an active listener, one truly engaged in the communication process, one who goes out of himself in search of significant cues emitted by others' (p. 229). Thus the good listener is aware of the selective nature of listening and of the possible obstacles to effective listening. There are a number of such obstacles.

Dichotomous listening

Dichotomous listening occurs when an individual attempts to assimilate information simultaneously from two different sources. This may occur when the listener attempts to listen to two people in a group who are speaking at the same time, when the listener attempts to conduct a telephone conversation while carrying on a face-to-face interaction with another person, or when the listener is distracted by some form of extraneous 'noise'. In all of these instances it is likely that the dichotomous nature of the listening will interfere with the ability of the listener to interact effectively, since messages may be either received inaccurately or not received at all. Effective listening is encouraged by paying attention to only one person at a time, and by manipulating the environment in order to ensure that extraneous distractions are minimised (e.g. by closing doors, switching off television or having telephone calls intercepted).

Inattentiveness

Inattentiveness is another obstacle to effective listening, where the listener for some reason may not be giving full attention to the speaker. If the listener is self-conscious, and concerned with the impression he is conveying to others, it is possible that he will not be listening closely to others. Similarly, if the listener has an important engagement looming ahead, his preoccupation with this may militate against the present situation, whereby the listener is thinking more about how he will handle the future encounter than about what the speaker is currently saying. A parallel case occurs where the listener has had an important meeting in the near past, and is still pondering the ramifications of this, at the expense of listening to the speaker in the present interaction. Effective listening occurs when the listener concentrates fully on the speaker and avoids such inattentiveness.

Individual bias

Individual bias can be an obstacle to effective listening, wherein an individual may, because of his personal circumstances, distort the message being conveyed by the speaker. This can occur in a number of contexts. If the listener has a limited period of time, he may not wish to get involved in lengthy dialogue with the speaker and therefore may choose to 'hear' only the less provocative or less difficult messages. Similarly someone who does not want to recognise difficult realities, may refuse to accept these when expressed by another — either by distorting the message or by refusing to listen to the speaker altogether (a common example where this often occurs is in bereavement where the bereaved may initially not accept the fact that a person close to them is actually dead).

At another level, people may not respond accurately to questions or statements, simply because they wish to make a separate point when 'given the floor'. One example of this is the politician who wants to ensure, at all costs, that he gets his message across, and when asked questions in public meetings frequently does not answer these questions accurately, but rather takes the opportunity to state his own point of view. These examples of individual bias are neatly encapsulated in the lyrics of the song 'The Boxer' by Simon and Garfunkel: 'a man hears what he wants to hear and disregards the rest'.

Mental set

The mental set of the listener may be an obstacle to effective, objective listening. The listener will be affected by previous experiences, attitudes, values and feelings, and these in turn will influence the way he is mentally set in any given situation. The listener will make judgements about the speaker based on his dress and appearance, his initial statements, or what he has said during previous encounters. These judgements can influence the way the speaker is heard by the listener, in that his statements may be filtered and only those aspects which fit with specific expectations be perceived.

By ascribing a stereotype to the speaker (e.g. racist, communist, delinquent, or hypochondriac) there is a danger that the listener will become less objective in judging what is being said. Judgements will tend to be based on who is speaking, rather than on what is being said. While it is often important to attempt to evaluate the motives and goals of the speaker, this can only be achieved by a reasoned, rational process, rather than by an irrational or emotional reaction to a particular stereotype. It is, therefore, important to listen carefully and as objectively as possible to everything that is being said, in order to be an effective listener.

Blocking

The process of blocking occurs when an individual does not wish to pursue a certain line of communication, and so various techniques are employed to end or divert the conversation. These blocking techniques are presented in Figure 8.4. On occasions, some of these techniques are quite legitimate. For example, a pharmacist would be expected to advise a patient to see the doctor if he suspected a serious illness before giving any advice himself. However, it is where blocking is used negatively that it becomes a serious obstacle to effective listening.

Figure 8.4: Blocking tactics to listening

—	Rejecting involvement	'I don't wish to discuss this with you' 'That has nothing to do with me'
—	Denial of feelings	'You've nothing to worry about' 'You'll be all right'
—	Selective responding	Focusing only on specific aspects of the speaker's message, while ignoring others
—	Admitting insufficient knowledge	'I'm not really qualified to say' 'I'm only vaguely familiar with that subject'
—	Topic shift	Changing the subject away from that expressed by the speaker
—	Referring	'You should consult your doctor about that' 'Your course tutor will help you on that matter
—	Deferring	'Come back and see me if the pain persists' 'We'll discuss that next week
—	Pre-empting any communication	'I'm in a terrible rush. See you later' 'I can't talk now, I'm late for a meeting'

ACTIVE LISTENING

In social interaction there are a number of behaviours which can be employed in order to demonstrate effective listening. Although verbal responses are the main indicators of successful listening, wherein person A responds in an appropriate verbal manner to person B to indicate that he has heard B's message, there are a number of related nonverbal behaviours which have become associated with the skill of listening. If these nonverbal behaviours are not displayed, it is usually assumed that an individual is not paying attention, and *ipso facto* not listening to what is being said. Thus while these nonverbal behaviours are not crucial to the assimilation of verbal messages, they are expected by others. Furthermore Harrigan (1985) found that there are clear nonverbal signals emitted by listeners, in terms of changes in posture, eye gaze and gestures, which serve to signal that they wish to move from listening to speaking. It should also be recognised that the nonverbal information conveyed by the speaker can often add to, and provide emphasis for, the verbal message (see Chapter 2). An example of this can be found in a study by Strong *et al.* (1971) who asked 86 college students to listen only, or both view and listen, to tapes of counsellors, and rate these counsellors on a 100-item checklist. Results indicated that when the counsellors in this study were both seen and heard they were described as more cold, bored, awkward, unreasonable and disinterested, than when they were heard only. This study highlights the importance of attending to both verbal and nonverbal information in judging social responses.

Verbal responses which are indicators of listening, have already been discussed to some extent in many of the social skills previously reviewed in this book. Within the skill of reinforcement, for example, *verbal reinforcers* are often regarded as being associated with attending and listening (see Chapter 3). In terms of listening, however, caution is needed when employing verbal reinforcement. Rosenshine (1971), for example, found that the curve of the relationship between amount of verbal reinforcement by teachers and degree of pupil participation in classroom lessons took the form of an inverted U-shape. While pure verbal reinforcement (e.g. 'very good', 'yes') initially had the effect of increasing pupil participation, if this reinforcement was continued in its pure form, pupils began to regard it with indifference. Rosenshine points out that it is simple to administer positive reinforcers without much thought, but in order to demonstrate genuine listening some reasons have to be given for the use of the reinforcers. Pupils need to be told why their responses are good, for the reinforcement to be regarded as genuine.

One aspect of reinforcement which is a potent indicator of effective listening is *reference to past statements* made by another person, and especially to the use of such statements in conversation. This can range from simply remembering someone's name, to remembering other details about facts, feelings or ideas they may have expressed in the past. By focusing on these aspects, where relevant during social encounters, it is possible to convey interest in another person, by showing an ability to listen and pay attention to what they have talked about previously. This is likely to encourage the person to participate more fully in the present interaction.

Another aspect of verbal responses which is indicative of careful listening is *verbal following*. This refers to the process whereby the listener matches his verbal comments closely to the responses of the speaker, so that they 'follow-on' in a coherent fashion from what the speaker has said. If the listener follows the comments of the speaker, by asking related questions, or making related statements which use the ideas expressed by the speaker, this is usually taken as an indication of attentiveness and interest. The ability to utilise verbal following to a high degree is vital in many contexts, such as interviewing, teaching and counselling, where it is important to follow certain lines of debate, discussion or guidance with other people, and demonstrate a willingness to listen to their points of view.

In discussing the issue of topic shifts, Crow (1983) distinguishes between *coherent topic shifts* which occur once the previous topic has been exhausted, and *noncoherent topic shifts* which are abrupt changes of conversation which are not explained. As Crow points out, we often use *disjunct markers* to signal a change of topic ('Incidentally', 'Can I ask you a different question?' 'Before I forget'). In the early stages of a relationship, individuals usually ensure that a disjunct marker is used before making a noncoherent topic shift, whereas once a relationship has been developed the need for such disjunct markers recedes. Thus Crow found that married couples used unmarked noncoherent topic shifts during conversation without this unduly affecting their interactions. However, in most professional interactions disjunct markers will be required where verbal following does not take place.

Within the skill of questioning (see Chapter 4) the use of *probing questions* is a direct form of listening, wherein the questioner follows up the responses of the respondent by asking related questions. Similarly, the skill of *reflecting* (see Chapter 5) represents a powerful form of verbal following. In order to reflect accurately the feeling, or the content, of what someone has said, it is necessary to listen carefully before formulating a succinct reflecting statement. Reflection of feeling, therefore, demands a much higher level of listening than does minimal verbal reinforcement, and it may be for this reason that it has been found to be more effective than reinforcement in increasing the participation of clients in interview situations.

Zuker (1983) argues that individuals have different dominant sensory channels, in that people are either predominantly visual, auditory or kinesthetic. A visual person will use expressions such as 'I see what you mean' or 'It's all become clear to me now'; an auditory person 'It doesn't sound quite right' or 'That rings a bell'; and a kinesthetic person 'It still doesn't feel right' or 'I've got to grips with it now'. Zuker suggests that we can facilitate the listening process by *using similar language to the speaker* when providing feedback, such as 'I've got the picture now' (visual), 'I hear what you're saying' (auditory), or 'I'm in touch with you now' (kinesthetic). While it is true that good listeners adjust their use of language to accommodate the speaker, research evidence linking this to the notion of predominant sensory channels is as yet lacking.

The use of *summarisation* during periods of closure is also evidence of prolonged listening throughout an interaction sequence (see Chapter 6). By using summarisation of the main points arising from the thoughts, ideas, facts and feelings expressed by the other person during an encounter, the impression conveyed is usually one of overall attentiveness and careful listening to what has been said.

Nonverbal responses are also important during listening. As Burley-Allen (1982) points out 'one of the most important skills of effective listening is listening to nonverbals . . . [and] to the pitch, rate, timbre and subtle variations that the tone of voice is communicating' (p. 56). In addition, certain nonverbal behaviours on the part of the listener are usually associated with attending, while other nonverbal behaviours are associated with lack of listening. Rosenfeld and Hancks (1980) found that head-nods, forward leaning posture, visual attention and eyebrow raises were all associated with positive ratings of listening responsiveness. They also report that the most prevalent nonverbal listening indicator is the head-nod, and the most frequent vocalisation is 'mm hmm'.

Thus a number of nonverbal responses are important, including:

(1) *Smiles* used appropriately as indicators of willingness to follow the conversation, or pleasure at what the speaker is saying.
(2) Direct *eye contact*, again to indicate interest in listening to what

is being said. In Western society, the listener will usually look more at the speaker than vice versa.
(3) Indicating enthusiasm for the speaker's thoughts and ideas, by using appropriate *paralanguage* when responding (e.g. tone of voice, emphasis on certain words, lack of interruption of speaker).
(4) Mirroring the *facial expressions* of the speaker, in order to reflect and express sympathy with the emotional message being conveyed.
(5) Adopting an attentive *posture*, such as a forward or sideways lean on a chair. This is taken as a sign of listening. Similarly a sideways tilt of the head (often with the head resting on one hand), is usually taken as an indicator of listening. In many situations, 'sympathetic communication' will involve the mirroring of overall posture, as well as facial expressions, and indeed where problems arise in communication such mirroring usually ceases to occur.
(6) *Nods* of the head to indicate readiness to listen to what the speaker is saying.
(7) Refraining from distracting mannerisms, such as doodling with a pen, fidgeting, or looking at a watch. This is also important in conveying an impression of attention and desire to listen.

While these nonverbal behaviours are usually regarded as signs of listening, there are a number of nonverbal cues which are taken as signs of inattentiveness or lack of listening. These negative behaviours are the opposite of the behaviours employed to signal positive listening. Nonverbal signs of non-listening include absence of head-nods, lack of eye contact, no smiles or appropriate facial expressions, poor use of paralanguage (e.g. flat tone of voice, interrupting the speaker, no emphasis), slouched posture, and the use of distracting behaviours such as rubbing the eyes, writing or reading while the speaker is talking, or yawning. (In fact, an effective technique to induce someone to stop talking is to use these indicators of non-listening.) It should be realised, however, that these nonverbal signals can be deceiving, in that someone may not appear to be listening as judged nonverbally, while in fact they are listening closely. In this respect the only true measure of listening is in terms of verbal responses. Most teachers will have experienced the situation where a pupil appears to be inattentive and not listening, and yet when asked a question is able to give an appropriate response.

Although it is quite possible to listen to another person without overtly indicating that listening is taking place, in most social settings it is desirable not only to listen but also to demonstrate such attentiveness. Thus both the verbal and nonverbal determinants of effective active listening are of importance in social interaction. In fact, the verbal and nonverbal signs of listening are integrated in such a fashion that, in most cases, if either channel of communication signals lack of attention, this will be taken as an indication of lack of listening.

OVERVIEW

Listening is a fundamental component of interpersonal communication, since in its absence communication will either be superficial or will break down completely. It is important to realise that listening is not something that just happens, but rather is an active process in which the listener decides to pay careful attention to the speaker. As Rogers and Farson (1973) point out, 'the listener has a very definite responsibility. He does not passively absorb the words which are spoken to him. He actively tries to grasp the facts and the feelings in what he hears' (p. 541). Listening involves focusing upon both the verbal and nonverbal messages being emitted by the speaker, while at the same time actively demonstrating both verbal and nonverbal signs of listening.

In professional contexts, the ability to listen effectively is of paramount importance. There are a number of basic guidelines which need to be borne in mind in order to ensure successful listening:

(1) Get physically prepared to listen. If the interaction is taking place in your own environment, ensure that it is conducive to effective listening, by providing an appropriate physical layout of furniture, ensuring adequate temperature and ventilation, and keeping intrusive noise and other distractions to a minimum.
(2) Be mentally prepared to listen objectively. Try to remove all other thoughts from your mind, and concentrate fully on the speaker. Be aware of your own biases, avoid preconceptions, and don't stereotype the speaker.
(3) Use spare thought time positively. Keep your thoughts entirely on the speaker and the message being delivered, by asking covert questions, constructing mental images of what is being said, or employing other concentration techniques.
(4) Avoid interrupting the speaker where possible. Develop a system of mental 'banking', where ideas you wish to pursue can be cognitively 'deposited' and 'withdrawn' later. This allows the speaker to have a continuous flow, and the fact that you can later refer back to what

has been said is a potent indicator of active listening.
(5) Organise the speaker's messages into appropriate categories and, where possible, into chronological order. Identify the main thrust and any supporting arguments. This process facilitates comprehension and recall of what has been said.
(6) Don't overuse blocking tactics. These are often used subconsciously to prevent the speaker from controlling an interaction. On occasions blocking is a legitimate option. For example, at the end of a counselling encounter a client may raise an important issue which the counsellor does not have time to deal with, and so may use the tactic of deferring discussion until the next session. However, the overuse of such tactics is indicative of a lack of desire to listen.
(7) Remember that listening is hard work. It takes energy to listen actively and demands a firm initial commitment to listen. Professionals who spend their working day listening, will testify that it is an exhausting activity, and one which requires discipline and determination.

Listening is therefore a core skill for professionals, and one that should be emphasised during training programmes. Professional educators have a particular responsibility in this respect, both to develop listening skills in trainees and to act as listening models since, as Conine (1976), in a discussion of the role of listening in physical therapy, remarks 'In the course of their education many physical therapy students have had little experience of being listened to, a factor contributing to a lack of appreciation for listening to others' (p. 160). The same criticism could apply to a number of professions, and where this is the case it is the responsibility of educators to rectify such a state of affairs.

9

Self-disclosure

INTRODUCTION

A great deal of social interaction consists of participants making statements, or disclosures, about a wide variety of issues. These disclosures may relate either to objective statements about other people, places or events, or they may be subjective disclosures about the speaker. This latter type of disclosure is referred to as self-disclosure, whereby the speaker reveals some personal information to others.

However, there is some disagreement about the exact meaning of the term 'self-disclosure'. Some definitions restrict the field of study to verbal disclosures only, for example: 'self-disclosure may be defined as any information about himself which Person A communicates verbally to Person B' (Cozby, 1973, p. 73). But this approach excludes the study of nonverbal self-disclosures, which can be an important channel for communicating personal information, especially about feelings and emotions. Thus Stewart (1977, p. 172) defines self-disclosure as: 'the act of verbally and non-verbally sharing with another some aspects of what makes you a person, aspects the other individual would not be likely to recognize or understand without your help.'

Other definitions highlight the importance of intentionality on the part of the discloser. The definition given by Worthy *et al.* (1969, p. 59) is: 'that which occurs when A knowingly communicates to B information about A which is not generally known.' A similar viewpoint is expressed by Fisher (1984) who argues that information disclosed unintentionally, or by mistake, is a self-revelation rather than a self-disclosure. Allen (1974, p. 198) limits the scope even further by defining self-disclosure as the 'uncoerced exchange of personal information in a positive relationship', thereby excluding, for example, disclosures made under interrogation.

In this chapter, however, a wider perspective is held and self-disclosure is defined as the process whereby person A verbally and/or nonverbally communicates to person B some item of personal information which was previously unknown to B. In this sense, telling a close friend your name would not be a self-disclosure since this information would be already known, whereas telling a complete stranger your name would be a self-disclosure. Likewise, nonverbal, disclosures, whether intentional or not, are included. As discussed in Chapter 2, facial expressions, posture, gaze, paralanguage and all the other features of nonverbal communication are the main means whereby we provide information about our emotional state. One important difference between verbal and nonverbal self-disclosure is that we have greater control over the former than the latter. For this reason, the nonverbal channel provides important information regarding the detection of deceptive communication from others (Zuckerman *et al.*, 1982).

The importance of self-disclosure, as a social skill, is usually associated with the work of Sidney Jourard (1964, 1971), who emphasised the value of this skill in helping situations. Jourard stressed the need for a high degree of openness between individuals in many contexts, and illustrated the potency of self-disclosure as a technique for encouraging deep levels of interpersonal sharing. Following the pioneering work carried out by Jourard, an enormous amount of interest has been generated in the field of self-disclosure, leading to a proliferation of research studies. A number of books have been devoted to this topic (e.g. Chelune, 1979; Derlega and Berg, 1987; Derlega and Chaikin, 1975), together with numerous book chapters and journal articles.

A knowledge of the nuances of self-disclosure is important to most professionals, for two main reasons. Firstly, it is vital for professionals to be aware of contexts in which it is appropriate for them to self-disclose to clients. Secondly, professionals also need to be aware of the benefits which accrue from, and the methods whereby they can encourage, full, open and honest self-disclosures from clients.

FEATURES OF SELF-DISCLOSURE

In interpersonal encounters there are a number of features of self-disclosure which influence the nature of the interaction that is taking place. Ivey and Authier (1978) highlight four of the main features of self-disclosure.

(1) Verbal self-disclosures involve the use of the personal pronoun 'I', or some other personal self-reference pronoun such as 'my', 'mine', or 'I'm'. While these words may be implied from the context of the speaker's utterances, their presence serves to remove any ambiguity about whether or not the statement being made is a self-disclosure. For this reason, the basic reference point for all self-disclosures should be a personal pronoun. Compare, for example, the statements:

A: 'Selection interviews can create a great amount of stress.'
B: 'I find selection interviews very stressful.'

In statement A it is not immediately clear whether the speaker is referring to selection interviews in general or to his feelings about attending selection interviews. The use of the personal pronoun 'I' in statement B, however, serves to clarify the nature of the statement as a self-disclosure. As Fisher (1984) points out, it is often necessary to ask for clarification about whether or not a statement is a self-disclosure, so that to the client statement 'You feel guilty when you don't do what others expect of you', the clarification probe (see Chapter 4) 'Are you saying *you* feel guilty when you don't do what others expect?' could be employed.
(2) Self-disclosures can be about either facts or feelings. When two people meet for the first time, it is more likely that they will focus upon factual disclosures (name, occupation, place of residence) while keeping any feeling disclosures at a fairly superficial level ('I hate crowded parties', 'I like rock music'). This is largely because the expression of personal feelings involves more risk and places the discloser in a more vulnerable position. At the same time, however, deep levels of disclosure may be made to a complete stranger providing we feel sure that we will never meet the person again (Chaikin and Derlega, 1974). Thus two strangers sitting beside one another on a long haul plane journey who discover that their encounter is likely to be 'one-off' may reveal personal information and feelings, which they would not do if they were planning to meet one another on a regular basis.

Falk and Wagner (1985) found that a gradual progression from low to high levels of self-disclosure leads to better relationship development. In this way the expression of deep feeling or of high

levels of factual disclosure (e.g. 'I was in prison for 5 years') will increase as a relationship develops. For this reason, professionals should expect clients to experience difficulties in self-disclosing at any depth at the early stage of an encounter. Even if the client has a deep-rooted need to 'tell someone', such an experience will inevitably be embarrassing, or at least awkward, where the disclosures relate to very personal details. The skilled helper will be aware of this and employ techniques which help the client to overcome such initial feelings of embarrassment. Factual and feeling disclosures at a deeper level can be regarded as a sign of commitment to a relationship (Newcomb, 1961). Two people who are in love will usually expect to give and receive disclosures about their feelings — especially towards one another. They will also want to know everything about one another. In such a relationship there will be a high level of trust, just as there will be in the confession box, a doctor's surgery or a counsellor's office (areas where disclosures will also be high).
(3) The third aspect of self-disclosure relates to the object of the statement. A self-disclosure can be about one's own personal experience, or it can be about one's personal reaction to the experiences being related by another person. Ivey and Authier contend that the latter type of self-disclosure is at a deeper level than the former, and that it can therefore serve to enhance the development of interpersonal relationships. Consider the following interaction:

John: I haven't been sleeping too well recently. I work until midnight every night, and yet nothing seems to sink in. I'm really worried about these exams. What would I do if I failed them?
Mary: You know John, I am very concerned about you. It seems to me that you are working too much, and not getting enough rest.

This is an example of a self-disclosure as a personal reaction to the experiences of another person, in which one individual is expressing concern and giving an opinion about the statements made by the other. In the example given, Mary could have chosen to give a self-disclosure about her own personal experience by saying something like 'I remember when I was sitting my final exams. I was worried about them too. What I did was to make sure I stopped working in time to get out of the house and meet other people. This took my mind off the exams . . . ' In this case, while Mary is reciprocating by self-disclosing she is taking the focus away from John and on to herself. Both types of self-disclosure are appropriate in different contexts, depending upon the nature of the interaction which is taking place and the goals of the interactors. If it is desirable to give concerted attention to an individual and encourage him to disclose fully, then the type of self-disclosure which concentrates upon reactions to the feelings or thoughts of the other person would probably be most successful. If, however, the intention is to demonstrate to someone that they are not alone in feeling as they do, then the use of a parallel self-disclosure relating one's own experience may be more effective. (4) Self-disclosure can be about the past (I was born in 1950; I was really grief-stricken when my father died), the present (I am a vegetarian; I am very happy), or the future (I hope to get promotion; I want to get married and have a family). One situation in which people are expected to self-disclose in terms of facts and feelings about the past, present and future, is in the selection interview. Candidates will be asked to talk about their previous experience or education, to say why they have applied for the job and to outline their aspirations. Not only will candidates be expected to give factual details about themselves, they will more often than not be expected to relate their attitudes and feelings towards these factual experiences. The depth of self-disclosure required will, of course, vary from one interview to another. In selection interviews at an executive level, for example, the candidate may even be asked to answer the question 'What type of person would you say you are?'

ELEMENTS OF SELF-DISCLOSURE

A number of important elements of self-disclosure have been identified by Derlega and Grzelak (1979) and these need to be taken into consideration in any evaluation of the effectiveness of self-disclosure.

Informativeness

This relates to the amount of information being provided by the discloser. As Figure 9.1 indicates, self-disclosures can be assessed along two dimensions, namely breadth and depth. The relationship between these two dimensions is such that as the depth (or intimacy) of disclosures increases, the breadth (or total number) decreases. Derlega and Chaikin (1975) give an example of a questionnaire designed to measure both breadth and depth of disclosures. Examples of shallow levels of disclosure given in this questionnaire include:

'How often my aunts and uncles and family get together', 'Whether or not I have ever gone to a church other than my own', and deeper levels such as 'Times that I have lied to my girlfriend (boyfriend)', 'The kinds of things I do that I don't want people to watch'.

Figure 9.1: The relationship between breadth and depth of self-disclosures

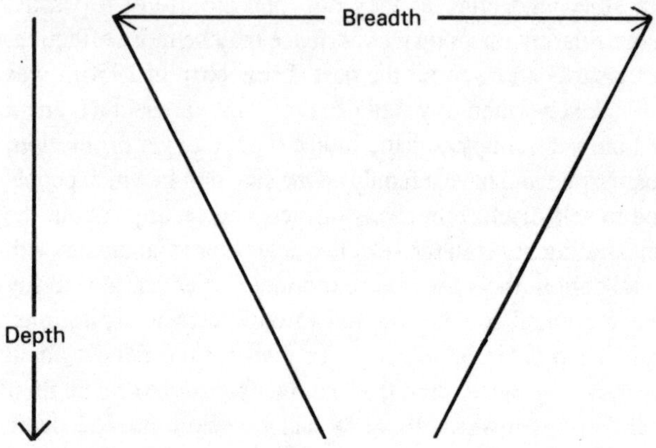

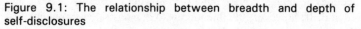

Appropriateness

This is perhaps the most crucial aspect of self-disclosure. Each disclosure needs to be evaluated in the light of the context in which it occurs. While there are no hard and fast rules about the exact appropriateness of self-disclosure in every situation, there are some general indicators. Self-disclosures are more appropriate:

— From low status to high status individuals but not vice versa. Thus workers may disclose personal problems to their supervisors, but the reverse does not usually happen. This is because for a supervisor to disclose personal information to a subordinate would cause a 'loss of face' which would affect the status relationship. Research findings tend to suggest, however, that self-disclosures are most often employed between people of equal status (Slobin *et al.*, 1968). While some self-disclosure from the professional to a client can be very appropriate, in most contexts clients will expect only minimal disclosures from professionals. Woolfolk (1979), for example, in a study of the use of self-disclosure by teachers, found that 'intimate teacher self-disclosure was viewed negatively by adult students and that superficial self-disclosure elicted a greater response' (p. 138).
— When the listener is not flooded with them. As Figure 9.2 illustrates there is a relationship between psychological adjustment and self-

disclosure in that individuals who are extremely high or low disclosers will have low adjustment.

Figure 9.2: Relationship between adjustment and disclosure

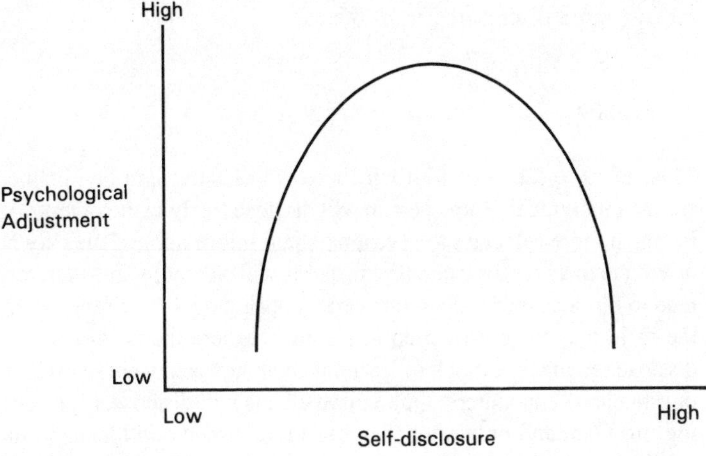

— Depending upon the roles of the interactors. For example, we may disclose information to our spouses which we would not disclose to our children. Similarly, clients will often discuss a problem with a 'neutral' counsellor, that they would not wish to discuss with their spouses or with close friends. Indeed most professionals will be reluctant to counsel close friends as part of their professional role, since to do so may well pose difficulties for both parties.
— Depending upon the setting. Thus we would not normally discuss bowel problems during an intimate dinner with a member of the opposite sex, but we would do so in a doctor's surgery.

Flexibility

Self-disclosure flexiblity refers to the ability of an individual to vary the breadth and depth of his disclosures across situations. Highly flexible disclosers are able to modify the nature and level of their self-disclosures whereas less flexible disclosers tend to disclose at the same level regardless of context. Fong *et al*. (1986) found that counsellors with high self-disclosure flexibility provided more effective counsellor responses. Furthermore, as Miller and Kenny (1986) point out, 'individuals who disclose across-the-board (not differentially) are not the recipients of disclosure across-the-board from others' (p. 718). They term this the 'blabber-mouth' effect, wherein an individual reveals all kinds of information readily, as opposed to the 'wise old owl' who will tend to disclose discreetly and will as a result tend to receive more disclosures from others.

Accessibility

This refers to the ease with which self-disclosures can be obtained from an individual. Some people will disclose freely while others will be much more reluctant to reveal personal information. This may be due to personality, for example extroverts will talk more, and therefore tend to disclose more, than introverts; upbringing and culture, where the child may have grown up in a context where the norm is not to disclose too much; or lack of learning about how and what to disclose during social encounters. Quite often clients will disclose a 'presenting' problem and only after they have established confidence in the professional will they reveal the real problem. This is particularly true where the problem is of an intimate or embarrassing nature.

Valence

This is the degree to which the disclosure is positive or negative for both the discloser and the listener. In the early stages of relationship development disclosures will be mainly positive, and negative self-disclosures will usually only emerge once a relationship has developed. This is another reason why some clients will find difficulty in disclosing negative information to an unfamiliar professional.

Honesty

Self-disclosures can be true or false. As mentioned earlier, an awareness of some of the nonverbal indicators of deception is important when considering the truth of self-disclosures. Rozelle *et al.* (1986) summarise the main deception indicators as including: speech errors, tone of voice, fidgeting with objects, less time spent looking at the other person, rocking, more leg movements, self-fidgeting and frequent head movements. However, it is necessary to be aware of the normal, or 'baseline', behaviour of the individual in order to judge whether or not these nonverbal behaviours are in fact deviations from the individual's normal pattern.

FUNCTIONS OF SELF-DISCLOSURE

The use of self-disclosure serves a number of functions depending upon whether this is carried out by the professional or the client. The main functions of self-disclosure by the professional are:

To overcome fear

Many people have a fear of disclosing too much about their thoughts and feelings, since they feel they may not be understood or will be subjected to ridicule. Indeed in many sub-cultures self-disclosure will be actively discouraged with the child being told 'whatever you say, say nothing' or 'tell people only what they need to know'. This attitude then persists into later life where respect is often given to the person who 'plays his cards close to his chest'. While in a game of poker it is wise not to disclose too much, either verbally or nonverbally, the attitude of avoiding self-disclosure can cause problems for people when they may have a need to talk about personal matters. However, the initial dangers of self-disclosure are such that we expect an equal commitment to this process from people with whom we may wish to develop a relationship. For this reason, reciprocation is expected in the early stages of everyday interaction. In relation to the poker analogy it is a case of the individual wanting to see all of the cards on the table! The fear of self-disclosure can sometimes be overcome partially by a self-disclosure from the professional to the effect that he has often dealt with this type of problem, or that he feels it is quite acceptable for the client to have the problem. This form of 'reassuring' self-disclosure will usually be appreciated by clients.

To encourage reciprocation

In everyday interaction, reciprocation of self-disclosures will usually occur in that if one person is prepared to reveal personal details about herself, this usually results in the listener also revealing personal details (Tubbs and Baird, 1976). In professional situations, clients can often be encouraged to 'open up' by receiving a self-disclosure from the professional. Such a disclosure can have a very potent effect on the client, who will then be more likely to begin to self-disclose more freely. O'Neill and O'Neill (1977) point out that where reciprocation of self-disclosures does not occur, one of three types of situations will usually prevail:

(a) The person making the disclosures is not really interested in the listener. This type of person's need is so great that he wants to tell all, without worrying about the effect this may have upon the listener. The speaker is simply using the listener as a receptacle into which he pours his disclosures. This is quite common when someone is undergoing some form of inner turmoil, and needs a friendly ear to encourage the ventilation of fears and emotions. To use another analogy, the listener becomes a 'wailing wall' for the speaker! In professional contexts this is often acceptable, as in counselling and therapy.
(b) The person who is receiving the disclosures does not care about the speaker. In this case the speaker is foolish to continue disclosing, since it is possible that the listener may use the disclosures against the speaker, either at the time of the disclosure or later.
(c) Neither one cares about the disclosures of the other. In this case there is no real relationship. If one person discloses, it is a monologue; if both disclose it is a dialogue in which exchanges are superficial. A great deal of everyday, fleeting conversation falls into the latter category.

To open conversations

When two people meet for the first time they will give and receive self-disclosures. Chaikin and Derlega (1976) identify three main stages or levels of relationship development. The first of these is *awareness* when two people have not actually interacted but are becoming aware of the presence of one another. At this stage, for example, a female may stand close to, or walk slowly past, a male whom she is interested in. The second stage is that of *surface contact*, when individuals give superficial information about themselves, and make judgements about whether or not to pursue the relationship. The final stage is *mutuality* where the two people begin to disclose personal feelings, and engage in more intimate self-disclosures. Many professionals will use self-disclosure to open interactions and establish surface contact. Thus a social worker visiting a family for the first time will usually begin by saying something like 'Hello. My name is John Whiteside. I'm a social worker from the . . . ' Such disclosures will be directly related to the job role.

To search for commonalities

At the surface contact stage of a relationship, people give self-disclosures in the hope that the other person may be able to identify with them. At this stage they search for shared interests or experiences in order to identify some common ground on which to build a conversation. This would usually occur in informal meetings between professionals and clients. It is also important in certain business contexts, such as selling, where the professional salesman may want to establish a common frame of reference with his client, in order to facilitate the development of a relationship (and the likelihood of a successful outcome in terms of sales!). On occasions, the professional may want to highlight commonalities. Thus a health visitor visiting a young mother who has just had her first child may say 'I know the problems associated with motherhood since I have three children myself', thereby establishing a common bond, and providing a good foundation for a discussion of the particular problems faced by this mother.

To express concern for the other person

This is the type of self-disclosure in which the professional expresses her feelings about the other person. Such self-disclosure can serve as a potent form of reinforcement for the client (see Chapter 3). Rackham and Carlisle (1978), however, also found that self-disclosure was a skill employed by effective negotiators. By making disclosures such as 'I am worried that we are so far apart on this', the negotiator gives an impression of openness and honest concern for the other side, which in turn is usually reciprocated.

To share experiences

In certain instances, the professional will have had similar experiences to the client, and can share these to underline the fact that there is a depth of understanding between the two. This helps to underline the fact that the professional is 'human'. For example, one situation where this can be of immense benefit is where a client has recently been bereaved, and the professional has also faced the pain of bereavement. The use of a self-disclosure here can be a valuable reassurance to the client that the pain will pass (e.g. 'I remember when my mother died I thought I would never get over it . . .').

To express one's point of view

In many contexts, such as at staff meetings, interviews, case conferences, the professional will be expected to put forward her thoughts, ideas and opinions. The ability to do so confidently and competently is therefore important.

These are the main functions of professional self-disclosure. However, self-disclosure by clients also serves a number of important functions including:

To facilitate self-expression

It can become a burden not being able to tell others about personal matters, and having to keep things 'bottled up'. Self-disclosure can have a therapeutic effect, by enabling us to 'get it off our chest', which is why counselling, the confessional or discussing something with a close friend can all make us feel better. Indeed, it is interesting to note that, when people may not be able to utilise one of these channels, they often use substitutes such as keeping a personal diary, talking to a pet, or conversing with God. Thus most of us have a strong need to express ourselves to others, and professionals should be aware both of the existence of this need and of ways to allow clients to satisfy it. (This need can be observed at an early stage in young children who often disclose to a teddy bear or doll.)

To heighten personal knowledge

This is exemplified by the saying 'How do I know what I think until I hear what I say?' As De Vito (1986, p. 105) puts it: 'while the individual is self-disclosing, she or he recognizes some facet of behaviour or some relationship that was not known before'. The value of the 'talking cure' in therapy is a good example of how the process of allowing someone freely to express their thoughts, ideas, fears, problems, etc., actually facilitates the individual's awareness of the type of person they are (Levin, 1977). It can also help people to understand their feelings and the reasons for them; in other words it encourages them to know themselves more fully. Thus Franzoi and Davis (1985) found that individuals who had a more accurate and detailed self-understanding engaged in more self-disclosure.

To promote social comparison

People who do not have access to a good listener may not only be denied the opportunity to heighten their self-awareness, they are also denied valuable feedback as to the validity and acceptability of their inner thoughts and feelings. By discussing such inner thoughts and feelings with others, we receive feedback as to whether these are experiences which others have as well, or whether they may be less common. Furthermore, by gauging the reactions of others to our self-disclosures, we learn what types of disclosures are acceptable or unacceptable with particular people and in specific situations. On occasions it is the fear that certain types of self-disclosure may be unacceptable to family or friends which motivates an individual to seek professional help. Counsellors, for example, will be familiar with client statements such as: 'I just couldn't talk about this to my husband'; 'I really can't let my mother know my true feelings'.

To develop relationships

The appropriate use of self-disclosure is crucial to the development and maintenance of long-term relationships. People who either disclose too much, or too little, will tend to have problems in establishing and sustaining relationships with others. Similarly, individuals who disclose at a deep level to relative strangers, or who make only negative disclosures, will find it difficult to make friends. By encouraging clients to self-disclose, and giving sensitive feedback, professionals can provide such clients with a valuable learning experience about how to use the skill of self-disclosure.

To ingratiate and manipulate

Some clients will use self-disclosures in an attempt to ingratiate themselves with the professional, for whatever reason. This type of client will tend to disclose quite a lot, and will say more positive things about the professional ('You are the only person who understands me'; 'I don't know what I would do without you'). In a sense, the client is 'coming on too strong', and this can be very difficult to deal with. It may be a technique used by the client to manipulate the professional for some form of personal gain. On the other hand, if this type of ingratiation is genuine, it can be a signal that the client is becoming over-dependent on the professional. Either way, it is advisable to be aware of this function of client self-disclosure.

These, then, are the main functions of self-disclosure by both the professional and the client. A number of these functions can be illustrated with reference to the Johari Window (Luft, 1970) developed by two psychologists, Joseph Luft and Harry Ingram (and named after the initial letters of both Christian names). As depicted in Figure 9.3 this indicates four dimensions of the self. There are aspects which are known both by the self and by others (A); aspects unknown by the self but known to others (B), including personal mannerisms, annoying habits and so on; aspects known by the self but not revealed to others (C), such as embarrassing personal details, thoughts or feelings; and aspects which are unknown both to the self and others (D). One of the effects of self-disclosing is that the size of segment A is increased and the size of the segments B, C and D reduced. In other words by encouraging clients to self-disclose, not only will they find out more about themselves, but the professional will also gain valuable knowledge about them, and thereby perhaps understand them more fully.

FACTORS INFLUENCING SELF-DISCLOSURE

There are a number of factors, pertaining to the nature of the discloser, the recipient, the relationship, and the context, which will influence the extent to which self-disclosure will be employed (for a full review see Archer, 1979).

The discloser

The following characteristics of the discloser are related to self-disclosure:

Figure 9.3: The Johari Window

	Known to self	Unknown to self
Known to others	A	B
Unknown to others	C	D

Age

Disclosure seems to increase with age. As Archer (1979) points out this finding has been reported in studies of children between the age of 6 and 12 years, and in college students between the ages of 17 to 55 years. However, Sinha (1972), in a study of adolescent females, found that 12–14-year-old girls disclosed most, followed by 17–18-year-olds, with 15–16-year-olds disclosing least. Sinha argues that at this latter stage the adolescent is at a stage of transition, from girl to woman, and may need more time to 'find herself'. This finding has obvious implications for professionals dealing with mid-adolescent individuals.

Feminity

Individuals, either male or female, who regard themselves as possessing female attributes will disclose more. Thus Bender *et al.* (1976) found that heterosexual females and homosexual males were more disclosing. Grigsby and Weatherley (1983), furthermore, found that women were significantly more intimate in their disclosures than men. It would seem that it is more acceptable in Western society for females to discuss personal problems and feelings. Males disclose more about their traits, work and personal opinions while females disclose more about their tastes, interests and relationships. Males also disclose less negative personal information than females (Naifeh and Smith, 1984). It is therefore important to be aware that males may find difficulty in discussing personal matters, and may need more help, support and encouragement to do so. Stokes *et al.* (1980) found that males will self-disclose more with strangers than will females, but at a shallow level, so the problem may be encouraging males to move from a shallow to a deeper level of disclosure.

Birth order

First-born children tend to disclose less than later born children. This difference has been attributed by Dimond and Hellkamp (1969) to the possibility that later-borns are more socially skilled, because their parents have more experience of child-rearing, and they have older siblings to interact with.

Ethnic group

Research evidence indicates that in the USA, whites disclose more than blacks, who in turn disclose more than hispanics. Americans have been found to be more disclosing generally than similar groups in Germany, Great Britain and the Middle East. Yet Wheeless *et al.* (1986), in a study of 360 students, found no difference in disclosure levels between American students and students of non-Western cultural origin studying in the USA. However, since the latter group of students had been studying in the USA for an average of 19 months, Wheeless *et al.* suggest that they may have learned to adapt their patterns of self-disclosure to the US cultural norm.

Personality

Introverts disclose less than extroverts. Also those with an external locus of control (who believe their destiny is shaped by events 'outside' themselves over which they have no control) disclose less than those with an internal locus of control (who believe they can largely shape their own destiny). Anxious people also tend to disclose more. It has further been found that neurotics tend to have low self-disclosure flexibility, in that they disclose the same amount, regardless of the situation.

The recipient

A number of characteristics of the listener will influence the amount of self-disclosure received, including:

Gender

It has been found that people tend to disclose more to members of the opposite sex (Brooks, 1974). However, this depends upon the context. For example, a female may prefer to discuss embarrassing health problems with a female, rather than a male, doctor.

Status

Generally, individuals disclose more to those of the same status than to people of higher status, and disclose least to lower status individuals (Burger and Vartabedian, 1985).

Attractiveness

The attractiveness of the listener is another important element in encouraging self-disclosures. Brundage *et al*. (1977) report findings which suggest that individuals will disclose more to a physically attractive, as opposed to an unattractive, recipient, irrespective of the sex of discloser and recipient. Similarly, there is evidence to indicate that more disclosures are made to individuals who are liked by the discloser. Interestingly, it has also been found that we tend to like people who disclose more to us. As Taylor (1979, p. 122) puts it 'self-disclosure leads to liking and liking leads to self-disclosure'. Not surprisingly, therefore, more self-disclosures tend to be made to individuals who are perceived as being similar (in attitudes, values, beliefs, etc.) to the discloser, since such individuals will usually be better liked.

Acceptance/empathy

Accepting/empathic people receive more disclosures. Miller *et al*. (1983) found that certain individuals, whom they term 'openers', are able to elicit intimate disclosures from others. They found particularly that those who demonstrated *perspective taking* ability received more self-disclosures. In other words, those who could demonstrate to the discloser that they could understand his perspective, thereby encouraged further self-disclosures to be made. Also, listeners who are accepting and supportive will receive more self-disclosures, since this acts as a form of reinforcement to the discloser.

Thus Purvis *et al*. (1984) found that individuals who used appropriate visual display and speech behaviour promoted more self-disclosure from others. In particular 'the appearance of comfort, interest, enjoyment and an attentive facial expression' (p. 65) is the visual display used by high openers, who also employ brief responsive utterances ('mm hmm', 'yeah', etc.). (See Chapter 3 for further information on reinforcement.)

The relationship

The following features of the relationship between discloser and recipient will influence the amount of self-disclosure used:

Trust

If the discloser trusts the recipient to keep his disclosures in confidence, and not use them against him in any way, then he will use more self-disclosure. This is the reason that deep disclosures tend to be given only when a relationship has been firmly established. In certain contexts the professional can be faced with an ethical dilemma when receiving self-disclosures. For example, if a client discloses that he has committed a crime of some sort, there may be a legal requirement for the professional to inform the police, yet to do so could well destroy the relationship of trust which has been developed. How such ethical dilemmas are resolved will, of course, depend upon the particular circumstances involved.

Reciprocation

As Archer (1979, p. 47) puts it 'the most frequently demonstrated determinant of disclosure is disclosure itself'. Thus those who reciprocate with self-disclosures will receive further self-disclosures. Also, in everyday interaction if Person A makes an intimate self-disclosure, this will influence the depth of disclosure reciprocated by person B. It is as if there is social pressure on the recipient to reciprocate intimacy with intimacy.

Role relationships

In certain relationships it is the norm that one person will demonstrate most, if not all, of the disclosures made. At a selection interview the candidate will be the discloser, and in most professional contexts the client will be the main discloser.

Anticipated length and commitment

As previously indicated, an awareness of the 'one-off' nature of an interaction can encourage self-disclosure in certain situations. This is referred to by Thibaut and Kelley (1959) as the 'stranger-on-the-train phenomenon'. This phenomenon can, however, apply to some professional situations. For example, a client may be reluctant to return to a counsellor, following an initial session in which deep self-disclosures may have been made to the counsellor, who is usually in effect a complete stranger. Counsellors should therefore employ appropriate closure skills in order to help overcome this problem (see Chapter 6).

Physical proximity

Johnson and Dabbs (1976) found that there was less intimate disclosure at close interpersonal distances (18 inches), and more tension felt by the discloser, than at a medium distance (36 inches). However, there is some evidence to suggest that it is males, but not females, who find close interpersonal distance a barrier to disclosure (Archer, 1979).

Gaze

Direct gaze from a stranger has been shown to decrease the intimacy of male disclosures, but to increase the intimacy of female disclosures.

Voluntary involvement

There is more self-disclosure in relationships where the client has volunteered to talk about some issue. An extreme example of the negative effects of coercion upon self-disclosure is the individual who is 'helping police with their enquiries'. However, this can also be a problem where a client has been referred to the professional and is present under some degree of duress. In such a relationship greater efforts need to be made to encourage self-disclosure.

The situation

Finally, the following aspects of the situation in which the interaction is taking place will influence the degree of self-disclosure which will occur:

Warmth

A 'warm' environment has been found to encourage more self-disclosures, in that if there are soft seats, gentle lighting, pleasant decor and potted plants in an office a client will be more likely to 'open-up' (Chaikin *et al.*, 1976). This finding is interesting, since interrogation sessions normally take place in 'cold' environments (bare walls, bright lights, etc). Presumably, the willingness of the person to self-disclose will be an important factor in determining the type of environment for the interaction.

Privacy

Solano and Dunnam (1985) found that self-disclosure was greater in dyads than in triads, which in turn was greater than in a four-person group. They further found that this reduction applied regardless of the gender of the interactors and concluded that 'there may be a general linear decrease in self-disclosure as the size of the group increases' (p. 186).

In an experimental study, Derlega *et al.* (1973) found that when student subjects were informed that their interaction with another subject (a confederate of the experimenter) was being video-recorded for later showing to an introductory psychology class, their depth of self-disclosures stayed at a superficial level, regardless of the intimacy of disclosures of the confederate subject. However, when no mention was made of being video-taped, the level of intimacy of disclosure from the confederate subject was reciprocated by the 'true' subject. This study highlights the importance of privacy for encouraging self-disclosure.

Crisis

People are more likely to self-disclose in situations where they are undergoing some form of crisis, especially if this stress is shared by both participants. Thus patients in a hospital ward who are awaiting operations will generally disclose quite a lot to one another.

Isolation

If individuals are 'cut off' from the rest of society they tend to engage in more self-disclosure. For example, two prisoners sharing a cell will often share a high degree of personal information. Indeed, for this reason the police will sometimes place a 'stooge' in a cell along with a prisoner from whom they want some information.

These, then, are the main findings relating to the influence which the characteristics of the discloser, the recipient, the relationship and the situation have upon the extent to which self-disclosure will be employed during interpersonal interaction. From this brief review of research findings, it is obvious that self-disclosure is affected by a wide range of variables, many of which will be operative in any particular social encounter. It is important for professionals to be aware of the importance of these variables when making decisions about giving and receiving self-disclosures.

OVERVIEW

From this analysis of self-disclosure, it will be clear that this is an important skill for professionals to be aware of, from two perspectives. Firstly, professionals need to be aware of the likely effects of any self-disclosures they may make upon the clients with whom they come into contact. Secondly, many professionals operate in contexts wherein it is vital that they are able to encourage clients to self-disclose freely, and so a knowledge of some of the factors which facilitate self-disclosure is very useful. Our impressions of other people can be totally wrong in many cases since we do not know what is 'going on inside them'. As Jourard (1964, p. 4) points out, 'Man, perhaps alone of all living forms, is capable of *being* one thing and *seeming* from his actions and talk to be something else'. The only method of attempting to overcome this problem of finding out what people are 'really like', is to encourage them to talk about themselves openly and honestly. If we cannot facilitate others to self-disclose freely, then we will never really get to know them.

When giving and receiving self-disclosures the following factors need to be considered:

— The total number of disclosures made
— The depth of these disclosures
— The nonverbal, as well as verbal, disclosures
— The physical environment
— The age, gender and personality of the interactors
— The status and role relationships between the interactors
— The timing of the disclosures
— How best to respond to client disclosures.

The general importance of self-disclosure in everyday interaction reflects the fundamental value of this skill in many professional contexts. It is therefore useful to conclude with a quote from Chaikin and Derlega (1976, p. 178), which neatly encapsulates the central role which this aspect has to play:

> The nature of the decisions concerning self-disclosure that a person makes will have great bearing on his life. They will help determine the number of friends he has and what they are like: they will influence whether he is regarded as emotionally stable or maladjusted by others: they will affect his happiness and the satisfaction he gets out of life. To a large extent, a

person's decisions regarding the amount, the type, and the timing of his self-disclosures to others will even affect the degree of his own self-knowledge and awareness.

10

Assertiveness

INTRODUCTION

Assertiveness is an area of study which has a long history within the field of behaviour therapy, dating back to the pioneering work of Salter (1949) and Wolpe (1958), who recognised that certain individuals in society had specific problems in standing up for their rights. As a result the skill of assertiveness was introduced during therapy in an attempt to help such individuals function more effectively in their everyday lives.

During the last few years the skill of assertiveness has attracted enormous interest, reflecting the importance of this aspect of social interaction across many areas. Within the past decade a large volume of research has also been conducted and, in fact, 'the amount of investigation has become a torrent permeating much of the professional literature' (McIntyre *et al.*, 1984, p. 311). It has increasingly been recognised that most groups of professionals can benefit from becoming more assertive, and so programmes of assertion training are now employed in the training of many such professionals.

While a knowledge of assertiveness will be of benefit to most professionals, for some it would seem to be of particular importance. For example, nurses apparently represent one particular profession with reported problems in being assertive (Clark, 1978; Porritt, 1984). In discussing this issue, McIntyre *et al.* (1984) attribute these problems to many of the values associated with nurses, in that they are expected to 'think of others first (even if they are tired or hurting), they should be humble, they should always listen and be understanding and they should never complain or confront' (p. 312). In a study of 26 nurses, McIntyre *et al.* found that, based upon a number of measures, nurses were clearly nonassertive (submissive) when compared to other professional groups. However, following an assertiveness training programme, the nurses demonstrated significant increases in assertiveness, which were maintained at a 2-month follow-up period.

Thus assertiveness is an aspect of interpersonal communication which can be developed and improved. It is a skill which is of importance when dealing with peers, superiors and subordinates. It is also pertinent to interactions between different groups of professionals, especially where differences of power and status exist (such as between nurses and doctors), and it is of relevance to interactions between professionals and clients.

Early definitions of assertiveness were fairly all-embracing in terms of interactional skills, and even more recently, Lazarus (1971), for example, regarded assertiveness as comprising four main components, namely the ability to:

(i) refuse requests;
(ii) ask for favours and make requests;
(iii) express positive and negative feelings; and
(iv) initiate, continue and terminate general conversations.

It is obvious that this conceptualisation of assertiveness is very wide, encompassing almost all forms of human interaction. Indeed, in the USA, as Kelly (1982) points out: 'Until somewhat recently, the terms "assertion training" and "social skills training" were often used in interchangeable fashion; it was not recognized that assertiveness represents one specific kind of interpersonal competency' (p. 172). Dissatisfaction with this approach has led to a more focused study of assertion, based specifically upon the theme of standing up for one's rights in a sensitive, competent, manner. This latter interpretation is the one given by most dictionaries, and a perspective held by most lay people, and it is the view adopted in this chapter.

Appropriate definitions of assertive behaviour can be found in two of the central texts in this area of study. Thus Lange and Jakubowski (1976) state that 'assertion involves standing up for personal rights and expressing thoughts, feelings and beliefs in direct, honest, and appropriate ways which respect the rights of other people' (p. 38). In like vein, Alberti and Emmons (1982) define assertion as behaviour which 'enables a person to act in his or her own best interests, to stand up for herself or himself without undue anxiety, to express honest feelings comfortably, or to exercise personal rights without denying the rights of others' (p. 13). Both of these definitions emphasise an important component of assertion, namely respect for the rights of other people, and the skilled individual should be able to achieve a balance between ensuring personal rights and not infringing the rights of others.

STYLES OF RESPONDING

In order to fully understand the concept of assertiveness, it is necessary to distinguish this style of responding from other approaches. Alberti and Emmons (1975) distinguished between three such styles, namely nonassertion, assertion and aggression, as follows:

Nonassertive responses involve expressing oneself in such a self-effacing, apologetic manner that one's thoughts, feelings and rights can easily be ignored. In this 'cap in hand' style, the person hesitates, speaks softly, looks away, avoids issues, agrees regardless of his own feelings, does not express opinions, values himself 'below' others, and hurts himself to avoid any chance of hurting others. The objective here is to appease others and avoid conflict at any cost.

Assertive responses involve standing up for oneself, yet taking the other person into consideration. The assertive style involves answering spontaneously, speaking with a conversational yet firm tone and volume, looking at the other person, addressing the main issue, openly expressing personal feelings and opinions, valuing oneself equal to others, and hurting neither oneself nor others. The objective here is to try to ensure fair play for everyone.

Aggressive responses involve threatening or violating the rights of the other person. Here the person answers before the other is finished speaking, talks loudly and abusively, glares at the other person, speaks 'past' the issue (accusing, blaming, demeaning), vehemently states feelings and opinions, values himself above others, and hurts others to avoid hurting himself. The objective here is to win, regardless of the other person.

These three styles can be exemplified in relation to a situation in which someone is asked for the loan of a book which he or she does not wish to lend:

(1) 'um . . . How long would you need it for? It's just that . . . ah . . . I might need it for an assignment. But . . . if it wasn't for long . . . ' (Nonassertion)
(2) 'I'm sorry. I'd like to help you out, but I bought this book so

I would always have it to refer to, so I never loan it to anyone.' (Assertion)
(3) 'No. Why don't you buy your own damn books!?' (Aggression)

From these examples, it can be seen that these three styles of responding form a continuum of:

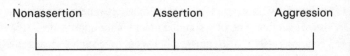

Nonassertion — Assertion — Aggression

Assertiveness forms the mid-point of this continuum, and is usually the most appropriate response. Aggressive individuals may initially get their own way by brow-beating others, but they will often be disliked and avoided. Alternatively, this style may provoke a similar response from others, with the danger that the verbal aggression may escalate and eventually lead to overt physical aggression. Nonassertive individuals, on the other hand, will often be viewed by others as weak, 'mealy-mouthed' creatures who can be easily manipulated, and as a result nonassertive people will frequently express dissatisfaction with their lives, owing to a failure to attain personal goals. Assertive individuals, however, tend to derive more satisfaction from their lives, and achieve their goals more often. They also will obtain more respect from those with whom they interact.

A number of research studies have verified the behavioural responses associated with these three styles. Rose and Tryon (1979) carried out a systematic, carefully controlled study, in which they found that assertive behaviour was clearly associated with louder voice [68 decibel (dB) level was viewed as nonassertive; 76dB level was the assertive ideal; 84dB level was towards the aggressive end of the continuum]; reduced response latency (pauses of 16 seconds before responding, were seen as nonassertive, whereas pauses of 3–4 seconds were viewed as assertive); increased use of gestures (although increased gestures coupled with approach behaviour were seen as aggressive); and increased vocal inflection. Similarly McFall *et al.* (1982), in a detailed research investigation, identified what they termed 'assertive body movements' the most salient being hands, arms and overall body cues. Assertive individuals used 'controlled, smooth, steady, and purposive movement as opposed to shifty, shaky, fidgety extraneous body activity' for nonassertive people (p. 137). Furthermore, Kolotkin *et al.* (1983) found that duration of eye contact was greater for assertive, as opposed to nonassertive individuals. They also found that the use of smiles can help to convey that a response is meant to be assertive rather than aggressive.

TYPES OF AGGRESSION

Although most texts on assertion differentiate between three styles of responding, some theorists have made a distinction between two types of aggression, namely open, direct aggression and passive, indirect aggression (for example, Phelps and Austin, 1975; De Giovanni, 1979). Recently, Del Greco (1983) has argued that these two types of aggression can be combined with nonassertion and assertion to form two continua, rather than one. As depicted in Figure 10.1, these two continua are coerciveness and directness.

The passive, or indirect, aggressive style of responding seems to embrace a range of behaviours including sulking, using emotional blackmail (such as crying in order to get your own way), pouting, and being subtly manipulative. Del Greco (1983) has developed an Inventory to measure all four response styles. Indirect, or passive, aggressive items include 'When I am asked for my preference I pretend I don't have one, but then I convince my friends of the advantages of my hidden preferences'; and 'When my friend asks me for my opinion I state that I have none, then I proceed to make my true preference seem the most attractive'. This type of Machiavellian approach is one clear example of indirect aggression. Another example would be where a person slams drawers and doors shut while refusing to discuss the reason for so doing.

Figure 10.1: Four styles of responding

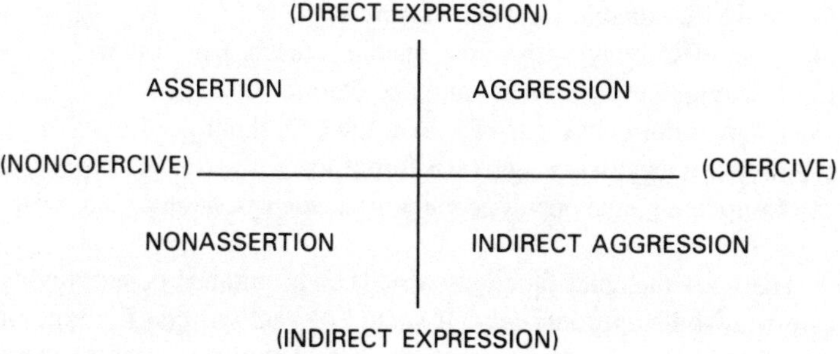

The four response styles can be illustrated with reference to alternative ways of responding to someone smoking in a 'no smoking' area:

(1) 'Hey, you, there's no smoking allowed in this area. Either put out or get out!' (Aggressive)
(2) 'Excuse me, but do you realise that this is a "no smoking" area? Cigarette smoke affects me quite badly, so I'd be grateful if you would not smoke here.' (Assertive)
(3) Not mentioning your discomfort, and hoping that someone else will confront the smoker. (Nonassertive)
(4) Coughing loudly and vigorously waving a hand towards the smoker as if to fan the smoke away. (Indirectly aggressive)

Once again, assertiveness is regarded as the optimal approach. While it is possible to be skilfully manipulative, there is always the danger of being found out, with resulting negative consequences. Similarly in the case of passive aggression, as in (4) above, this can also lead to a negative evaluation, and may simply be ignored by the other person.

FUNCTIONS OF ASSERTIVENESS

The skill of assertion serves a number of purposes, depending upon the situation in which one has to assert oneself. Generally, however, the skilled use of assertive responses will help individuals to:

(1) Ensure that their personal rights are not violated.
(2) Withstand unreasonable requests from others.
(3) Make reasonable requests of others.
(4) Deal effectively with unreasonable refusals from others.
(5) Recognise the personal rights of others.
(6) Change the behaviour of others towards them.
(7) Avoid unnecessary aggressive conflicts.
(8) Confidently, and openly, communicate their position on any issue.

These are the chief functions which can be attained by employing assertion skills appropriately. It should be realised that the type of assertiveness used can determine the extent to which each of these functions may be fulfilled, and so a knowledge of types of assertiveness is of vital importance during social encounters. Furthermore, personal and contextual factors also play a crucial role in determining the effectiveness of assertive responses.

TYPES OF ASSERTIVENESS

There are a number of different types of assertive behaviour which can be employed. Lange and Jakubowski (1976) identify five types of assertiveness as follows:

Basic assertion

This involves a simple expression of standing up for personal rights, beliefs, feelings or opinions. For example, when interrupted a basic assertive expression would be: 'Excuse me, I would like to finish what I was saying'.

Empathic assertion

This type of assertion conveys some sensitivity to the other person, by making a statement that conveys some recognition of the other person's situation or feelings before making the assertive statement. Thus an empathic assertion to an interruption might be: 'I know you are keen to get your views across, but I would like to finish what I was saying'.

Escalating assertion

Here the individual begins by making a minimal assertive response, and, if the other person fails to respond to this, gradually increases or escalates the degree of assertiveness employed. An example of escalating assertiveness may occur where a professional in his or her office is being pressurised by a very determined sales person, and the escalation may proceed as follows:

(i) 'No, I've decided that I don't wish to purchase any of these products.'
(ii) 'No, as I've already said, I'm not buying any of them.'
(iii) 'Look, I've told you twice that the answer is no. I'm going to have to ask you to leave now.'

Confrontive assertion

This is used when someone's words contradict his actions, and involves clearly telling the person what he said he would do, and what he actually did. The speaker then expresses what he now wants. An example would be: 'You said you would have the report typed by Tuesday. It is now Thursday and you still haven't typed it. I would like you to type it for me now please.'

I-language assertion

Here the speaker objectively describes the behaviour of the other person, how this affects the speaker's life or feelings and why the other person should change his behaviour. In the case of being interrupted, an I-language assertive response would be: 'You know, this is the fourth time you've interrupted me in the past few minutes. This makes me feel that you aren't interested in what I am saying, and I feel a bit hurt and annoyed. I would like you to let me finish what I want to say.'

Linehan and Egan (1979) distinguish between a direct, and an indirect, style of assertiveness. They argue that a direct, unambiguous assertive style may not always be most effective, especially for those individuals for whom it is important to be liked and regarded positively by others. Rather, a more ambiguous, indirect style of response seems more appropriate in some instances (despite the fact that most texts recommend a direct style). An example of these two styles can be seen in relation to the following question:

Q.: 'Could you loan me that new LP you bought yesterday?'
Direct: 'No, I never loan my LPs to anyone.'
Indirect: 'Oh, you mean The Oceans — You know, I'm still trying to get a chance to sit down and listen to it at length myself. I usually take ages listening to a new LP.'

However, Linehan and Egan also point out that the direct style can be less abrasive if turned into a complex-direct style. This latter approach would involve the use of an embellishment associated with a refusal. They identify five main embellishments which can be employed, namely empathy, helplessness, apology, flattery and outright lying (although this one would need to be used with caution). The idea here is to 'soften' the refusal and so maintain a relationship. Thus using this style a response to the above question might be:

Complex-Direct: 'I know you would look after it really well, but I've recently had three LPs that I loaned ruined, so I've just had to make the general decision never to loan my LPs to anyone again. That way I hope no one will feel personally offended.'

Fry (1983) identifies three types of assertiveness which she refers to as 'protective skills', and which are a form of verbal defence commonly used against manipulation, nagging or rudeness. The first of these skills is the *broken record* where the person simply makes an assertive statement and keeps repeating this statement (as if the 'needle had stuck') until it is accepted by the other person. For example, to repeated pleas for a loan the individual may just keep saying 'No, I'm not going to give you any money'. The second protective skill is known as *fogging*, wherein the person appears to accept negative criticism without changing his behaviour. An example of a fogging sequence would be:

A: 'You always look down in the dumps.'
B: 'Yes, I probably do.'
A: 'Could you not try to look a bit happier?'
B: 'I suppose I could.'
A: 'If you did, you would be a bit more pleasant to work with.'
B: 'Yes, you're probably right.'

The idea here is that eventually the other person will become tired getting no real response to the criticisms and will eventually give up.

It should be realised that these two skills are basic forms of assertion which should really only be used as a form of protection from prolonged or unwarranted criticism. They are not intended as general methods for expressing one's rights. The third type of skill listed by Fry is that of *metalevel* assertion whereby someone, who realises that a solution is unlikely, suggests that wider perspectives should be considered rather than specific issues. One example of this approach, of moving from the particular to the general, would be where someone involved in an argument with a colleague says 'We obviously are not going to agree about this, and I think this is typical of what is happening to our whole working relationship.'

COMPONENTS OF ASSERTIVENESS

In order to execute assertiveness skills effectively, there are a number of central components which need to be mastered. Rakos (1986) has identified four main components of assertion:

Content

The actual content of an assertive response should include both an expression of rights, and a statement placing this expression of rights within the context of socially responsible and appropriate behaviour. Rakos identified five possible accompanying statements. We will illustrate in relation to a refusal to a request from a colleague to go to the bar at lunchtime:

(i) An explanation for the necessity to assert oneself — 'I can't go today because I have some work to finish off during the lunch break.'
(ii) An empathic statement recognising the other person's situation — 'I can't go today. I know you are disappointed . . . '
(iii) Praise for the other person — 'It's very nice of you to ask, but I can't go today . . . '
(iv) An apology for any resulting consequence — 'I can't go today. I'm sorry if you are on your own over lunch.'
(v) An attempt to identify a mutually acceptable compromise — 'I haven't time to go out to the bar today. How about just having a quick snack in the canteen?'

These content statements, which are similar to the embellishments recommended by Linehan and Egan, could obviously be combined to soften the assertion, and distinguish the response from aggression. Rose and Tryon (1979) make a distinction between three types of assertion content, which can be exemplified in relation to complaining about a meal in a restaurant, as follows:

(i) Description of the behaviour — 'Excuse me, this meal is cold.'
(ii) Description of behaviour plus indication of your noncompliance — 'Excuse me, this meal is cold. I couldn't eat it.'
(iii) Description, noncompliance, plus request for behaviour change — 'Excuse me, this meal is cold. I couldn't eat it. Could you please replace it?'

Rose and Tryon found that ratings of assertiveness increased as individuals moved from simply giving a description, through to using all the above three types of content.

Kolotkin *et al.* (1983) also found that assertiveness was associated with requests for behaviour change. In addition, they found that it was associated with use of 'I' statements, whereas use of 'you' statements (which imply accusatory content) were associated with aggression. They identified other important aspects of assertion as including: cognitive statements (what the person thought about the situation), orienting statements (indicating the topic or issue that is going to be raised), and statements of feeling. Galassi *et al.* (1981) emphasise the importance of recognising the separate sub-elements of assertion, which they summarise as: statement of rights, refusal behaviour, request for behaviour change, empathy statement, threat or conflict statement, and giving reasons for behaviour.

Covert elements

This refers to the influence of thoughts, ideas and feelings upon the ability to be assertive. Rakos identifies the following covert elements:

Knowledge

In order to be assertive it is necessary to know both what one's rights are, and how to enforce them. It is not always clear in many situations exactly what one's rights are, and it is therefore sometimes necessary to consult with others in order to gauge their views about whether personal rights have been infringed. This process of consultation is termed *reality testing* (Dawley and Wenrich, 1976), which may involve asking other people either for advice about what exactly your rights are (e.g. 'Has he the right to ask me to do that?'), or about their perceptions of your behaviour (e.g. 'Have I upset you in some way?', 'Do you mind doing this?').

In terms of actual rights, Zuker (1983) has produced a general Assertive Bill of Rights for individuals which includes the right to:

- be treated with respect
- have and express personal feelings and opinions
- be listened to and taken seriously
- set one's own priorities
- say no without feeling guilty
- ask for what one wants

— get what one pays for
— make mistakes
— assert oneself even though it may inconvenience others
— choose not to assert oneself.

Beliefs

Submissiveness can result from mistaken beliefs. For example, someone may believe that they should always do what their superiors tell them to do or negative consequences may accrue. Before such a person could effectively be assertive, he would have to replace this belief with a new one, for example that it is always valid to ask for a good reason if requested to do anything that seems unreasonable. Kuperminc and Heimberg (1983) found that submissive individuals expected negative consequences to follow from noncompliance and positive consequences from compliance, with unreasonable requests, whereas assertive individuals expected positive outcomes from non-compliance and negative consequences from compliance. This research finding lends further support to the view that changes in beliefs and expectations may well be a prerequisite for changes in assertive behaviour.

Dawley and Wenrich (1976) refer to this as a process of *cognitive restructuring* for people with inappropriate beliefs. Such restructuring would include changes in self-instructions, the covert behaviour-guiding self-statements we employ when making decisions about which responses to carry out. Kern (1982) found that nonassertive individuals have 'a high frequency of negative self-statements and expectations that their behaviour will yield a relatively large number of negative consequences' (p. 496). Thus submissive individuals would use self-statements such as 'She will not like me if I refuse', rather than 'I have the right to refuse'.

Social perception

Nonassertive people are more likely to perceive the behaviour of others inaccurately by, for example, perceiving unreasonable requests as being reasonable. Such people will be viewed by others as 'easy touches', in terms of borrowing items, doing extra work, etc., since they are always ready to be helpful. There comes a time when being helpful develops into being used, and people need to learn not only to be able to draw the line between these two, but also to actually learn to perceive the behaviour of others more accurately, in order to distinguish reasonable and unreasonable requests.

Process

The way in which assertive responses are carried out can be crucial to their success. Thus the correct timing of vocalisations and nonverbal responses is vital. As mentioned earlier, assertive responses should be given without undue delay or hesitation. On occasions, we may have our rights infringed because we are unsure about whether they actually have been violated. If we later discover this to be the case then it is necessary to reconstruct the situation in which the infringement occurred ('Yesterday you asked me to do X. I have since discovered that it is not my job to do X. I would therefore be grateful if you would not ask me to do this again'.)

Stimulus control skills are also important. These refer to manipulations of the environment, or other people, to make the assertive response more successful. For example, asking someone to come to your room (where you will feel more in charge) rather than discussing an issue in the corridor; requesting that you seek the opinion of another person to help settle the matter (where you already know the views of this third person); or simply asking for time to think over a request (which allows you to think through the ramifications thereof).

The use of reinforcement (see Chapter 3) is also important, for two reasons. Firstly, rewarding another person is a positive use of assertion. If someone has performed a task well, then he or she has the right to expect reward. Secondly, the use of reward for a person who has complied with an assertive response can help to minimise any negative feelings resulting from the assertion, and it can encourage the person to behave more appropriately in the future.

Nonverbal responses

The final component of assertiveness identified by Rakos relates to the nonverbal behaviour of the asserter. This includes: medium levels of eye contact; avoidance of inappropriate facial expressions; smooth use of gestures while speaking, yet inconspicuous while listening; upright posture; direct body orientation; appropriate paralinguistics (short response latency, medium response length, good fluency, medium volume and inflection, increased firmness).

PERSONAL AND CONTEXTUAL FACTORS

There are a number of factors which influence the degree, nature and effectiveness of assertion.

Gender

The skill of assertiveness has attracted a great deal of interest within women's movements. As Linehan and Egan (1979) point out, females often report that they find it difficult to be assertive. Kahn (1981) has suggested that this is because:

> People expect women to behave unassertively. Women may not only accept this judgement of others and behave so as to fulfill prophecies based on stereotyped beliefs, but . . . may avoid behaviours that do not fit 'the feminine role' and when they do engage in 'masculine assertiveness', they are likely to encounter disbelief or even hostility from others . . . A common attack against females is the labelling of women who assert themselves as aggressive (p. 349).

However, Kern *et al.* (1985) found that, in a review of 14 studies comparing the reactions to male and female assertiveness, 10 found no significant difference, 3 found male assertions to be more favourably evaluated, and 1 found female assertions more favourably evaluated. In their ensuing study, Kern *et al.* found that how female assertion was evaluated was a function of the individual's attitude towards females. Males or females holding a conservative, low attitude towards women (LATW) devalued females' assertions, whereas those with a liberal, high attitude towards women (HATW) were not influenced by the gender of the asserter. This would suggest that females might gainfully employ different types of assertive responses patterns when dealing with those with LATW as opposed to those with HATW.

In a separate study, Nix *et al.* (1983) concluded that assertiveness is a masculine sex-role characteristic. They found that females achieving high masculinity scores in the Bem Sex Role Inventory scored significantly higher on measures of assertiveness than those high in feminity. Lewis and Gallois (1984) further discovered that both males and females were more assertive towards those of the same gender; that expression of negative feeling was more acceptable from a member of the opposite sex; and that aggressive encounters were more prevalent in same-sex dyads.

Situation

The situation in which assertiveness is required is another important factor. Following a detailed research investigation, Eisler *et al.* (1975) concluded that 'an individual who is assertive in one interpersonal context may not be assertive in a different interpersonal environment. Further, some individuals may have no difficulty responding with negative assertions but may be unable to respond when the situation requires positive expressions' (p. 339). Thus some people may find it easy to be assertive at home, but difficult to be assertive at work, or vice versa. In such instances, attention needs to be devoted to the difficult situation, and strategies evolved to overcome particular difficulties.

Furthermore, the cultural context is also important. As Furnham (1979) points out, the concept of assertiveness tends to be culture bound. Assertive responses which may be appropriate in Europe or the USA, may not be so appropriate in other countries where values of humility, tolerance or subservience may be prevalent. Conversely, Margalit and Mauger (1985) found that Israelis generally respond more aggressively than Americans. Israelis were found to express anger more readily and more frequently ignored the rights of others, while Americans were more ready to give and accept praise.

Certain types of assertiveness may well be more appropriate in some settings than in others. Cianni-Surridge and Horan (1983) found this to be the case in the job interview. They had 276 employers rate the efficacy of 16 'frequently advocated assertive job-seeking behaviours' in terms of whether or not each would enhance the applicant's chances of being offered employment. They found that some behaviours were advantageous and some disadvantageous. Thus, for example: 'Following an interview, an applicant writes you a letter thanking you for interviewing him/her and expressing his/her continued interest in the position' was regarded by 54 employers as greatly enhancing, by 176 as enhancing, by 46 as having no effect, and by 0 as diminishing or greatly diminishing job prospects. On the other hand: 'An applicant feels his/her interview with you went poorly. He/she requests a second interview with another interviewer' was regarded by 44 employers as greatly diminishing, by 100 as diminishing, by 119 as having no effect, by 10 as enhancing, and by 3 as greatly enhancing job prospects.

From our own evaluation of a range of professional groups, we have ascertained a number of situations in which it can be more difficult to be assertive. These include: when interacting in someone else's home or office; when in a strange country or sub-culture; when alone as opposed to when with friends or colleagues; when dealing with superiors at work; when promoted to a position of authority over those who were formerly friends and colleagues; when dealing with elderly people; when dealing with those who are physically or mentally handicapped; when interacting with those who are seriously or terminally ill, and with their relatives; when dealing with people who are in poverty or in severe social deprivation; when interacting with other professionals of higher status and power; with friends or close work colleagues; and when dealing with members of the opposite sex.

The Assertee

Gormally (1982) found that assertive behaviour was rated more favourably by individuals who were assertive themselves, while Kern (1982) discovered that low assertive subjects reacted negatively to assertive behaviour whereas high assertive subjects generally devalued nonassertive behaviour. These findings suggest that decisions about when and how to apply assertion should be moderated by the assertive nature of the other person.

Lewis and Gallois (1984) investigated the influence of friendship on assertiveness. They found that certain types of negative assertions (expression of anger, or difference of opinion) were more acceptable when made by friends as opposed to strangers. However, refusal of a request from a friend was perceived to be less socially skilled and more hurtful, than refusal from a stranger. As a result, they recommend that with strangers it is 'wise to refrain from assertively expressing a difference of opinion or negative feelings, at least until the relationship is well established' (p. 366).

OVERVIEW

Assertiveness is a very important social skill both in professional contexts and in everyday interactions. We feel hurt, aggrieved and upset if our rights have been violated. Some individuals find it difficult to be assertive. This is often related to upbringing in that they may have been raised under a very strict regime by parents in which as children they were 'seen and not heard', and learned in school that the quiet child who did as it was told was most approved of by the teacher. It can then be difficult in later life to overcome this residue of parental and educational upbringing. However, research evidence clearly indicates that it is possible to improve assertion skills.

Where such changes in assertiveness occur, it is useful to be aware of some possible reactions of other people to new-found assertiveness. Alberti and Emmons (1975) identify four such reactions:

(1) Back-biting. Making statements behind the person's back, which they ensure are overheard ('Who does she think she is', 'All of a sudden he's now a big fellow').
(2) Aggression. Others may try to negate the assertion by using threatening or aggressive behaviour in an attempt to regain dominance.
(3) Overaplogising. Some people may feel they have caused offence and as a result will apologise profusely.
(4) Revenge-seeking. The assertion may be accepted but the person will retain hidden resentment and hold a desire to 'get their own back'.

It is important to be alert to such possible consequences of changing from nonassertion to assertion, and to help reduce any negative outcomes by ensuring skilful use of assertiveness. It should also be realised that assertion may not always be the most appropriate response in every situation. There are at least three contexts in which it may be more skilled to be nonassertive:

(1) Seeing that someone is in a difficult situation. If you are in a busy restaurant and you know that a new waitress has just been employed, you are more likely to overlook certain issues, such as someone who came in later being served before you. Here it is appropriate to be nonassertive, since personal rights are not deliberately being denied, and to be assertive may cause undue stress to the other person.
(2) Interacting with a highly sensitive individual. If by being assertive someone is liable to burst into floods of tears, or physically attack you, it may be wise to be nonassertive, especially if the encounter is 'one-off'.
(3) Manipulating others. Some females will deliberately employ a helpless style in order to achieve their goals, for example to encourage a male to change a flat tyre on their car. Equally, males may

do likewise. For example, if stopped by police following a minor traffic misdemeanour it may be wise to be nonassertive ('I'm terribly sorry officer, but I've just bought this car . . . '). Such behaviour is more likely to achieve positive benefits.

Nevertheless, a pattern of continued nonassertion will not be the most productive approach for the majority of people. Quite often what happens is that individuals will move from prolonged nonassertion straight into aggression, feeling they can no longer put up with being used, taken for granted, or having their rights ignored. It is therefore more appropriate to employ assertiveness at an early stage during social interaction. The advantages of so doing have been underlined by Zuker (1983) who points out that assertiveness is:

> not a mysterious, mystical gift that some have and others don't. Rather it's a series of skills that anyone can master with a little practice. The exciting thing about acquiring these skills is that you will suddenly find yourself being able to say no without guilt, to ask for what you want directly, and in general to communicate more clearly and openly in all your relationships. Most important, your self-confidence will improve dramatically (p. 12).

11

Group Interaction and Leadership

INTRODUCTION

This book is about people and how they behave when interrelating and communicating with each other. This can take place either in dyadic, or one-to-one interactions, or alternatively in larger gatherings. The various social skills which have occupied the preceding chapters, questioning, nonverbal communication, reinforcing, reflecting, listening, and so on, are applicable regardless of the number of individuals involved. Some, however, e.g. reflecting and self-disclosure, are more likely to be made use of in smaller, more intimate encounters. Consequently, much of this book, including various examples of skill deployment, has concentrated, at least implicitly, upon what happens when two people communicate. Interaction in the group context has not been directly considered. While many of the communication skills which form part of dyadic interaction can also be used when people get together in groups, there are added complexities associated with the latter which must be appreciated. As Applbaum *et al.* (1973, p. 63) pointed out:

> Research has shown that communication patterns between two people are different from those that occur with three or more people in face-to-face interaction. The difference is not just a matter of size . . . Many of the principles of intrapersonal and interpersonal communication apply as well to group communication, but many new factors affect the communication between individual members.

It is with such factors that the first half of this chapter is concerned. The remainder concentrates upon the characteristics and skills associated with a rather special and particularly important position within the group — that of leader.

Before progressing, however, it may be a useful and interesting exercise to pause, momentarily, to reflect upon the ubiquity of the group in social life. The individual is born into a social group and, as he develops, comes to play a more active part in an increasing range of them. Apart from the family he may be a member of a staff group, a sports team, study group, choir, appreciation society, yoga class, trade union committee, parent-teacher association, amateur photographic club, political party executive, to mention but a very few of the possibilities. (It may be worthwhile and illuminating for the reader, at this point, to list the various groups to which he or she belongs, to reflect upon the amount of time spent actively involved in each and the extent to which, collectively, they account for the various social activities engaged in. The outcome will probably be quite surprising!) Argyle (1983a) suggested that the three most important types of group in terms of everyday interaction are family, friendship and work groups. Other types of small group activity identified by Argyle include committees, problem-solving and creative groups and, secondly, T-groups and therapy groups. Each category could, of course, be further differentiated. Dealing solely with groups in the therapeutic context, Massarik (1972), for instance, listed no less than 39 identifiable variants. Since it is highly unlikely that being involved in this particular type will feature prominently in the daily routine of the typical individual, this figure serves to underscore the plethora of groups which abound and their pervasion in social life.

Focusing upon work groups it is evident that an important part of the service provided by such interpersonal professionals as doctors, nurses, social workers, teachers, etc., entails group involvement. Commenting upon the group with which the social worker is involved, Brown (1979) made an initial distinction between direct work with clients and indirect work for clients. The former may include dealing with natural groups, such as the family, as the target of intervention rather than an individual member of that family; secondly, institutionalised groups in, for example, psychiatric hospitals, prisons or residential centres; thirdly, community groups such as self-help, pressure or action groups. The second dimension of group involvement, while not directly encompassing the client, nevertheless plays an important part in enabling professional duties to be discharged effectively. Here can be listed meetings: with colleagues; in association with further training; during inter-professional case conferences; with voluntary groups; and in connection with professional associations. Such a system of classification could, no doubt, be applied with varying degrees of flexibility to other professions apart from that of social work and again serves to emphasise the range of group contexts within which the professional is called upon to operate. By so doing, it also vindicates the inclusion, in a book of this type, of a consideration of at least some of the underlying structures and processes which influence group functioning. But perhaps more thought needs to be given to the concept of group and to matters of definition before continuing further.

WHAT IS A GROUP?

The word 'group' has occurred several times in the preceding pages without, presumably, causing undue confusion. It is highly unlikely, however, that each reader will have attached the same meaning to it. If asked to attempt to produce a formal definition, many would probably find the task more difficult than it might have seemed at first blush. (You can test this for yourself by closing the book at this point and committing your deliberations on the issue to paper.) Most would probably agree that a group necessarily involves a plurality of individuals — but how many? While four or five people would probably be acceptable would 40 or 50 — and what about four or five thousand?

A common distinction is that between small groups and larger aggregations with the lower limits of the former being in the region of two to five and the upper limits, 15 to 20. There is little agreement on precise numbers, however, leading many to agree with Hare (1976) that attempts to define small groups purely in terms of size are fruitless. Size *per se* is not the key factor but rather availability for face-to-face interaction. This characteristic also forms the basis of the distinction between 'primary' and 'secondary' groups, first drawn by Cooley (1929). Primary groups are typified by the potential for close and frequent face-to-face association. It is with groups of this type that this chapter will be concerned to the exclusion of larger assemblies.

This notion of face-to-face contact has been extended by a number of authors who stress the importance of interaction and interpersonal influence among members in defining group existence. Bales (1950), for instance, regarded a small group as 'any number of persons engaged in interaction with one another in a single face-to-face meeting or series of such meetings, in which each member receives some impression or perception of each other member . . . ' (p. 33). In a similiar vein, Shaw (1981, p. 8), wrote that, ' . . . two or more persons who are interacting with one another in such a manner that each person influences and is influenced by each other person', constitutes a group and that small groups, for practical reasons, tend to have an upper limit of about 20 members.

In addition to interacting with and influencing each other, the interdependence of group members has been noted (Lewin, 1951; Fiedler, 1967). Thus events that affect one person will have a bearing on the rest of the group and group outcomes will affect each individual member.

The fact that groups are typically formed for some identifiable purpose and that those who belong share at least one common goal, has been regarded as an essential characteristic by many authors (Hare, 1976). In the case of a formal group, this goal is often reflected in its name (e.g. Eastham Branch of the Campaign for Nuclear Disarmament; Eastham F C Supporters Club; Eastham Brass Band). Interestingly, when a group's goal has been attained or rendered obsolete, members may direct their energies in other directions, thus ensuring the continued existence of the group. Eastham F C Supporters Club may still meet to have a drink and play snooker even though Eastham F C has long since ceased to exist! New goals have come to dominate group activities. This does not always happen, of course. In many cases the achievement of the group goal or goals results in its disbandment.

Apart from acting to maintain the group and directing its activities, goals also influence the development of particular structures and procedures within the group. Such considerations will be dealt with more fully in a later section of the chapter.

While interaction and interpersonal influence, interdependence, and the pursuit of a common goal or goals are commonly accepted as the quintessence of the concept, various other defining features of groups can be found in the literature. Campbell (1958), for example, pointed out that groups are reasonably enduring units and that any aggregate, in order to be so regarded, must have a certain permanency. But how long must it last? As with questions of size, no easy, absolute or commonly accepted answer can be given. Perhaps one way around this problem is to invoke members' perceptions of their 'groupness'. Thus in order to merit the label 'group', members must see themselves as forming a group, and extending the notion, be so perceived by outsiders (Feldman, 1985).

WHY DO PEOPLE JOIN GROUPS?

Accepting the universality of group involvement, the next question to tackle is why should this be so? Why should this prevalence to associate closely with others in social units exist? One reasonable attempt at explanation suggests that individuals rely upon group membership in order to satisfy certain felt needs. These needs may be interpersonal, informational, or material and in some cases, by their nature, may only be capable of being met in a social context. While we may not have to join a group in order to gain knowledge of our physical environment it is only through association with others that we come to an understanding of the social world which we inhabit and, indeed, of ourselves. Festinger (1954) proposed that individuals engage in a process of social comparison in order to establish where they stand in certain respects. For example, it is only possible to decide if you are a good, average or poor student by comparing your marks with others on your course. By so doing you gradually create an impression of yourself, including your strengths and weaknesses.

When it comes to satisfying interpersonal needs, the necessity to establish some form of group contact is obvious. These particular needs, according to Schutz (1955), may be for varying degrees of, firstly, inclusion — to want to belong or feel part of a social entity; secondly, control — to dominate or be controlled; and thirdly, affection — at the extremes, to love or hate. Argyle (1983b) also proposed that much of interpersonal behaviour is in response to social drives for affiliation, dominance, dependency or aggression. But, of course, being able to, for example, dominate depends upon one or more others who are prepared to be submissive. There is some evidence that groups comprised of members whose needs are complementary rather than conflicting, tend to be more satisfying and enduring. In a study involving student nurses, Bermann and Miller (1967) reported that those who complemented each other in terms of dominance formed more stable and satisfying associations.

Groups may also be established for material reasons. It may be to their mutual benefit for a number of individuals to pool their various resources in order to complete some task. Trade union and co-operative movements are some of the more contemporary examples of collectives being formed to further the material wellbeing of members. Man's gregarious nature is thought to have stemmed from the advantages of hunting in groups and sharing the kill, experienced by our early ancestors.

HOW ARE GROUPS ORDERED AND REGULATED?

Given that groups are made up of individuals each with particular, and perhaps contrasting, personalities, opinions and preferences, it seems reasonable to ask how they manage to become sufficiently organised and ordered for goals to be pursued efficiently. The emergence of group *norms* is of crucial importance in this respect. As groups evolve, regularities of operation begin to emerge reflecting the creation of expectations on the part of members. This has been expressed by Applbaum *et al.* (1973, p. 60), in the following way: 'As group members interact, they tend to standardize their activities to create customary ways of behaving that the whole group can recognize as norms. A group norm is the shared acceptance of a rule prescribing how members perceive, think, feel and act'. It should be noted that it is not only overt behaviour which is subject to a normative influence but also the characteristic perceptions, thoughts and feelings which members entertain. Not all aspects of group life are governed to the same extent by norms. Those most stringently subjected to this type of influence include activities: directly concerned with the achievement of group goals and the satisfaction of members' needs, especially the needs of the most powerful in the group; commonly associated with group membership both by those within and outwith the group; amenable to public scrutiny. Thus strict norms govern the examination of patients but not the colour of underpants which the doctor should wear! Secord and Backman (1974) pointed out that behaviours which have a strong physiological basis and those which could only be performed at considerable personal cost to the individual are less likely to come under normative control.

Apart from facilitating goal achievement, norms serve to increase regularity and predictability in the operation of the group. Members can determine, with reasonable accuracy, what is likely to happen in most situations. This also means that they have certain guidelines as to the nature and extent of their own involvement. Personal needs for status and esteem can also be satisfied through the operation of norms. Thus many of the tacit rules of everyday conversation are intended to avoid causing offence or embarrassment in public. A further advantage of having certain actions norm-governed is that it obviates the necessity of frequently having to rely upon personal influence (Secord and Backman, 1974). It can be pointed out, for example, that student nurses are expected to behave in a deferential manner to *all* ward sisters. Again the fact that certain norms have to do with the maintenance and integrity of the group must not be overlooked. Their importance is reflected in the level of disapprobation associated with terms such as traitor, scab, etc.

Norms may be communicated directly to those in the group. A case in point would be giving a new club member a set of formal rules and regulations governing club activities — or a landlady informing a new lodger, in no uncertain terms, what he can and cannot do. More often, however, such expectations are conveyed indirectly by, perhaps, watching what established members do and following their example. It is sometimes only when a violation occurs that one realises the existence of the norm. This information is often conveyed by subtle verbal and nonverbal cues.

Regardless of how they are communicated, norms are prescriptive. They must, to varying degrees, be complied with — members, to varying degrees, must conform. The origins of these pressures to conform to the expectations of the group may be internal. Feelings of shame or guilt may be sufficient to force the errant member to mend his ways. If not, external pressures in the form of positive and negative group sanctions may be brought to bear. In extreme cases, recalcitrance may result in boycott or indeed expulsion from the group.

Conformity to the commonly held views and practices of the majority has a number of advantages for the group. It tends to increase efficiency and facilitate group maintenance as well as reduce uncertainty and confusion among members and project a strong group image to the rest of society. Intense pressures to conform can, however, result in less desirable outcomes. One of these was identified by Janis (1972) and labelled 'Groupthink' which was defined as the 'deterioration of mental efficiency, reality testing, and moral judgement that results from in-group pressures' (p. 9). When such pressures militate against the reasoned and objective consideration of the range of available options and discourage frank expression of individual points of view, the decision reached by the group is frequently seriously flawed.

Norms, as we have seen, apply to all group members. In any group, however, it would be highly undesirable for everyone to act in exactly the same way. Specific sets of expectations concerning the behaviour of those in particular positions in the group are referred to as *roles* (Sarbin and Allen, 1968). Thus we would expect, even demand, that the committee secretary behave differently from the chairperson and the smooth operation of a committee meeting, leading to a fruitful outcome, would be dependent upon it.

Roles, in part, reflect status differences which exist between various positions in the group. *Status* represents the evaluation of a position in terms of, for example, the importance, prestige, etc., associated with it. Most groups are hierarchically structured in this respect with high-status positions affording greater opportunities to exercise social power and influence. As shall be seen in the following section, one facet of intra-group communication has to do with the acknowledgement and confirmation of these differences. This frequently operates at a covert level; for example, the chairperson *directs* the secretary while the secretary *advises* the chairperson. Further ramifications of status and the role of the group leader will be detailed in the second part of the chapter.

The actual roles which evolve are a function of a number of determinants, including the nature of the specific group and its tasks. Nevertheless it would seem that there are certain roles which typify small group interaction and some of these have been identified and labelled by Benne and Sheats (1948). It should not, of course, be assumed that they will be found in each and every case. Apart from that of leader they include the information or opinion giver, harmoniser, critic, tension releaser, isolate and scapegoat. All are readily recognisable. The information or opinion giver has a wealth of information, not necessarily always accurate or relevant, which he insists in divulging. He tends, as a consequence, to be one of the more vociferous members of the group. The harmoniser, like the tension releaser, tends to be more concerned with harmonious internal relationships than substantive issues and as a result operates, for the most part, at the socio-emotional rather than the task level. He, or she, is likely to be the person who intervenes during heated disputes to suggest compromise, identify areas of commonality and diffuse the situation. The critic tends not to be one of the more popular members of the group. Frequently this person is regarded as being obstructive and bloody-minded, yet he can have a more positive role to play in, for example, identifying difficulties overlooked by the rest with proposed courses of action. Groupthink is less likely to occur when there are several critics in the group.

Some groups have a member who tends to be much more reticent than the rest, who interacts minimally with others and fails to participate fully in group activities. This individual is commonly labelled the isolate and, indeed, in larger groups may, for the most part, go unnoticed. The fact that this individual does not become fully involved does not mean that he has nothing to offer as tactful handling by an adroit leader can often demonstrate. When a group is beset by set-back and failure it is not uncommon for some member to be singled out as the cause and accused of not 'pulling his weight' or letting the group down. By 'identifying' the source of failure members can have their flagging beliefs in the worth of the group reaffirmed and redouble their efforts to achieve the goal. The projection of unacceptable personal feelings or tendencies upon the scapegoat can also assuage feelings of guilt among the others.

Through the establishment and operation of norms and roles, therefore, regular and predictable patterns of activity come to characterise much of group life. Communication between members is a necessary prerequisite for the emergence and perpetuation of such norms and roles. At the same time, the communication process is heavily influenced by them as will be seen in the next section.

INTRA-GROUP COMMUNICATION

The essential part which communication among members plays in the group is widely acknowledged. Applbaum *et al.* (1973, p. 61) made this point forcefully when they wrote, 'The importance of communication in the group cannot be overestimated. Initially communication unites the collection of individuals when they interact to fulfil some common purpose. The pressures to communicate are induced by the need to resolve internal and external problems that arise when the group tries to meet that goal.' Thus communication makes it possible for those belonging to the group to organise themselves, pool resources and through co-operative action solve some common difficulty or reach a desired goal. But, in addition, the resolution of interpersonal and indeed personal difficulties within the group and the creation and maintenance of harmonious relationships relies upon effective communication. These two functions, which will be discussed further in relation to the role of the leader later in the chapter, have been noted by several researchers and labelled, respectively, *task* and *psyche* communication (Littlejohn, 1978; Luft, 1984). The former, as the name suggests, concerns substantive group activities and typically operates in accordance with reason and logic. Psyche communication, on the other hand, '. . . refers to feelings and attitudes of people who are interacting, to how people relate to one another' (Luft, 1984, p. 126). This does not necessarily mean, though, that each communicative act must either be task or psyche in function. While ostensibly discussing how to solve a task issue, members may, contemporaneously, be forming impressions of where they stand in relation to the others in terms of status, positive regard, etc. Such judgements are often heavily influenced by nonverbal as well as verbal communication.

(The reader may wish to turn back to Chapter 2 to reconsider some of the features and functions of NVC.)

Task and Socio-emotional (roughly comparable to psyche communication) aspects of group communication have also been identified by Bales (1950, 1970). Using a system which he developed known as Interaction Process Analysis, Bales found that interpersonal behaviour during small group interaction could be located in some one of twelve distinct categories. Six of these were concerned with task functions. Of these, two involved the asking or giving of opinions, evaluations, etc.; another two, the asking or giving of information, repetition or clarification; and the final two the asking or giving of suggestions or directions. A further three categories related to positive socio-emotional reactions. These were, firstly, showing solidarity, helping or rewarding; secondly, showing tension release (e.g. joking, laughing) or satisfaction; and thirdly, showing agreement, acceptance, understanding, etc. The final three categories were also in the socio-emotional area but were negative in character. They were, firstly, showing antagonism; secondly, showing tension, withdrawing, or asking for help; and, thirdly, disagreeing or rejecting. By analysing the communication between members in this way a number of interesting discoveries can be made. It can be established, for example, whether most of what takes place is concerned with task or socio-emotional issues, and, if the latter, the types of relationship which seem to predominate in the group. Different types of difficulty in group operation can also be detected. At the level of the individual, the extent and nature of the contribution of each member can also be ascertained.

A common finding to emerge from this sort of detailed analysis is that some members participate markedly more than others in group discussion. This seems to be a function of several factors including: (1) Position in the group and status — high status members, particularly group leaders, tend to contribute extensively. (2) Knowledge — those with relevant information are frequently vociferous and indeed may be encouraged to be so by other group members. (3) Personality — extroverts, almost by definition, are more communicative than their more introverted colleagues. There is some evidence to suggest that individuals have their characteristic levels of participation, although these are not immutable. (4) Physical location — those centrally located in the group frequently take a more active part. (5) Group size — it has been found that differences between members in their contributions to group interaction are much greater in large than in small groups.

As well as quantitative differences existing between high and low participants, disparities in the typical form of their communications have also been identified (Bales, 1970). While high participators tend to provide information, give opinions and make suggestions, low participators, when they do contribute, do so by asking questions or expressing agreement. Again the target of such communication is frequently different. While low contributors, for the most part, direct contributions to individual members, high contributors are more inclined to address their remarks to the group. This is frequently associated with attempts to exert influence and exercise power. (This will be dealt with further, in the second part of the chapter, in relation to group leadership.) Those who contribute most are also likely to be the recipients of frequent messages from others.

As those forming groups begin to interact with one another, regularities begin to emerge in the form of identifiable patterns of communication. The effects of these patterns, or communication networks, on a number of variables, including group efficiency and member satisfaction, have been investigated by a number of researchers. As initially described by Bavelas (1950), five subjects were each given a number of cards, each containing several symbols. Their task was to identify the symbol common to each member's card. Since the subjects were located in separate booths, channels of communication between them could be carefully controlled by the experimenter, creating the four networks outlined in Figure 11.1.

In each of the four diagrams in Figure 11.1, the circles represent particular group members and the adjoining lines are available channels of communication. Thus in the Circle arrangement, for example, (a) and (b) could communicate but not (a) and (e) — at least not directly. It should also be appreciated that members do not necessarily have to bear the particular spatial relationships to each other depicted in each of the diagrams in order for those networks to pertain. It is rather the communication channels in each case which is the telling feature.

Networks differ in two important respects. The first is in terms of Connectivity; the second, Centrality. Connectivity refers to the number of channels available to members, in the network. The Circle in Figure 11.1 contains five channels and is therefore a more highly connected structure than any of the others. Centrality is defined as a function of the number of channels from a given position to each other's position (Raven and Rubin, 1983). Thus of the four alternatives in Figure 11.1, the Circle, although the most highly connected, is the least centralised structure, followed by the Chain, Y and Wheel, in order. With the Wheel it can be seen that one person (c) can

Figure 11.1: Communication networks

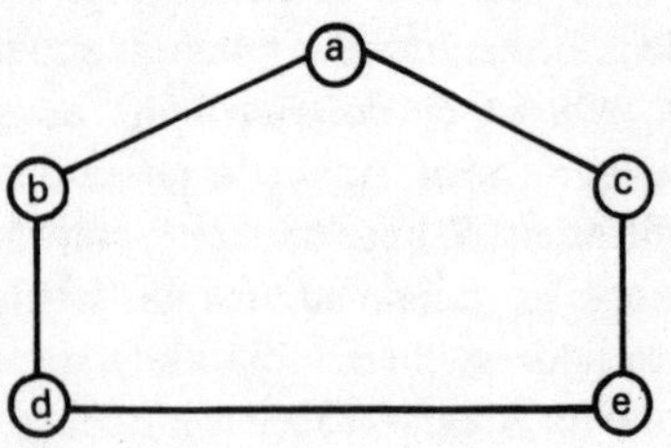

(b) CHAIN

(c) Y

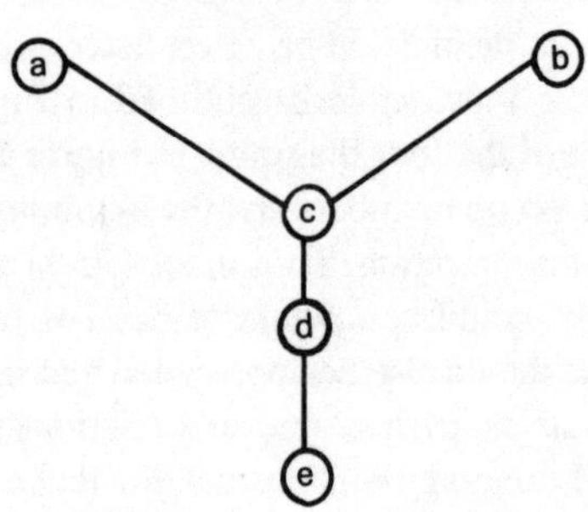

(d) WHEEL

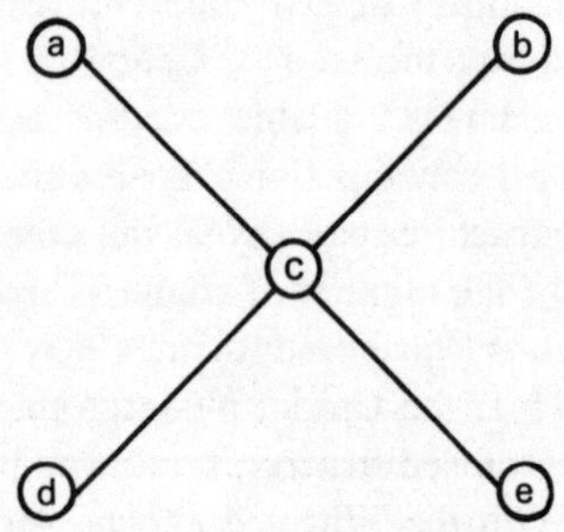

communicate directly with a total of four others.

Results from a number of research studies suggest that these networks have a significant impact on group efficiency and member satisfaction. Group productivity in terms of the number of tasks completed, and efficiency measured by time taken to complete each and the number of messages needed, were found to increase with increases in group centrality. The Wheel was, therefore, more productive and efficient followed by the Y, the Chain and the Circle. The likelihood of emerging as group leader was also found to be directly related to the centrality of that person's position in the arrangement. Such findings led Guetzkow and Simon (1955) to propose organisational development as an explanatory concept. The increased productivity and efficiency of more centralised structures was regarded as a consequence of the greater opportunities which they afford for groups to organise themselves. Upon reviewing some of the research, Shaw (1981) concluded, however, that it was not entirely in keeping with this hypothesis. Rather, the concept of saturation would seem to have greater explanatory power. Indeed with tasks which are much more complex than those investigated by Bavelas, highly centralised networks may be less, rather than more, effective due to the unreasonable demands placed upon the individual in the most central position — this position becomes saturated.

While more centrally organised groups tend to be more productive and efficient (especially when dealing with simple problems), members frequently manifest low morale and express little satisfaction with group activities. Subjects operating in the Circle typically express much greater satisfaction with their involvement in the group than those in the Wheel, in spite of the fact that they may not, collectively, achieve as much. Shaw (1981) proposed that this is most likely a result of the greater independence of action which members enjoy in the former.

In naturally operating groups though, the communication channels between members are not limited in the contrived fashion described by Bavelas. Networks are completely connected, in principle, with each individual free to communicate with each other. In practice, however, it has been found that those which actually emerge frequently resemble one of the more restricted configurations (Secord and Backman, 1974). A range of factors (including the roles being played by different individuals) may serve to reduce the number and sequence of channels typically used. Physical arrangement determining visual accessibility of certain members to others may also play a part. Cary(1978) demonstrated that likelihood of initiation of conversation was dependent upon the prior engagement, by those individuals, in eye contact.

Having considered the defining characteristics of groups, some of the reasons for their existence, the mechanisms by which they become ordered and regulated, and the types and patterns of communication between members, the chapter will continue by examining a particularly influential position within the group — that of leader — and the characteristics and skills associated with leadership.

LEADERS AND LEADERSHIP

What is a leader? What is leadership? Are individuals born to be leaders or are they created by the society in which they live? The concepts *leader* and *leadership* have been examined and defined in more different ways than almost any other concept associated with group dynamics. Preoccupation with the role of leader has not merely been confined to the investigations of social scientists. Although not studied extensively and scientifically until the last three or four decades leadership has intrigued philosophers and historians for centuries. Such famous leaders as Benjamin Franklin, Disraeli, George Washington, Ghandi and Hitler, have intrigued and tested the ability of historians to clarify the qualities and behaviours which these persons exuded. Despite the fact that so many people have studied this phenomenon there is still no precise or commonly agreed definition of leadership. Instead there are a range of definitions which have a fair degree of concordance.

DEFINITION OF LEADERSHIP

One of the earliest definitions of leadership is provided by Stogdill (1950) who claimed that, 'Leadership may be considered as the process (act) of influencing the activities of an organized group in its efforts toward goal setting and goal achievement' (p.3). Stogdill spent the next 20 years or so attempting to identify, analyse and develop the concept of leadership using a range of perspectives such as leadership as a focus of group dynamics, a feature of personality, the art of inducing compliance, a function of the situation, to name but a few. In other words, many of the diverse definitions were a result of the researcher's *a priori* selection of one perspective rather than another (Stogdill, 1974).

Nevertheless, more recent authors appear to endorse Stogdill's original claim that leadership is concerned with the act of influencing others, whether the influence is strong or overt, as in the case of a supervisor or teacher, or more facilitating or subtle, as in the case of a moderator or counsellor. Hollander (1978), for instance, maintained that 'leadership is a process of influence between a leader and those who are followers' (p. 1). Rauch and Behling (1984) define leadership as 'the process of influencing the activities of an organized group toward goal achievement' (p. 46). Continuing this theme of 'influencing', Hosking and Morley (1985) define leaders as 'those who are both perceived, and expected, to make consistent, influential contributions to decision-making processes' (p. 11). The common elements in these definitions imply that leadership involves a process of social influence in which a person guides group members towards a goal.

But how does one person influence others? According to Goffman (1967) and Strauss (1977), a leader invests considerable attention, practice, energy and time in learning to manage the impression he makes on others. Even by appearance alone, stated Stone (1962), 'a person (leader) announces his identity, shows its value, expresses his mood or proposes his attitude' (p. 101). The latter part of this chapter will examine in more detail how leadership can influence the decision-making process in groups.

Using the context of a discussion group, it is fair to say that each statement or question put forward by an individual group member could be identified as an act of leadership. However, some individuals appear to be more effective than others at directing a group toward the attainment of its goals. These persons can be described as focal persons or leaders since their contributions to the accomplishment of group goals are significantly greater than any other members' contribution. Although a leader may be appointed either formally or informally to lead a group, seldom does that person completely dominate the group's procedures. Instead, in most discussion or decision-making groups, other members can be called upon occasionally to perform certain acts of leadership. Thus although certain individuals are elected to provide group leadership, acts of leaderships can be exhibited by any other group member.

THEORIES OF LEADERSHIP

Whilst most researchers have been centrally concerned with the problems of why or how leaders emerge, their investigations have been conducted using a range of perspectives. As a result, a number of theories have emerged which attempt to provide a better understanding about the character of leadership or about the effects of different styles of leadership in different situations. What follows is a brief outline of three of the most notable of these theories, namely trait, situation and need theory.

Trait theory

Throughout history many people have believed that leaders are born, not made, and that truly great leaders are discovered, not developed. The assumption underlying this belief is that a leader is a unique person possessing some innate ability which allows him or her to assume a leadership position no matter the social situation. Thus the trait approach attempted to distinguish leaders from non-leaders on the basis of how they differ on personal characteristics.

Since the early twentieth century, hundreds of research studies have been conducted to identify the personal attributes of leaders, such as physical factors (height, weight, physique, appearance and age), ability characteristics (intelligence, fluency of speech, scholarship and knowledge) and personality features (conservatism, introversion-extroversion, dominance, emotional control, etc.). The most influential review of literature on leadership 'traits' (Stogdill, 1948), came to the conclusion that general qualities or abilities could not be discerned. Instead, the qualities and skills which leaders require are largely determined by the demands of the situation in which the leader is to function. Since these early reviews were generally pessimistic about this line of research, many researchers abandoned the search for innate characteristics of leaders. Despite a number of recent studies (England, 1975; Bass, 1981; and Yukl, 1981) aimed at identifying 'traits' in relation to managerial ability, no trait has been consistently associated with leadership. To date, the traits approach has failed to provide a coherent set of personal characteristics which differentiates between effective and ineffective leaders.

Situation theory

As stated earlier, researchers began to turn from studying traits of leaders to studying the situation in which leadership was located. In other words, it was assumed that as situations varied, so did the amount and type of leadership required. Thus the traits or skills which constituted an effective leader in one group did not necessarily transfer to another. The situationally contingent approach explicitly claims there are no universally appropriate styles of leadership; rather the leader's behaviour is contingent upon the demands of the situation.

In the work of Fiedler (see especially 1967, 1971 and 1978) can be found the earliest systematic attempt to develop a contingency approach to the study of leadership style. Using a variety of group situations, ranging from sports groups through to military and industrial settings, Fiedler's starting point was that some leaders were more committed to the nature or structure of the task whilst others were more orientated to achieving good personal relationships within the group. He concluded that it was unusual to find individuals who were equally orientated to both group needs and task completion. (This aspect will be dealt with more fully later in the chapter.)

Very briefly, Fiedler, using a questionnaire technique, as opposed to direct observation, examined the attitudes of the leader towards his or her co-workers. A scale, known as the least preferred co-worker (LPC) and comprising 18 pairs of adjectives (e.g. cold-warm, boring-interesting, kind-unkind, etc.) enabled researchers to distinguish between leaders who provided favourable depictions ('high LPC' leaders) and those whose descriptions were unfavourable ('low LPC' leaders). On the basis of his own and other research evidence, Fiedler maintained that high LPC leaders extract superior performances from their subordinates in some situations whilst, in other contexts, low LPC leaders do better.

For instance, a task-oriented leader appears to be most effective when he or she is on very good terms with group members, the task is clearly structured and he or she is held in high esteem within the group. Alternatively, a task-oriented leader is equally effective when he or she is on poor terms with group members, the task is ambiguous and she or he is held in low esteem. However, it would appear that when moderate relationships exist between leader and group members, when the task is moderately clear and when the leader has a moderate position of esteem, the leader who emphasised good relationships within the group was the most effective at achieving member participation in the problem-solving or decision-making process. In other words, Fielder maintained that the type of leader required in order for group performance to be enhanced, is situationally contingent.

One major criticism of this approach is that group performance is measured in terms of its task or goal completion. Output is only one measure of a group's value, however. Individual group members' satisfaction may be equally important yet not contribute to the achievement of the extrinsic goal. It will be recalled from earlier in the chapter that the most satisfied members don't necessarily belong to the most productive groups. Fielder's model leaves questions relating to group relationships unresolved.

Need theory

According to need theory, leadership arises out of the necessity for the group to perform certain functions or roles in order that its goals be achieved. The leader who emerges has the skills and ability to ascertain what the group needs are and he or she is most capable at providing the means for their achievement. Groups have at least two basic objectives: to complete a task and to maintain effective social relationships among the members.

The work of Hollander is most closely associated with this idea which he tends to refer to as a 'transactional approach'. According to Hollander and Julian (1969) in order for a leader to continue his position of leadership he must be responsive to the needs of the group members. That is, leaders must pay attention to maintaining good working relationships while at the same time moving the group towards successful task completion. In other words, it does no good to complete a task if the manner of doing so alienates most of the group members. Thus if a number of group members refuse to come to the next meeting, the group has not been successful.

Hollander (1978) claimed that this theoretical approach to understanding leadership effectiveness includes two basic ideas. Firstly, any member of a group may become a leader by taking actions that assist the group to *complete its task* and *maintain effective relationships*. Secondly, any leadership function may be fulfilled by different members performing a variety of relevant behaviours such as suggesting how the group's work can be improved, relieving tension when it gets too high, listening carefully and respecting other people's views and facilitating interaction between group members by asking questions and reinforcing responses.

This need approach to leadership is one of the most concrete and direct approaches available for improving a person's leadership skills and so improving the effectiveness of a group. However, it must be noted that this approach is not without its critics who claim that there are so many diverse and varied actions that individual members can make when trying to accomplish task completion and group maintenance that defining specific skills for every situation is hard to achieve. Morley and Hosking (1985) recognised that 'the literature on leadership has not been informed by attempts systematically to articulate the nature of the skills which make leaders effective' (p. 2). Despite an absence of empirical research into leadership skills *per se*, insights can be gained from an analysis of studies in allied areas such as teaching which have drawn their inspiration from and added to interaction theory. Some of these skills will be identified and examined later in the chapter.

LEADER PERFORMANCE

The performance of the leader can be examined at two different but related levels. Firstly, at the macro level; observing leaders in action has revealed that leadership style can affect group productivity and the attitudes of group members. Secondly, at the micro level; specific skills can be identified as depicting a particular leadership style.

Leadership styles

In what is now considered a classical study, Lewin, Lippitt and White (1939) distinguished three different group climates produced by these distinct styles of leadership; the autocratic (authoritarian), democratic and the laissez-faire (lax). Briefly, the researchers requested three adult leaders to adopt an autocratic (dictating orders and determining all policy), democratic (encouraging and helping group members to interact), or laissez-faire (no participation in the group's decision-making process) style with groups of ten and eleven year old boys engaged in a recreational youth centre. The results revealed that when the groups were led by an autocratic leader, they were more dependent on the leader and did not co-operate freely with their peers. When the leaders adopted a democratic approach, the same boys showed more initiative and responsibility for the progress of the group and were more friendly towards each other, even when the leader left the room. In the laissez-faire or leaderless group, the boys lacked interest in their tasks and failed to complete successfully any of the tasks they had been set. Aggressive acts were more frequent under autocratic and laissez-faire leaders than they were under a democratic leader. There was more scape-goating in the autocratic group, in the form of boys occasionally being made a target of hostility until they eventually left the group. This hostility among the boys was three times as great in the autocratic group as it was in the democratic group. Finally, when a measure of 'liking' the leader was collected it was found that the most liked was the democratic leader, the least liked being the autocratic leader.

Since this study a number of researchers have investigated the relative impact of leadership styles on group functioning (Likert, 1967; Stogdill, 1974; Martinko and Gardner 1984). From the findings it can be concluded that different styles are effective under different conditions. For example, autocratic leadership appears to be more effective when an urgent decision has to be made (a pilot giving orders to his crew to avert an air disaster, or a surgeon ordering his medical team to carry out specific procedures to save a patient's life). In such crucial circumstances leaders would be ill advised to stop and take a vote. On the other hand, when formal groups are meeting to establish or perhaps change certain operational rules or procedures (e.g. a school principal meeting with his staff to decide on school rules) it would be more appropriate to adopt a democratic approach since there is a greater chance of group members complying with the group findings.

Since we live in a democratic society, we would like to believe that all decisions should be made democratically and that the autocratic leader should not be acknowledged. However, this belief would be erroneous. A more constructive means of describing leadership styles is to suggest that a leader's behaviour invariably ranges from autocratic to democratic to laissez-faire on different occasions.

Leadership skills

There are a number of behaviours which can be employed in order to be an effective leader in contexts ranging from the captaincy of a sporting group to the chairmanship of an organisation. These behaviours can be related to the task function of the leader or the maintenance function. Cartwright and Zander (1968) noted that this kind of division can be problematic. For instance,

> a member who helps a group to work co-operatively on a difficult problem may inadvertently help it to develop solidarity . . . (alternatively) an eager member may spur the group on in such a way that friction develops among the members, and even though the

goal is achieved efficiently, the continued existence of the group is seriously endangered (pp. 306–7).

However, Harnack, Fest and Jones (1977) suggested that it matters little how these functions are labelled, what is important is the understanding that both these functions need to be performed if the group is to succeed.

Task skills

It has been necessary to be selective given the vast amount of literature available on leadership behaviour (Douglas, 1976; Johnson and Johnson, 1982; Zander, 1982; and Bryman 1986). What follows is a checklist of four basic task skills, gathered from a variety of sources, which a leader can use to produce effective group functioning.

Initiating/focusing

From the outset, it is important that the leader establishes aims for the group, proposes tasks or goals for its members and suggests procedures or ideas for the group's functioning. Halpin and Winer (1957) conducted a factor analysis of the results of 300 air crew men's descriptions of leadership behaviour and found that 'consideration and initiating structure' were central ingredients of the measurement of leader behaviour. This factor contained statements such as 'emphasizing the mission or job to be done', 'assigns crew members to particular tasks' and 'talks about how much should be done'. More recently Tjosvold (1984) found that leader directiveness and warmth (corresponding to Halpin and Winer's consideration and initiating structure) had a pronounced impact on group performance. Whittington (1986) advocated that chairpersons, at the beginning of a meeting, should 'clarify the objectives of the meeting, deal with any procedural matters and introduce the main business' (p. 299). In addition, it is useful for the leader or chairperson to provide transitional summaries at the end of each phase of the meeting or discussion before introducing the next issue as this alerts the group to where they have been, where they are now, and where they are going. (See Chapter 6 for further information on set induction.)

Clarifying/elaborating

Once a meeting is underway or discussion of a topic begun, it is important that the group leader interprets or reflects ideas or suggestions by 'clearing-up' confusion which may have arisen, indicating alternatives which may be considered or by giving appropriate examples so that the group gains a clearer understanding. Turney *et al.* (1976) suggest there are three separate but interrelated skills that are important in keeping a discussion full and to the point. The first is paraphrasing or summarising a member's contribution which has been rather involved or lengthy so that it is clearer both to him or herself and to the group (see Chapter 5 on Reflection). A good example of this skill in practice can be found in some TV programmes set up with a panel of academic experts to discuss profound philosophical problems related to modern-day living. Often the chairperson of such a programme will clarify or simplify the contributions of such academics for the understanding of a lay audience. Secondly, leaders who use probing questions invariably help the group clarify, support or develop an idea (see Chapter 4 on Questioning). Finally, leaders should elaborate on contributions, by providing further information or appropriate examples, when the group has reached an impasse. (see Chapter 7 on Explanation).

Promoting contributions

Most of us have at some time had the experience of engaging in animated conversation after the conclusion of a meeting with people who hardly spoke at all during the meeting. When asked why they kept interesting or perhaps novel ideas or suggestions to themselves they are apt to say, 'I couldn't get a word in edgeways', or 'I wasn't sure whether my idea was appropriate or not'. If one of the main purposes of a leader is to encourage maximum participation in the decision-making or problem-solving process, it is imperative that all members have an equal chance of contributing regularly in the group's proceedings. The leader can achieve this in a number of ways. If a member has appeared to be interested but has not made many contributions, the leader may be able to secure participation by tactfully asking for an opinion. However, emphasis must be placed on tact. It is more useful to say 'Before we go on, I would like to make sure that we have heard everyone's views or opinions', than bluntly asking, 'What do you think Harry?' where nothing is received at all because Harry has been caught off his guard. By warning everyone that their opinions are going to be solicited, there is a better chance of securing a response when attending to the non-participant.

The opposite of a 'non-talker', of course, is an 'over-talker'. Often one or two discussants monopolise proceedings, and leaders are sorely tempted to rebuke them. Instead, the leader should sensitively discourage such monopolisation by using phrases such as 'John, if we're not careful, this will end up as a two-person conversation' or words to that effect. It is important to be aware that while John's participation needs to be curtailed in no way should it be nullified.

Abercrombie (1974) and Turney *et al.* (1976) emphasise the point that members should be encouraged to comment on each other's contribution and suggest that one of the best ways this can be achieved is for the leader to remain silent and curb his or her nonverbal behaviour such as withdrawal of eye contact. There may be times when individual contributions are not being made as readily. In such circumstances, it is important that the leader remains quietly waiting and expectant rather than filling in periods of silence with talk (see Chapter 4 on Questioning).

Finally, the use of controversial or provocative questions or comments can on occasions help to revive a 'flagging' discussion.

Summarising

A number of studies have been set up to investigate the specific communicative behaviours which leaders use to achieve their desired goals (Mortensensen, 1966; Cartwright and Zander, 1968; and Rackham and Morgan, 1977). One category which emerges from these research findings is that of 'integrating and summarising group activity'. This ability to summarise clearly and briefly the main group findings can differentiate effective from non-effective leaders. Rackham and Morgan (1977), comparing chairman behaviour with that of other group members, found that the difference on this summarising category between the two groups was significantly greater than on any other category, emphasising how strongly associated summarisation is with the role of chairman. These same authors go on to suggest that, 'the association is so strong that if another member of the meeting attempts to summarise, this is frequently seen as a personal challenge to the chairman and his authority' (p. 273).

In addition to the summary, it can be advantageous for the group to be encouraged to think further about some of the issues or ideas which have been explored during a meeting. The leader can achieve this by relating these issues to other areas not previously covered.

Finally, having the group evaluate how it functioned and what it has achieved is an appropriate way of checking the efficiency of the original goals which were set. In the light of this evaluation, goals can be maintained, extended or refined in order to enhance their realism.

Maintenance skills

There is some evidence to suggest that while formal leaders are the most sensitive to the task needs of the group, maintenance needs are more likely to be accurately perceived by ordinary group members (Gordon, 1955; McGregor, 1960). If groups are to function effectively and with commitment, it is important that the leader is sensitive to maintaining good interpersonal relations within the group. Two basic skills can be applied to achieve this.

Relieving group tension

There are occasions when individuals within a group have ideologically opposing views regarding a particular issue, resulting in a tense situation, particularly when both participants are putting forward their views forcefully. There are two techniques which the leader can apply in such a situation. Firstly, the leader may alleviate the situation by perhaps focusing on the ideas and away from personalities, with a view to draining off negative feelings between the two main protagonists and so putting a tense situation into a wider context.

Alternatively, the leader can introduce humour into the situation. Foot (1986) advocated the use of humour to

> defuse a tense or hostile situation prevailing between two other interactants, thus enabling the contesting parties to back off from the confrontation without loss of face. . . The humour serves not only as a corrective to restore the normal boundaries of social etiquette, but as an admonition that the argument has gone quite far enough (p. 362).

Supporting or encouraging

If members are to become totally involved in the group's activity, they must feel that any contribution they make will be accepted. Nothing will cool the eagerness of a discussant more quickly than having a contribution ignored or summarily dismissed. While it is apparent that not all contributions are equally valuable, the leader must administer supportive, encouraging statements appropriate to the individual (see Chapter 3 on Reinforcement).

On the other hand, not only can rewards help an individual member to participate more willingly if encouraged to do so by the leader, but it can also enhance the leader's control over the group. Bass (1981) suggested that those leaders who employed rewards as a way of influencing people felt they had a great deal of social control in the group situation. Alternatively, leaders who were more coercive and threatening in their approach felt they were a product of forces over which they had no control. In other words, the leader's administration of rewards and punishments appeared to influence their social control.

OVERVIEW

This chapter has been concerned with small groups, how they operate and the manner in which leaders emerge and leadership is exercised within them. Groups, in this sense, can be thought of as involving a plurality of individuals who influence each other in the course of interaction and share a relationship of interdependence in pursuit of some common goal or goals. Members also characteristically develop a sense of belonging to this particular social entity. People come together to form groups to satisfy needs which may be interpersonal, informational or material. In so doing they become part of an ordered and regulated system which evolves through the establishment of, for example, norms, or commonly expected and accepted ways of perceiving, thinking, feeling and acting; the enactment of roles including that of leader, and the creation of identifiable forms and patterns of communication between members.

Additionally, an attempt has been made to show leadership as virtually synonymous with the act of influencing others in a range of group contexts. However, it is important to bear in mind the distinction between leadership and leader. While specific individuals are elected leaders, acts of leadership can be manifested by any group member.

Recent theories of leadership, notably situation and need theories, offer some scope in attempting to explain the emergence of leaders and their functioning. These theories suggest that leaders display specific skills and ability in order to help the group achieve its goals; the skills and abilities exhibited being dependent upon the demands of the situation. Focusing on the actual performance of leaders, their behaviour can be examined on two levels: leadership styles at the macro level and leadership skills at the micro level. While at least three styles have emerged, notably autocratic, democratic and laissez-faire, it is important to note that a leader's behaviour can be exemplified using all three styles either at different points on the same occasion or on distinctly different occasions.

Six basic skills were identified, examined and defined and it was propounded that leaders who execute these skills can increase the productivity of the group and at the same time ensure the longevity of the group's life. As Zander (1982) succinctly writes, 'We are not directly interested in changing individuals except where changes in their information, skill, experience or confidence may help them to be more effective on behalf of their group' (p. xiii).

12

Concluding Comments

This book has been concerned with an examination of the central components of interpersonal communication, namely the social skills which individuals employ in order to achieve their goals in social encounters. The skills selected for inclusion in this text were: nonverbal communication, reinforcement, questioning, reflecting, set induction, closure, explanation, listening, self-disclosure, assertiveness, and group interaction. It is recognised that this selection is not exhaustive, since other specialised skills may be employed in particular settings. However, we believe that the skills included do represent the core behavioural elements of interpersonal communication and, for this reason, the practising professional needs to have a sound working knowledge of them.

It has not been our intention, however, to offer a cook-book approach to the study of interpersonal interaction. There are no 'right' or 'wrong' ways to communicate with others. Rather, there are a range of alternative approaches which can be employed in any particular interactive episode, and it is up to the individual to select what he or she considers to be the most appropriate. Such selection, however, demands an extensive knowledge of the range of alternatives available and their likely effects in any given context. It is at this level that the present book has been geared. An understanding of the skills covered, and of their behavioural determinants, should enable the individual to increase his or her understanding of the process of interpersonal communication. It provides the reader with a language which can be used to study, and interpret, this process more fully.

In the final analysis, however, improvements in skilled performance necessitate practical action. In other words, it is only by converting knowledge of skills into skilled behaviour that increases in social skills can occur. Thus we would encourage the reader to experiment with various social techniques in order to develop, refine and extend their existing repertoire of social skills. Once a wide repertoire has been developed, the individual thereby becomes a more effective communicator with the ability to adjust and adapt to varying social situations. For most professionals, this is an essential prerequisite to effective functioning.

Bibliography

Abercrombie, M.L.J. (1974) 'Aims and techniques of group teaching', *Society for Research in Higher Education*, London

Abrami, P., Leenthal, L. and Perry, R. (1982) 'Educational seduction', *Review of Educational Research*, 52, 446–64

Adams, R. (1969) 'Location as a feature of instructional interaction', *Merrill Palmer Quarterly*, 15, 309–21

Alberti, R. and Emmons, M. (1975) *Stand up, speak out, talk back: the key to assertive behaviour*, Impact, San Luis Obispo, California

— and Emmons, M. (1982) *Your perfect right: a guide to assertive living*, Impact, San Luis Obispo, 4th edition, California

Allen, D.I. (1970) 'Some effects of advance organizers and level of questions on the learning and retention of written social studies material', *Journal of Educational Psychology*, 61, 333–9

Allen, J.G. (1974) 'When does exchanging personal information constitute self-disclosure?, *Psychological Reports*, 35, 195–8

Altman, I. (1977) 'The communication of interpersonal attitudes: an ecological approach' in T.L. Houston (ed.), *Foundations of interpersonal attraction*, Academic Press, London

Applbaum, R.L., Anatol, K., Hays, E.R., Jenson, O.O., Porter, R.E. and Handel, J.E. (1973) *Fundamental concepts in human communication*, Cranfield Press, New York

Archer, R. (1979) 'Role of personality and the social situation', in G. Chelune (ed.), *Self-Disclosure*, Jossey-Bass, San Francisco

Arenson, S.J., (1978) 'Age and dress of experimenter in verbal conditioning', *Psychological Reports*, 43, 823–7

Argyle, M. (1975) *Bodily communication*, Methuen, London

— (1981) *Social skills and health*, Methuen, London and New York

— (1983a) 'Five kinds of small social group', in H.H. Blumberg, A.P. Hare, V. Kent and M.F. Davies (eds), *Small groups and social interaction*, vol. 1, Wiley, Chichester

— (1983b) *The psychology of interpersonal behaviour*, Penguin, Harmondsworth, Middlesex

— (1983c) *The psychology of interpersonal behaviour*, 4th edition, Penguin, Harmondsworth

— and Cook, M. (1976) *Gaze and mutual gaze*, Cambridge University Press, Cambridge

— and Ingham, R. (1972) 'Gaze, mutual gaze and proximity', *Semiotica*, 6, 32–49

— and McHenry, R. (1971) 'Do spectacles really increase judgements of intelligence?', *British Journal of Social and Clinical Psychology*, 10, 27–9

Aronson, E. (1984) *The social animal*, W.H. Freeman and Co., New York

Arvey, R. and Campion, J. (1984) 'Person perception in the employment interview', in M. Cook (ed.), *Issues in person perception*, Methuen, London and New York

Aubertine, H.E. (1968) 'The set induction process and its application to teaching', *Journal of Educational Research*, 61, 363–7

Auerswald, M.C. (1974) 'Differential reinforcing power of restatement and interpretation on client production of affect', *Journal of Counselling Psychology*, 21, 9–14

Bakken, D. (1977) 'Saying goodbye: an observational study of parting rituals', *Man-Environment Systems*, 7, 95–100

Baldock, J. and Prior, D. (1981) 'Social workers talking to clients: a study of verbal behaviour', *British Journal of Social Work*, 11, 19–38

Baldwin, J.D. and Baldwin, J.I. (1981) *Behaviour principles in everyday life*, Prentice-Hall, Englewood Cliffs, NJ

Bales, R.F. (1950) *Interaction process analysis: a method for the study of small groups*, Addison-Wesley, Cambridge, Mass.

—— (1970) *Personality and interpersonal behaviour*, Holt, Rinehart and Winston, New York

Balsam, P.D. and Bondy, A.S. (1983) 'The negative side-effects of reward', *Journal of Applied Behaviour Analysis* 16, 283–96

Bandura, A. (1971) *Social learning theory*, General Learning Press, Morristown, NJ

—— Lipsher, D.H. and Miller, P.E. (1960) 'Psychotherapists' approach avoidance reactions to patients' expressions of hostility', *Journal of Consulting Psychology* 24, 1–8

Banks, D.L, (1972) 'A comparative study of the reinforcing potential of verbal and non-verbal cues in a verbal conditioning paradigm', unpublished doctoral dissertation, University of Massachusetts

Barnabei, F., Cormier, W.H. and Nye, L.S. (1974) 'Determining the effects of three counsellor verbal responses on client verbal behaviour', *Journal of Counselling Psychology*, 21, 355–9

Barnes, D., Britton, J. and Rosen, H. (1971) *Language, the learner and the school*, Penguin, Harmondsworth

—— and Rosenthal, R. (1985) 'Interpersonal effects of experimenter attractiveness, attire and gender, *Journal of Personality and Social Psychology*, 48, 2, 435–46

Bass, B.M. (1981) *Stogdill's handbook of leadership*, Free Press, New York

Bavelas, A. (1950) 'Communication patterns in task-oriented groups', *Journal of the Acoustical Society of America*, 22, 725–30

Baxter, J. and Rozelle, R. (1975) 'Nonverbal expression as a function of crowding during a simulated police-citizen encounter', *Journal of Personality and Social Psychology*, 32, 40–54

Beattie, G. (1978) 'Floor apportionment and gaze in conversational dyads', *British Journal of Social and Clinical Psychology*, 17, 7–15

—— (1979) 'Contextual constraints on the floor-apportionment function of speaker-gaze in dyadic conversations', *British Journal of Social and Clinical Psychology*, 18, 390–2

—— (1981) 'A further investigation of the cognitive interference hypothesis of gaze patterns during conversation', *British Journal of Social Psychology*, 20, 243–8

Becker, H.S. (1963) *Outsiders*, Collier-Macmillan, New York

Beezer, R. (1956) 'Research on methods of interviewing foreign informants', George Washington University, Hum RRO Technical Reports, No. 30

Beharry, E.A. (1976) 'The effect of interviewing style upon self-disclosure

in a dyadic interaction', *Dissertation Abstracts International*, 36, 4677B
Bellack, A.S. and Hersen, M. (eds) (1979) *Research and practice in social skills training*, Plenum, New York
Bender, V., Davis, Y., Glover, O. and Stapp, J. (1976) 'Patterns of self-disclosure in homosexual and heterosexual college students', *Sex Roles*, 2, 149–60
Benjamin, A. (1974) *The helping interview*, Houghton Mifflin, Boston
Benne, K.D. and Sheats, P. (1948) 'Functional roles of group members', *Journal of Social Issues*, 4, 41–9
Berlyne, D.E. (1951) 'Attention to change', *British Journal of Psychology*, 42, 269–79
—— (1960) *Conflict, arousal and curiosity*, McGraw-Hill, New York
Bermann, E. and Miller, D.R. (1967) 'The matching of mates', in R. Jessor and S. Feshback (eds), *Cognition, personality and clinical psychology*, Jossey-Bass, San Francisco
Berne, E. (1964) *Games people play*, Grove Press, New York
Bernstein, B. (1971, 1972) *Class codes and control*, vols. 1 and 2, Routledge and Kegan Paul, London
Berscheid, E. and Walster, E. (1978) *Interpersonal attraction*, Addison-Wesley, Reading, Mass.
Bickman, L. (1974) 'Social roles and uniforms: clothes make the person', *Psychology Today*, 7, 48–51
Birdwhistell, R.L. (1970) *Kinesics and context*, University of Pennsylvania Press, Philadelphia
Blackman, D., Howe, M. and Pinkston, E. (1976) 'Increasing participation in the social interaction of the institutionalized elderly', *The Gerontologist*, 16, 69–76
Bligh, D. (1971) *What's the use of lectures?*, Penguin, Harmondsworth
Boddy, J., Carvier, A. and Rowley, K. (1986) 'Effects of positive and negative verbal reinforcement on performance as a function of extroversion-introversion: some tests of Gray's theory', *Personality and Individual Differences*, 7, 81–8
Bond, M. and Ho, H. (1978) 'The effect of relative status and the sex composition of a dyad on cognitive responses and non-verbal behaviour of Japanese interviewees', *Psychologia*, 21, 128–36
Boore, J. (1979) *Prescription for recovery*, R.C.N., London
Boy, A.V. and Pine, G.J. (1963) *Client-centered counselling in the secondary school*, Houghton Mifflin, Boston
Bradburn, N. and Sudman, S. (1980) *Improving interview method and questionnaire design: response effects to threatening questions in survey research*, Aldine, Chicago
Brammer, L.M. (1973) *The helping relationship: process and skills*, Prentice-Hall, Englewood Cliffs, NJ
—— and Shostrom, E.L. (1977) *Therapeutic psychology: fundamentals of counseling and psychotherapy*, Prentice-Hall, Englewood Cliffs, NJ
Brimer, M. (1971) 'Sex differences in listening comprehension' in S. Duker (ed.), *Listening: readings*, Scarecrow Press, Metuchen, New Jersey
Brokaw, D.W. and McLemore, C.W. (1983) 'Toward a more rigorous definition of social reinforcement: some interpersonal clarifications', *Journal of Personality and Social Psychology*, 44, 1014–20

Brooks, L. (1974) 'Interactive effects of sex and status on self-disclosure', *Journal of Counseling Psychology*, 21, 469–74

Brophy, J. (1981) 'Teacher praise: a functional analysis', *Review of Educational Research*, 51, 5–32

Brown, A. (1979) *Groupwork*, Heinneman, London

Brown, G. (1982) 'Two days on explaining and lecturing', *Studies in Higher Education*, 2, 93–104

—— (1986) 'Explaining', in O. Hargie (ed.), *A handbook of communication skills*, Croom Helm, London/New York University Press, NY

—— and Hatton, N. (1982) *Explaining and explanations*, Macmillan, London

—— and Bakhtar, M. (eds) (1983) *Styles of lecturing*, Loughborough University Press, Loughborough

—— and Armstrong, S. (1984) 'On explaining', in E.C. Wragg (ed.), *Classroom teaching skills*, Croom Helm, London/Nichols, New York

Brundage, L., Derlega, V. and Cash, T. (1977) 'The effects of physical attractiveness and need for approval on self-disclosure', *Personality and Social Psychology Bulletin*, 3, 63–6

Bruner, J.S., Goodnow, J.J. and Austin, G.A. (1956) *A study of thinking*, Wiley, New York

Bryman, A. (1986) *Leadership and organizations*, Routledge and Kegan Paul, London and New York

Buckwalter, A. (1983) *Interviews and interrogations*, Butterworth, Stoneham, USA

Bugental, D., Kaswan, J.W., Love, L.R. and Fox, M.N. (1970) 'Child versus adult perception of evaluative messages in verbal, vocal and visual channels', *Developmental Psychology*, 2, 267–375

Bull, P. (1983) *Body movement and interpersonal communication*, Wiley and Sons, Chichester

Burger, J. and Vartabedian, R. (1985) 'Public self-disclosure and speaker persuasiveness', *Journal of Applied Social Psychology*, 15, 153–65

Burley-Allen, M. (1982) *Listening: the forgotten skill*, Wiley, New York

Burton, M. (1985) 'The environment, good interactions and interpersonal skills in nursing', in C. Kagan (ed.), *Interpersonal skills in nursing: research and applications*, Croom Helm, Beckenham

Busch, P. and Wilson, D. (1976) 'An experimental analysis of a salesman's expert and referent bases of social power in the buyer-seller dyad', *Journal of Market Research*, 13, 3–11

Cairns, L. (1986) 'Reinforcement', in O. Hargie (ed.), *A handbook of communication skills*, Croom Helm, London/New York University Press, NY

Campbell, D.T. (1958) 'Common fate, similarity and other indices of the status of aggregates of persons as social entities', *Behavioural Science*, 3, 14–25

Cannell, C.F., Oksenberg, L. and Converse, J.M. (1977) 'Striving for response accuracy; experiments in new interviewing techniques', *Journal of Marketing Research*, 14, 306–21

Canter, D. and Wools, R. (1970) 'A technique for the subjective appraisal of buildings', *Building Science*, 5, 187–98

Carkhuff, R.R. (1973) *The art of helping: an introduction to life skills*, Human Resource Development Press, Amherst, Mass.

Carnevale, J.P. (1971) 'Shaping of verbal behaviour in an interview',

Dissertation Abstracts International, 31, 6340A

Cartwright, D. and Zander, A. (1968) *Group dynamics*, 3rd ed., Harper and Row, New York

Cary, M. (1978) 'The role of gaze in the initiation of conversation', *Social Psychology*, 41, 269–71

Chaikin, A. and Derlega, V. (1974) *Self-disclosure*, General Learning Press, New Jersey

—— and Derlega, V. (1976) 'Self-disclosure', in J. Thibaut, J. Spence and R. Carson (eds), *Contemporary topics in social psychology*, General Learning Press, New Jersey

——, Derlega, V. and Miller, S. (1976) 'Effects of room environment on self-disclosure in a counseling analogue', *Journal of Counseling Psychology*, 23, 479–81

Chelune, G. (ed.) (1979) *Self-disclosure*, Jossey-Bass, San Francisco

Cianni-Surridge, M. and Horan, J. (1983) 'On the wisdom of assertive job-seeking behavior', *Journal of Counseling Psychology*, 30, 209–14

Citkowitz, R.D. (1975), 'The effects of three interview techniques — paraphrasing, modelling, and cues — in facilitating self-referent affect statements in chronic schizophrenics', *Dissertation Abstracts International*, 36, 2462B

Clark, C. (1978) *Assertive skills for nurses*, Contemporary Publishing, Wakefield, Mass.

Cline, V.B., Mejia, J., Coles, J., Klein, N. and Cline, R.A. (1984) 'The relationship between therapist behaviors and outcome for middle and lower-class couples in marital therapy', *Journal of Clinical Psychology*, 40, 691–704

Clore, G.L. (1977) 'Reinforcement and affect in attraction', in S. Duck (ed.), *Theory and practice in interpersonal attraction*, Academic Press, London

Collier, G. (1985) *Emotional expression*, Lawrence Erlbaum Associates, Hillsdale, NJ

Conine, N. (1976) 'Listening in the helping relationship', *Physical Therapy*, 56, 159–62

Cook, M. (1970) 'Experiments on orientation and proxemics', *Human Relations*, 23, 61–76

—— (1977) 'The social skill model and interpersonal attraction', in S. Duck (ed.), *Theory and practice in interpersonal attraction*, Academic Press, London

Cooley, C.H. (1929) *Social organization*, Scribner, NY

Corey, S. (1940) 'The teachers out-talk the pupils', *School Review*, 48, 745–52

Cozby, P. (1973) 'Self-disclosure: a literature review', *Psychological Bulletin*, 79, 73–91

Crow, B. (1983) 'Topic shifts in couple's conversations', in B. Craig and K. Tracy (eds), *Conversational coherence: form, structure and strategy*, Sage, Beverly Hills, California

Dabbs, J. (1985) 'Temporal patterns of speech and gaze in social and intellectual conversation', in H. Giles and R. St Clair (eds), *Recent advances in language, communication and social psychology*, Lawrence Erlbaum Associates, London

Danish, S.J. and Hauer, A.L. (1973) *Helping skills: a basic training program*, Behavioral Publications, NY

Davitz, J.R. (1964) *The communication of emotional meaning*, McGraw-Hill, NY

Dawley, H. and Wenrich, W. (1976) *Achieving assertive behaviour: a guide to assertive training*, Brooks/Cole, Monterey, California

De Giovanni, I. (1979) 'Development and validation of an assertiveness scale for couples', *Dissertation Abstracts International*, 39 (9-B), 4573

Delefes, P. and Jackson, B. (1972) 'Teacher-pupil interaction as a function of location in the classroom', *Psychology in the Schools*, 9, 119–23

Del Greco, L. (1983) 'The Del Greco assertive behavior inventory', *Journal of Behavioral Assessment*, 5, 49–63

Dell, D.M. and Schmidt, L.D. (1976) 'Behavioral cues to counselor expertness', *Journal of Counseling Psychology*, 23, 197–201

Derlega, V. and Berg, J. (eds), (1987) *Self-disclosure; theory, research and therapy*, Plenum Press, New York

—— and Chaikin, A. (1975) *Sharing intimacy: what we reveal to others and why*, Prentice-Hall, Englewood Cliffs, NJ

—— , Chaikin, A., Easterling, R. and Furman, G. (1973) 'Potential consequences and self-disclosure reciprocity', unpublished mimeo, Old Dominion University, Norfolk, Virginia

—— and Grzelak, J. (1979) 'Appropriateness of self-disclosure', in G. Chelune (ed.), *Self-disclosure*, Jossey-Bass, San Francisco

De Vito, J.A. (1986) *The interpersonal communication book*, 4th edition, Harper and Row, New York

Dickson, A. (1985) *Assertiveness and you — a woman in your own right*, Quartet Books, London

Dickson, D.A. (1981) 'Microcounselling: an evaluative study of a programme', unpublished PhD thesis, Ulster Polytechnic

—— (1986) 'Reflecting', in O. Hargie (ed.), *A handbook of communication skills*, Croom Helm, London/New York University Press, NY

Dillon, J.T. (1981) 'To question and not to question during discussion 1. Questioning and discussion', *Journal of Teacher Education*, 32, 51–5

—— (1982) 'The multidisciplinary study of questioning', *Journal of Educational Psychology*, 74, 147–65

—— (1986) 'Questioning', in O. Hargie (ed.), *A handbook of communication skills*, Croom Helm, London/New York University Press, NY

Dimond, R. and Hellkamp, D. (1969) 'Race, sex, ordinal position of birth, and self-disclosure in high school students', *Psychological Reports*, 25, 235–8

Dohrenwend, B. (1965) 'Some effects of open and closed questions on respondents' answers', *Human Organization*, 24, 175–84

—— and Richardson, S. (1964) 'A use for leading questions in research interviewing', *Human Organization*, 3, 76–7

Donohue, G.B. and Tryon, W.W. (1985) 'A functional analysis of social reinforcement in vicarious verbal conditioning', *Pavlovian Journal*, 20, 140–48

Douglas, T. (1976) *Groupwork practice*, Tavistock, London

Duck, S. (ed.), (1977) *Theory and practice in interpersonal attraction*, Academic Press, London

Dudley, W.H.C. and Blanchard, E.B. (1976) 'Comparison of experienced and inexperienced interviewers on objectively scored interview behaviour',

Journal of Clinical Psychology, 32, 690–7

Duncan, S. (1972) 'Some signals and rules for taking speaking turns in conversations', *Journal of Personality and Social Psychology*, 23, 283–92

—— and Fiske, D.W. (1977) *Face-to-face interaction: research, methods and theory*, Lawrence Erlbaum Associates, Hillsdale, NJ

Egan, G. (1977) 'Listening as empathic support', in J. Stewart (ed.), *Bridges not walls*, Addison-Wesley, Reading, Mass.

—— (1982) *The skilled helper*, Brooks/Cole, Monterey, California

Ehrlich, R.P., D'Augelli, A.R. and Danish, S.J. (1979) 'Comparative effectiveness of six counselor verbal responses', *Journal of Counseling Psychology*, 26, 390–8

Eisler, R., Hersen, M., Miller, P. and Blanchard, D. (1975) 'Situational determinants of assertive behavior', *Journal of Consulting and Clinical Psychology*, 43, 330–40

—— and Frederiksen, L.W. (1980) *Perfecting social skills. A guide to interpersonal behavior development*, Plenum Press, New York

Ekman, P. and Friesen, W.V. (1967) 'Head and body cues in the judgement of emotion: a reformulation', *Perceptual and Motor Skills*, 24, 711–24

—— and Friesen, W.V. (1969) 'The repertoire of non-verbal behaviour: categories, origins, usage and coding', *Semiotica*, 1, 49–98

—— and Friesen, W.V. (1975) *Unmasking the face: a guide to recognising emotions from facial cues*, Prentice-Hall, Englewood Cliffs, NJ

—— , Friesen, W.V. and Tomkins, S.S. (1971) 'Facial affect scoring technique: a first validity study', *Semiotica*, 3, 49–98

—— and Oster, H. (1979) 'Facial expressions of emotion', *Annual Review of Psychology*, 30, 527–55

Ellis, R. and Whittington, D. (1981) *A guide to social skill training*, Croom Helm, London/Brookline Books, Cambridge, Mass.

—— and Whittington, D. (eds) (1983) *New directions in social skill training*, Croom Helm, London/Methuen, New York

Ellison, C.W. and Firestone, I.J. (1974) 'Development of interpersonal trust as a function of self-esteem, target status and target style', *Journal of Personality and Social Psychology*, 29, 655–63

England, G.W. (1975) *The manager and his values: an international perspective*, Ballinger, Cambridge, Mass.

Ennis, R. (1969) *Logic in teaching*, Prentice-Hall, New York

Falk, D. and Wagner, P. (1985) 'Intimacy of self-disclosure and response processes as factors affecting the development of interpersonal relationships', *Journal of Social Psychology*, 125, 557–70

Feigenbaum, W.M. (1977) 'Reciprocity in self-disclosure within the psychological interview', *Psychological Reports*, 40, 15–26

Feldman, R.S. (1985) *Social psychology: theories, research and applications*, McGraw-Hill, New York

Festinger, L. (1954) 'A theory of social comparison processes', *Human Relations*, 7, 117–40

Fiedler, F.E. (1967) *A theory of leadership effectiveness*, McGraw-Hill, New York

—— (1971) 'Validation and extension of the contingency model of leadership effectiveness: a review of empirical findings', *Psychological Bulletin*, 76, 128–48

—— (1978) 'Recent developments in research on the contingency model', in L. Berkowitz (ed.), *Group processes*, Academic Press, New York

Field, S., Draper, J., Kerr, M. and Hare, M. (1982) 'A consumer view of the health visiting service', *Health visitor*, 55, 299–301

Fisch, H., Frey, S. and Hirsbrunner, H. (1983) 'Analyzing nonverbal behavior in depression', *Journal of Abnormal Psychology*, 92(3), 307–18

Fish, M.C. and White, M.A. (1979) 'The effects of verbal reinforcement, interest, and usable performance feedback upon task performance', *Journal of Experimental Psychology*, 47, 144–8

Fisher, D. (1984) 'A conceptual analysis of self-disclosure', *Journal for the Theory of Social Behaviour*, 14, 277–96

Fisher, J., Rytting, M. and Heslin, R. (1975) 'Hands touching hands: affective and evaluative effects of interpersonal touch', *Sociometry*, 39, 416–21

Flanders, N.A. (1970) *Analyzing teaching behaviour*, Addison-Wesley, Reading, Mass.

Floyd, J. (1985) *Listening: a practical approach*, Foresman, Glenview, Illinois

Fong, M., Borders, L. and Neimeyer, G. (1986) 'Sex role orientation and self-disclosure flexibility in counselor training' *Counselor Education and Supervision*, 25, 210–21

Foot, H. (1986) 'Humour and laughter', in O. Hargie (ed.), *A handbook of communication skills*, Croom Helm, London/New York University Press, NY

Forbes, R.J. and Jackson, P.R. (1980) 'Nonverbal behaviour and the outcome of selection interviews', *Journal of Occupational Psychology*, 53, 65–72

Foxman, R., Moss, P., Boland, G. and Owen, C. (1982) 'A consumer view of the health visitor at six weeks post practicum', *Health Visitor*, 55, 302–8

Franzoi, S. and Davis, M. (1985) 'Adolescent self-disclosure and loneliness: private self-consciousness and parental influences', *Journal of Personality and Social Psychology*, 48, 768–80

French, P. (1983) *Social skills for nursing practice*, Croom Helm, London

Friedman, H. (1979) 'Non-verbal communications between patients and medical practitioners', *Journal of Social Issues*, 35, 82–99

Friedman, N. and Hoffman, S.P. (1967) 'Kinetic behaviour in altered clinical states: approach to objective analysis of motor behaviour during clinical interviews', *Perceptual and Motor Skills*, 24, 525–39

Friesen, W., Ekman, P. and Wallblatt, H. (1980) 'Measuring hand movements', *Journal of Nonverbal Behaviour*, 4, 97–113

Fry, L. (1983) 'Women in society', in S. Spence and G. Shepherd (eds), *Developments in social skills training*, Academic Press, London

Furnham, A. (1979) 'Assertiveness in three cultures: multidimensionality and cultural differences', *Journal of Clinical Psychology*, 35, 522–7

Gage, N.L., Belgard, M., Dell, D., Hiller, J.E., Rosenshine, B. and Unruh, W.R. (1968) 'Explorations of the teachers' effectiveness in explaining', Technical Report 4, Stanford University Center for Research and Development in Teaching, Stanford

Galassi, J., Galassi, M. and Vedder, M. (1981) 'Perspectives on assertion as a social skills model', in J. Wine and M. Smye (eds), *Social competence*, Guilford Press, New York

Gall, M. (1970) 'The use of questions in teaching', *Review of Educational*

Research 40, 709–21

Gallagher, J. (1965) 'Expressive thought by gifted children in the classroom', *Elementary English*, 42, 559–68

Garramone, G. (1984) 'Audience motivation effects', *Communication Research*, 11, 79–96

Geller, D.M., Goodstein, L., Silver, M. and Sternberg, W.C. (1974) 'On being ignored: the effects of the violation of implicit rules of social interaction', *Sociometry*, 37, 541–56

Gleason, J. and Perlmann, R. (1985) 'Acquiring social variation in speech', in H. Giles and R. St Clair (eds), *Recent advances in language, communication and social psychology*, Lawrence Erlbaum Associates, London

Goffman, E. (1956) *The presentation of self in everyday life*, Edinburgh University Press, Edinburgh

—— (1961) *Encounters*, Bobbs-Merrill, Indianapolis

—— (1967) *Interaction ritual*, Aldine, Chicago

—— (1972) *Relations in public: micro-studies of the public order*, Penguin, Harmondsworth

Goldfried, M.R. and Davison, G.C. (1976) *Clinical behavior therapy*, Holt, Rinehart and Winston, New York

Goldman, M. (1980) 'Effect of eye-contact and distance on the verbal reinforcement of attitude', *Journal of Social Psychology*, 111, 73–8

Gordon, T. (1955) *Group-centred leadership*, Houghton Mifflin, Boston

Gormally, J. (1982) 'Evaluation of assertiveness: effects of gender, rater involvement and level of assertiveness', *Behavior Therapy*, 13, 219–25

Graesser, A. and Black, J. (1985) *The psychology of questions*, Lawrence Erlbaum Associates, Hillsdale, NJ

Graham, J. and Heywood, S. (1976) 'The effects of elimination of hand gestures and of verbal codability on speech performance', *European Journal of Social Psychology*, 5, 189–95

Green, R.T. (1977) 'Negative reinforcement as an unrewarding concept — a plea for consistency', *Bulletin of the British Psychological Society*, 30, 219–22

Greenbaum, P. and Rosenfeld, H. (1980) 'Varieties of touching in greetings: sequential structure and sex-related differences', *Journal of Nonverbal Behavior*, 5, 13–25

Greenspoon, J. (1955) 'The reinforcing effect of two spoken sounds on the frequency of two responses', *American Journal of Psychology*, 68, 409–16

Gregg, V. (1986) *Introduction to human memory*, Routledge and Kegan Paul, London and New York

Grigsby, J. and Weatherley, D. (1983) 'Gender and sex-role differences in intimacy of self-disclosure', *Psychological Reports*, 53, 891–97

Guetzkow, H. and Simon, H.A. (1955) 'The impact of certain communication acts upon organization and performance in task-oriented groups', *Management Science*, 1, 233–50

Haase, R.F. and Di Mattia, D.J. (1976) 'Spatial environment and verbal conditioning in a quasi-counselling interview', *Journal of Counseling Psychology*, 23, 414–21

Haines, J. (1975) *Skills and methods in social work*, Constable, London

Hall, E.T. (1959) *The silent language*, Doubleday, Garden City, New York

—— (1966) *The hidden dimension*, Doubleday, Garden City, New York

Halpin, A.W. and Winer, B.J. (1957) 'A factorial study of the leader behaviour descriptions', in R.M. Stogdill and A.E. Coons (eds), *Leader behaviour: its description and measurement*, Bureau of Business Research, Ohio State University, Ohio

Hare, A.P. (1976) *Handbook of small group research*, Free Press, NY

Hargie, O. (1980) 'An evaluation of a microteaching programme', unpublished doctoral dissertation, Ulster Polytechnic, Northern Ireland

—— (1983) 'The importance of teacher questions in the classroom', in M. Stubbs and H. Hiller (eds), *Readings on language, schools and classrooms*, Methuen, London

—— (1984) 'Training teachers in counselling skills: the effects of microcounselling', *British Journal of Educational Psychology*, 54, 214–20

—— (1986a) 'Communication as skilled behaviour', in O. Hargie (ed.), *A handbook of communication skills*, Croom Helm, London/New York University Press, NY

—— (1986b) 'From teaching to counselling: an evaluation of the role of microcounselling in the training of school counsellors', Proceedings of the First International Conference on Psychological Teacher Education, Universidade de Minho, Braga, Portugal

—— and McCartan, P. (1986) *Social skills training and psychiatric nursing*, Croom Helm, London

Harnack, R.V., Fest, T.B. and Jones, B.S. (1977) *Group discussion: theory and technique* 2nd edition, Prentice-Hall, Englewood Cliffs, NJ

Harper, R., Wiens, A. and Matarrazo, J. (1978) *Nonverbal communication: the state of the art*, Wiley, Chichester

Harrigan, J. (1985) 'Listeners' body movements and speaking turns', *Communication Research*, 12, 233–50

Harris, C.W. (ed.) (1960) *Encyclopedia of educational research*, 3rd edition, Macmillan, New York

Harris, J. (1973) 'Answering questions containing marked and unmarked adjectives and adverbs', *Journal of Experimental Psychology*, 97, 399–401

Haviland, J. and Malatesta, C. (1981) 'The development of sex differences in nonverbal signals: fallacies, facts and fantasies', in C. Mayo and N. Henley (eds), *Gender and nonverbal behavior*, Springer-Verlag, New York

Hekmat, H. (1974) 'Three techniques of reinforcement modification: a comparison', *Behavior Therapy*, 5, 541–8

—— and Lee, Y.B. (1970) 'Conditioning of affective self-references as a function of semantic meaning of verbal reinforcers', *Journal of Abnormal Psychology*, 3, 427–33

Henry, S.E., Medway, F.J. and Scarbo, H.A. (1979) 'Sex and locus of control as determinants of children's responses to peer versus adult praise', *Journal of Educational Psychology*, 71, 604–12

Heslin, R. (1974) 'Steps toward a taxonomy of touching', paper presented at the Convention of the Midwestern Psychological Association, Chicago, May

—— and Alper, T. (1983) 'Touch, a bonding gesture', in J. Wiemann and R. Harrison (eds), *Nonverbal interaction*, Sage Annual Reviews of Communication Research, vol. 11, Sage Publications, London

—— and Patterson, M.L. (1982) *Nonverbal behavior and social psychology*, Plenum Press, NY

Higgins, S.T. and Morris, E.K. (1985) 'A comment on contemporary definitions of reinforcement as a behavioural process', *Psychological Record*, 35, 81–8

Highlen, P.S. and Baccus, G.K. (1977) 'Effects of reflection of feeling and probe on client self-referenced affect', *Journal of Counseling Psychology*, 24, 440–3

—— and Nicholas, R.P. (1978) 'Effects of locus of control, instructions, and verbal conditioning on self-referenced affect in a counseling interview', *Journal of Counseling Psychology*, 25, 177–83

Hildum, D.C. and Brown, R.W. (1956) 'Verbal reinforcement and interviewer bias', *Journal of Abnormal Psychology*, 53, 108–11

Hill, C.E. and Gormally, J. (1977) 'Effects of reflection, restatement, probe and nonverbal behaviors on client affect', *Journal of Counseling Psychology*, 24, 92–7

Hiller, J. (1971) 'Verbal response indicators of conceptual vagueness', *American Educational Research Journal*, 8, 151–61

—— Fisher, G. and Kaess, W. (1969) 'A computer investigation of verbal characteristics of effective classroom lecturing', *American Educational Research Journal*, 6, 661–75

Hoffnung, R.J. (1969) 'Conditioning and transfer of affective self-references in a role-played counseling interview', *Journal of Consulting and Clinical Psychology*, 33, 527–31

Holahan, C.J. (1979) 'Redesigning physical environments to enhance social interactions', in R. Munoz, L. Snowden, J. Kelly *et al. (eds), Social and psychological research in community settings*, Jossey-Bass, San Francisco

Hollander, E.P. (1978) *Leadership dynamics: a practical guide to effective relationships*, Free Press, New York

—— and Julian J.W. (1969) 'Contemporary trends in the analysis of leadership processes', *Psychological Bulletin*, 71, 387–97

Honing, W.K. and Staddon, J.E.R. (1977) *Handbook of operant behaviour*, Prentice-Hall, Englewood Cliffs, NJ

Hore, T. (1971) 'Assessment of teaching practice: an "Attractive" Hypothesis', *British Journal of Educational Psychology*, 41, 3, 302–5

Hosking, D.M. and Morley, I.E. (1986) 'The skills of leadership', paper presented at Aston University Management centre, Birmingham

Hyman, R.T. (1974) *Teaching: vantage points for study*, Lippincott Press, New York

—— (1979) *Strategic questioning*, Prentice-Hall, Englewood Cliffs, NJ

Ivey, A. (1971) *Microcounseling: innovations in interviewing training*, C.C. Thomas, Springfield, Illinois

—— and Authier, J. (1978) *Microcounseling: innovations in interviewing, counseling, psychotherapy and psychoeducation*, C.C. Thomas, Springfield, Illinois

—— and Gluckstern, N. (1976) *Basic influencing skills: leader and participant manuals*, Microtraining Associates Inc., Mass.

Jaffe, J., Anderson, S. and Stern, D. (1979) 'Conversational rhythms', in D. Aaronson and R. Rieber (eds), *Psycholinguistic research*, Lawrence Erlbaum, Hillsdale, NJ

Janis, I.L. (1972) *Victims of groupthink: a psychological study of foreign-policy decisions and fiascoes*, Houghton-Mifflin, Boston

Jesudason, S. (1976) 'Open-ended and closed-ended questions: are they complementary?', *Journal of Family Welfare*, 25, 66–8

Johnson, C. and Dabbs, J. (1976) 'Self-disclosure in dyads as a function of distance and the subject-experimenter relationship', *Sociometry*, 39, 257–63

Johnson, D.W. and Johnson, F.P. (1982) *Joining together*, 2nd edition, Prentice-Hall, Englewood Cliffs, NJ

Jones, S.E. and Yarbrough, A.E. (1985) 'A naturalistic study of the meanings of touch', *Communication Monographs*, 52, 19–56

Jones, W.H., Hobbs, S.A. and Hockenbury, D. (1982) 'Loneliness and social skill deficits', *Journal of Personality and Social Psychology*, 42, 682–9

Jourard, S. (1964) *The transparent self*, Van Nostrand Reinhold, New York

—— (1971) *Self-disclosure*, Wiley, New York

Kahn, R. and Cannell, C. (1957) *The dynamics of interviewing*, Wiley, New York

Kahn, S. (1981) 'Issues in the assessment and training of assertiveness with women', in J. Wine and M. Smye (eds), *Social competence*, Guilford Press, New York

Kelly, J.A. (1982) *Social skills training: a practical guide for interventions*, Springer Publishing Co., New York

Kendon, A. (1967) 'Some functions of gaze direction in social interaction', *Acta Psychologica*, 26, 22–63

—— (1978) 'Looking in conversation and the regulation of turns at talk: a comment on the papers of G. Beattie and D.R. Rutter et al', *British Journal of Social and Clinical Psychology*, 17, 23–4

—— (1981) 'Geography of gesture', *Semiotica*, 37, 129–63

—— (1983) 'Gesture and speech: how they interact', in J. Wiemann and R. Harrison (eds), *Nonverbal interaction*, Sage Annual Reviews of Communication Research, vol. 11, Sage Publications, London

—— and Ferber, A. (1973) 'A description of some human greetings', in R. Michael and J. Crook (eds), *Comparative ecology and behaviour of primates*, Academic Press, London

Kennedy, J.J. and Zimmer, J.M. (1968) 'Reinforcing value of five stimulus conditions in a quasi-counseling situation', *Journal of Counseling Psychology*, 15, 357–62

Kennedy, T.D., Timmons, E.O. and Noblin, C.D. (1971) 'Nonverbal maintenance of conditioned verbal behavior following interpretations, reflections and social reinforcers', *Journal of Personality and Social Psychology*, 20, 112–17

Kennedy, W.A. and Willcutt, H.C. (1964) 'Praise and blame as incentives', *Psychological Bulletin*, 62, 323–32

Kennelly, K.J. and Mount, S.A. (1985) 'Perceived contingency of reinforcements, helplessness, locus of control and academic performance', *Psychology in the Schools*, 22, 465–9

—— Dietz, D. and Benson, P. (1985) 'Reinforcement schedules, effort vs. ability attributions, and persistence', *Psychology in the Schools*, 22, 459–64

Kern, J. (1982) 'Predicting the impact of assertive, empathic-assertive and non-assertive behavior: the assertiveness of the assertee', *Behavior Therapy*, 13, 486–98

—— Cavell, T. and Beck, B. (1985) 'Predicting differential reactions to males' versus females' assertions, empathic assertions and nonassertions', *Behavior Therapy*, 16, 63–75

Kestler, J. (1982) *Questioning techniques and tactics*, McGraw-Hill, Colorado Springs, Colorado

Kiefer, F. (ed.) (1982) *Questions and answers*, D. Reidel, Dordrecht, Holland

King, G. (1972) 'Open and closed questions: the reference interview', *RQ — Reference and Adult Sciences Division*, 12, 157–60

Kittell, J.E. (1957) 'An experimental study of the effect of external direction during learning in transfer and retention of principles', *Journal of Educational Psychology*, 48, 391–405

Kleck, R. (1969) 'Physical stigma and task orientated interaction', *Human Relations*, 22, 51–60

Klein, K., Kaplan, K.J. and Firestone, I.J. (1975) 'Reciprocity, compensation and mediation in verbal and visual distancing', paper presented at the 83rd Annual Meeting of the American Psychological Association, Chicago

Kleinke, C.L. (1980) 'Interaction between gaze and legitimacy of request on compliance in a field setting', *Journal of Nonverbal Behavior*, 5, 3–12

—— (1986) *Meeting and understanding people*, W.H. Freeman, New York

—— Staneski, R.A. and Berger, D.E. (1975) 'Evaluation of an interviewer as a function of interviewer gaze, reinforcement of subject gaze and interviewer attractiveness', *Journal of Personality and Social Psychology*, 31, 115–22

Knapp, M.L. (1972) *Nonverbal communication in human interaction*, Holt, Rinehart and Winston, New York

—— Hart, R., Friedrich, G. and Schulman, G. (1973) 'The rhetoric of goodbye: verbal and nonverbal correlates of human leave-taking', *Speech monographs*, 40, 182–98

Knapper, C. (1981) 'Presenting and public speaking', in M. Argyle (ed.), *Social skills and work*, Methuen, London

Kolotkin, R., Wielkiewicz, R., Judd, B. and Weisler, S. (1983) 'Behavioral components of assertion: comparison of univariate and multivariate assessment strategies', *Behavioral Assessment*, 6, 61–78

Korda, M. (1976) *Power in the office*, Weidenfeld and Nicolson, London

Krasner, L. (1958) 'Studies of the conditioning of verbal behaviour', *Psychological Bulletin*, 55, 148–70

Krivonos, P. and Knapp, M. (1975) 'Initiating communication: what do you say when you say hello?', *Central States Speech Journal*, 26, 115–25

Kuperminc, M. and Heimberg, R. (1983) 'Consequence probability and utility as factors in the decision to behave assertively', *Behavior Therapy*, 14, 637–46

L'Abate, L. and Milan, M. (eds) (1985) *Handbook of social skills training and research*, Wiley, New York

Land, M. (1984) 'Combined effect of two teacher clarity variables on student achievement', *Journal of Experimental Education*, 50, 1, 14–17

—— (1985) 'Vagueness and clarity in the classroom', in T. Husen and T. Postlethwaite (eds), *International encyclopedia of education: research studies* Pergamon Press, Oxford

Lange, A. and Jakubowski, P. (1976) *Responsible assertive behavior*, Research Press, Champaign, Illinois

Laver, J. (1981) 'Linguistic roles and politeness in greeting and parting', in F. Coulmas (ed.), *Conversational routine: explorations in standardized communication situations and prepatterned speech*, Mouton, The Hague
—— and Hutcheson, S. (eds) (1972) *Communication in face-to-face interaction*, Penguin, Harmondsworth
Lazarsfield, P. (1944) 'The controversy over detailed interviews — an offer for negotiation', *Public Opinion Quarterly*, VIII, 38–60
Lazarus, A. (1971) *Behavior therapy and beyond*, McGraw-Hill, New York
Levin, M. (1977) 'Self-knowledge and the talking cure', *Review of Existential Psychology and Psychiatry*, 15, 95–111
Lewin, K. (1951) *Field theory in social science*, Harper, New York
—— Lippitt, R. and White, R.K. (1939) 'Patterns of aggressive behaviour in experimentally created social climates', *Journal of Social Psychology*, 10, 271–99
Lewis, P. and Gallois, C. (1984) 'Disagreements, refusals, or negative feelings: perception of negatively assertive messages from friends and strangers', *Behavior Therapy*, 15, 353–68
Ley, P. (1983) 'Patients' understanding and recall in clinical communication failure', in D. Pendleton and J. Hasler (eds), *Doctor-patient communication*, Academic Press, London
Likert, R. (1967) *The human organization*, McGraw-Hill, New York
Linehan, M. and Egan, K. (1979) 'Assertion training for women', in A. Bellack and M. Hersen (eds), *Research and practice in social skills training*, Plenum, New York
Littlejohn, S.W. (1978) *Theories of communication*, Merrill, Columbus, Ohio
Loftus, E. (1975) 'Leading questions and the eyewitness report', *Cognitive Psychology*, 7, 560–72
—— (1982) 'Interrogating eyewitnesses — good questions and bad', in R. Hogarth (ed.), *Question framing and response consistency*, Jossey-Bass, San Francisco
—— and Palmer, J. (1974) 'Reconstruction of automobile destruction: an example of the interaction between language and memory', *Journal of Verbal Learning and Verbal Behaviour*, 13, 585–9
—— and Zanni, G. (1975) 'Eyewitness testimony: the influence of the wording of a question', *Bulletin of the Psychonomic Society*, 5, 86–8
Long, L., Paradise, L. and Long, T. (1981) *Questioning: skills for the helping process*, Brooks/Cole, Monterey, California
Lott, A.J. and Lott, B.E. (1968) 'A learning theory approach to interpersonal attitudes', in A.G. Greenwald, T.C. Brock and T. McOstrom (eds), *Psychological foundations of attitudes*, Academic Press, New York
Lott, D.F. and Sommer, R. (1967) 'Seating arrangements and status', *Journal of Personality and Social Psychology*, 7, 90–95
Luft, J. (1970) *Group processes: an introduction to group dynamics*, National Press Books, Palo Alto, California
—— (1984) *Group processes: an introduction to group dynamics*, 2nd ed., Mayfield, San Francisco
Lundsteen, S. (1971) *Listening: its impact on reading and other language acts*, National Council of Teachers of English, New York
Lysakowski, R.S. and Walberg, H.J. (1981) 'Classroom reinforcement

and learning. a quantitative synthesis', *Journal of Educational Research*, 75, 69–77
Maguire, P. (1984) 'Communication skills and patient care', in A. Steptoe and A. Mathews (eds), *Health care and human behaviour*, Academic Press, London
— (1985) 'Deficiencies in key interpersonal skills', in C. Kagan (ed.), *Interpersonal skills in nursing*, Croom Helm, London
Maguire, G.P. and Rutter, D. (1976) 'History taking for medical students', *Lancet*, 2, 556–8
Margalit, B. and Mauger, P. (1985) 'Aggressiveness and assertiveness: a cross-cultural study of Israel and the United States', *Journal of Cross-Cultural Psychology*, 16, 497–511
Marisi, D.Q. and Helmy, K. (1984) 'Intratask integration as a function of age and verbal praise', *Perceptual and Motor Skills*, 58, 936–9
Marshall, K., Kurtz, D. and Associates (1982) *Interpersonal helping skills*, Jossey-Bass, London
Martin, J.R. (1970) *Explaining, understanding and teaching*, McGraw-Hill, New York
Martinko, M.J. and Gardner, W.L. (1984) 'The observation of high-performing managers: methodological issues and managerial implications', in J.C. Hunt, D.M. Hosking, C.A. Schriesheim and R. Stewart (eds), *Leaders and managers: international perspectives on managerial behavior and leadership*, Pergamon Press, New York
Maslow, A.H. (1970) *Motivation and personality*, Harper and Row, New York
Massarik, F. (1972) 'Standards for group leadership', in L.N. Solomon and B. Berzon (eds), *New perspectives on encounter groups*, Jossey-Bass, San Francisco
Matarazzo, J.D. and Wiens, A.N. (1972) *The interview: research on its anatomy and structure*, Aldine-Atherton, Chicago
— Wiens, A.N. and Saslow, G. (1965) 'Studies in interview speech behaviour', in L. Krasner and L. Ullman (eds), *Research in behavior modification: new developments and implications*, Holt, Rinehart and Winston, New York
Mayfield, E. (1972) 'Value of peer nominations in predicting life insurance', *Journal of Applied Psychology*, 46, 6–13
Mayo, C. and Henley, N. (1981) 'Nonverbal behavior: barrier or agent for sex role change', in C. Mayo and N. Henley (eds), *Gender and nonverbal behavior*, Springer-Verlag, New York
McFall, M., Winnett, R., Bordewick, M. and Bornstein, P. (1982) 'Nonverbal components in the communication of assertiveness', *Behavior Modification*, 6, 121–40
McGrade, B.J. (1966) 'Effectiveness of verbal reinforcers in relation to age and social class', *Journal of Personality and Social Psychology*, 4, 555–60
McGregor, D. (1960) *The human side of enterprise*, McGraw-Hill, New York
McGuire, J. and Priestley, P. (1981) *Life after school: a social skills curriculum*, Pergamon, Oxford
McHenry, R. (1981) 'The selection interview', in M. Argyle (ed.), *Social skills and work*, Methuen, London
McIntyre, T., Jeffrey, D. and McIntyre, S. (1984) 'Assertion training: the

effectiveness of a contemporary cognitive-behavioral treatment package with professional nurses', *Behavior Research and Therapy*, 22, 311–18

McKeown, R. (1977) 'Accountability in responding to classroom questions: impact on student achievement', *Journal of Experimental Education*, 45, 24–30

Mehrabian, A. (1968) 'Inference of attitudes from the posture, orientation and distance of a communicator', *Journal of Consulting and Clinical Psychology*, 32, 296–308

—— (1972) *Nonverbal communication*, Aldine-Atherton, Chicago

—— and Ferris, S.R. (1967) 'Influence of attitudes from nonverbal communication in two channels', *Journal of Consulting Psychology*, 31, 248–52

Merbaum, M. (1963) 'The conditioning of affective self-references by three classes of generalized reinforcers', *Journal of Personality*, 31, 179–91

Metzler, K. (1977) *Creative interviewing: the writer's guide to gathering information by asking questions*, Prentice-Hall, Englewood Cliffs; NJ

Michelson, L., Sugai, D., Wood, R. and Kazdin, A. (1983) *Social skills assessment and training with children*, Plenum, New York

Miller, J. and Eller, B.F. (1985) 'An examination of the effect of tangible and social reinforcers on intelligence test performance of middle school students', *Social Behaviour and Personality*, 13, 147–57

Miller, L. and Kenny, D. (1986) 'Reciprocity of self-disclosure at the individual and dyadic levels: a social relations analysis', *Journal of Personality and Social Psychology*, 50, 713–19

—— Berg, J. and Archer, R. (1983) 'Openers: individuals who elicit intimate self-disclosure', *Journal of Personality and Social Psychology*, 44, 1234–44

Mills, M.C. (1983) 'Adolescents' self-disclosure in individual and group theme-centred modelling, reflecting and probing interviews', *Psychological Reports*, 53, 691–701

Miltz, R.J. (1972) 'Development and evaluation of a manual for improving teachers' explanations', *Technical Report*, 26, Stanford University Center for Research and Development in Teaching, Stanford

Mock, J.F. (1957) 'The influence of verbal and behavioural cues of a listener on the verbal productions of the speaker', cited in L. Krasner (1958) 'Studies of the conditioning of verbal behaviour', *Psychological Bulletin*, 55, 148–70

Montagu, M.F.A. (1971) *Touching: the human significance of the skin*, Columbia University Press, New York

Montgomery, R. (1981) *Listening made easy*, AMACOM, New York

Morley, I.E. and Hosking, D.M. (1985) 'The skills of leadership', paper presented at the West European Conference on the Psychology of Work and Organization, Aachen, FRG, 1–3 April

Morris, D., Collett, P., Marsh, P. and O'Shaughnessy, M. (1979) *Gestures: their origins and distribution*, Stein and Day, New York

Mortensensen, C.D. (1966) 'Should the discussion group have an assigned leader?' *Speech Teacher*, 15, 34–41

Mucchielli, R. (1983) *Face-to-face in the counselling interview*, Macmillan, London

Munro, E.A., Manthei, R.J. and Small, J.J. (1983) *Counselling: a skills approach*, Methuen, New Zealand

Nagata, D.K., Nay, W.R. and Seidman, E. (1983) 'Nonverbal and verbal content behaviors in the prediction of interviewer effectiveness', *Journal of Counseling Psychology*, 30, 83–6

Naifeh, S. and Smith, G. (1984) *Why can't men open up?*, Clarkson N. Potter, New York

Nelson-Jones, R. (1983) *Practical counselling skills*, Holt, Rinehart and Winston, London

Newcomb, T. (1961) *The acquaintance process*, Holt, Rinehart and Winston, New York

Newman, H. (1982) 'The sounds of silence in communicative encounters', *Communication Quarterly*, 30, 142–9

Nix, J., Lohr, J. and Mosesso, L. (1983) 'The relationship of sex-role characteristics to self-report and role-play measures of assertiveness in women', *Behavioral Assessment*, 6, 89–93

Norton, R. (1983) *Communicator style: theory, applications and measures*, Sage, Beverly Hills, California

Novak, J.D., Ring, D.G. and Tanir, P. (1971) 'Interpretation of research findings in terms of Ausubel's Theory and implications for science education', *Science Education* 55, 483–526

Nuthall, G.A. (1968) 'Studies of teaching: 11 types of research on teaching', *New Zealand Journal of Educational Studies*, 3, 125–47

O'Brien, J.S. and Holborn, S.W. (1979) 'Verbal and nonverbal expressions as reinforcers in verbal conditioning of adult conversation', *Journal of Behaviour Psychiatry*, 10, 267–9

O'Donnell, P.J., Kennedy, B. and McGill, P. (1983) 'Verbal operant conditioning, extinction trials and types of awareness statement', *Psychological Reports*, 53, 991–7

O'Leary, K. and O'Leary, S. (eds) (1977) *Classroom management: the successful use of behaviour modification*, Pergamon, New York

O'Neill, N. and O'Neill, G. (1977) 'Relationships' in B. Patton and K. Giffin (eds), *Interpersonal communication in action*, Harper and Row, New York

Owens, R.G. (1986) 'Handling strong emotions', in O. Hargie (ed.), *A handbook of communication skills*, Croom Helm, London/New York University Press, NY

Pansa, M. (1979) 'Verbal conditioning of affect responses of process and reactive schizophrenics in a clinical interview situation', *British Journal of Medical Psychology*, 52, 175–82

Paradowski, W. (1967) 'Effects of curiosity on incidental learning', *Journal of Educational Psychology*, 58, 50–5

Passons, W.R. (1975) *Gestalt approaches in counselling*, Holt, Rinehart and Winston, New York

Pate, R. and Bremer, N. (1967) 'Guiding learning through skilful questioning', *Elementary School Journal*, 67, 417–22

Patterson, C.H. (1980) *Theories of counselling and psychotherapy*, Harper and Row, New York

Patterson, M. (1983) *Nonverbal behavior: a functional perspective*, Springer Verlag, New York

Pattison, J. (1973) 'Effects of touch on self-exploration and the therapeutic relationship', *Journal of Consulting and Clinical Psychology*, 40, 170–75

Pavlov, I.P. (1927) *Conditioned reflexes*, Dover Reprint, New York

Peeck, J. (1970) 'Effects of prequestions on delayed retention of prose material', *Journal of Educational Psychology*, 51, 241–6

Pendleton, D. and Bochner, S. (1980) 'The communication of medical information in general practice consultations as a function of patients' social class', *Social Science Medicine*, 14, 669–73

Phelps, S. and Austin, N. (1975) *The assertive woman*, Impact, San Luis Obispo, California

Phillips, E. (1978) *The social skills basis of psychopathology*, Grune and Stratton, New York

Pietrofesa, J.J., Hoffman, A., Splete, H.H. and Pinto, D.V. (1978) *Counseling: theory, research and practice*, Rand McNally, Chicago

Pinney, R.H. (1969) 'Presentational behaviors related to success in teaching', PhD thesis, Stanford University, *Dissertation Abstracts International*, 30, 1970

Pope, B. (1979) *The mental health interview: research and applications*, Pergamon Press, Oxford

—— (1986) *Social skills training for psychiatric nurses*, Harper and Row, London

Poppleton, S. (1981) 'The social skills of selling', in M. Argyle (ed.), *Social skills and work*, Methuen, London

Porritt, L. (1984) *Communication: choices for nurses*, Churchill Livingstone, Melbourne, Australia

Powell, W.J. (1968) 'Differential effectiveness of interviewer interventions in an experimental interview', *Journal of Consulting and Clinical Psychology*, 32, 210–15

Purvis, J., Dabbs, J. and Hopper, C. (1984) 'The "Opener": skilled user of facial expression and speech pattern', *Personality and Social Psychology Bulletin*, 10, 61–6

Raben, C.S., Wood, M.T., Klimoski, R.J. and Hakel, M.D. (1974) 'Social reinforcement: a review of the literature', US AFHRL Technical Report, 74–9 (1)

Rachlin, H. (1970) *Introduction to modern behaviorism*, W.H. Freeman, San Francisco

Rackham, N. and Carlisle, J. (1978) 'The effective negotiator — Part 1', *Journal of European Industrial Training*, 2, 6–10

—— and Morgan, T. (1977) *Behaviour analysis in training*, McGraw-Hill, Maidenhead, Berks.

Rakos, R. (1986) 'Asserting and confronting', in O. Hargie (ed.) *A handbook of communication skills*, Croom Helm, London/New York University Press, NY

Rauch, C.F. and Behling, O. (1984) 'Functionalism: basis for an alternative approach to the study of leadership', in J. Hunt, D. Hosking, C. Schriesheim and R. Stewart (eds), *Leaders and managers: international perspectives on managerial behavior and leadership*, Pergamon, New York

Raven, B.H. and Rubin, J.Z. (1983) *Social psychology*, Wiley, New York

Reece, M.M. and Whitman, R.N. (1962) 'Expressive movements, warmth and verbal reinforcement', *Journal of Abnormal and Social Psychology*, 64, 234–6

Reid, L.S., Henneman, R. and Long, E. (1960) 'An experimental analysis of set: the effect of categorical instruction', *American Journal of Psychology*, 73, 568–72

Resnick, L. (1972) 'Teacher behaviour in an informal British infant school', *School Review*, 81, 63–83

Reynolds, J.H. and Glaser, R. (1964) 'Effects of repetition and spaced review upon retention of a complex learning task', *Journal of Educational Psychology*, 5, 297–308

Richardson, S. (1960) 'The use of leading questions in non-schedule interviews', *Human Organization*, XIX, 86–9

— Dohrenwend, N. and Klein, D. (1965) *Interviewing: its forms and functions*, Basic Books; New York

Rierdan, J. and Brooks, R. (1978) 'Verbal conditioning of male and female schizophrenics as a function of experimenter proximity', *Journal of Clinical Psychology*, 34, 33–6

Riggio, R. and Friedman, H. (1986) 'Impression formation: the role of expressive behavior', *Journal of Personality and Social Psychology*, 50, 2, 421–7

Riseborough, M. (1981) 'Physiographic gestures as decoding facilitators: three experiments exploring a neglected facet of communication', *Journal of Nonverbal behavior*, 5, 172–83

Robinson, J. (1982) *An Evaluation of Health Visiting*, CETHV, London

Rogers, C.R. (1951) *Client-centred therapy*, Houghton Mifflin, Boston

— (1961) *On becoming a person: a therapist's view of psychotherapy*, Houghton Mifflin, Boston

— (1977) *On personal power: inner strength and its revolutionary impact*, Delacante Press, New York

— (1980) *A way of being*, Houghton Mifflin, Boston

— and Farson, R. (1973) 'Active listening', in R. Huseman, C. Logue and D. Freshley (eds), *Readings in interpersonal and organizational communication*, 2nd edition, Holbrook Press, Boston, Mass.

Rogers, W. (1978) 'The contribution of kinesic illustrators toward the comprehension of verbal behaviour within utterances', *Human Communication Research*, 5, 54–62

Rose, Y. and Tryon, W. (1979) 'Judgements of assertive behavior as a function of speech loudness, latency, content, gestures, inflection and sex', *Behavior Modification*, 3, 112–23

Rosenblatt, P.C. (1977) 'Cross-cultural perspective on attraction', in T.L. Huston (ed.), *Foundations of interpersonal attraction*, Academic Press, London

Rosenfeld, H. and Hancks, M. (1980) 'The nonverbal context of verbal listener responses', in M. Kay (ed.), *The relationship of verbal and nonverbal communication*, Mouton, The Hague

Rosenshine, B. (1968) 'Objectively measured behavioural predictors of effectiveness in explaining', Technical Report 4, Stanford Unviersity Center for Research and Development in Teaching, Stanford

— (1971) *Teaching behaviour and student achievement*, National Foundation for Educational Research in England and Wales, Windsor, Berks.

— and Furst, N. (1973) 'The use of direct observation to study teaching', in R. Travers (ed.), *Second handbook of research on teaching*, Rand McNally, New York

Roth, H.L. (1889) 'On salutations', *Journal of the Royal Anthropological Institute*, 19, 164–81

Rothkopf, E.Z. (1972) 'Variable adjunct question schedules, interpersonal interaction and incidental learning from written material', *Journal of Educational Psychology*, 63, 87–92

Rotter, J.B. (1966) 'Generalized expectancies for internal versus external control of reinforcement', *Psychological Monographs*, 80, No. 609

Rousseau, E. and Redfield, D. (1980) 'Teacher questioning', *Evaluation in Education*, 4, 51–2

Rowe, M. (1969) 'Science, silence and sanctions', *Science and Children*, 6, 11–13

Rozelle, R., Druckman, D. and Baxter, J. (1986) 'Nonverbal communication', in O. Hargie (ed.), *A handbook of communication skills*, Croom Helm, London/New York University Press, NY

Russell, J.L. (1971) *Motivation*, W.C. Brown, Dubuque, Iowa

Russo, N.F. (1975) 'Eye-contact, interpersonal distance, and the equilibrium theory', *Journal of Personality and Social Psychology*, 31, 497–502

Rutter, D., Stephenson, G., Ayline, K. and White, P. (1978) 'The timing of looks in dyadic conversation', *British Journal of Social and Clinical Psychology*, 16, 191–2

Ryan, E. (1972) 'Differentiated effects of levels of questioning on student achievement', *Journal of Experimental Education*, 41, 63–7

Saigh, P.A. (1981) 'Effects of nonverbal examiner praise on selected WAIS subtest performance of Lebanese undergraduates', *Journal of Nonverbal Behaviour*, 6, 84–8

Salter, A. (1949) *Conditioned reflex therapy*, Capricorn Books, New York

Salzinger, K. and Pisoni, S. (1960) 'Reinforcement of verbal affect responses of normal subjects during the interview', *Journal of Abnormal and Social Psychology*, 60, 127–30

Sarbin, T.R. and Allen, V.L. (1968) 'Role theory', in G. Lindzey and E. Aronson (eds), *Handbook of social psychology*, vol. 1, Addison-Wesley, Reading, Mass.

Saunders, C. (1986) 'Opening and closing', in O. Hargie (ed.), *A handbook of communication skills*, Croom Helm, London/New York University Press, NY

Schatzman, L. and Strauss, A. (1956) 'Social class and modes of communications', *American Journal of Sociology*, LX, 329–38

Schegloff, E.A. and Sacks, H. (1973) 'Opening-up closings', *Semiotica*, 8, 289–327

Scherer, K. (1979) 'Acoustic concomitants of emotional dimensions: judging affect from synthesized tone sequences', in S. Weitz (ed.), *Nonverbal communication: readings with commentary*, 2nd edition, Oxford University Press, New York

—— and Ekman, P. (eds) (1982) *Handbook of methods in nonverbal behaviour research*, Cambridge University Press, Cambridge

Schlundt, D. and McFall, R. (1985) 'New directions in the assessment of social competence and social skills', in L. L'Abate and M. Milan (eds), *Handbook of social skills training and research*, Wiley, New York

Schneider, D., Hastorf, A. and Ellsworth, P. (1979) *Person perception*, Addison-Wesley, Reading, Mass.

Schuck, R.F. (1969) 'The effect of set induction upon pupil achievement, retention and assessment of effective teaching', *Educational Leadership*, 2, 785–93

Schulman, L. (1979) *The skills of helping*, Peacock Publishers, Illinois

Schultz, C.B. and Sherman, R.H. (1976) 'Social class, development and differences in reinforcer effectiveness', *Review of Educational Research*, 46, 25–59

Schutz, W.C. (1955) 'What makes groups productive?', *Human Relations*, 8, 429–65

—— (1967) *Joy*, Grove Press, New York

Scofield, M.E. (1977) 'Verbal conditioning with a heterogeneous adolescent sample: the effects on two critical responses', *Psychology*, 14, 41–9

Scott, M., McCroskey, J. and Sheahan, M. (1978) 'The development of a self-report measure of communication apprehension in organizational settings', *Journal of Communication*, 28, 104–11

Secord, P.F. and Backman, C.W. (1974) *Social psychology*, McGraw-Hill, New York

Seligman, M.E.P. (1975) *Helplessness: on depression, development, and death*, W.H. Freeman and Co., San Francisco

Shapiro, J.G. (1968) 'Responsivity to facial and linguistic cues', *Journal of Communication*, 18, 11–17

Shaw, M.E. (1981) *Group dynamics: the psychology of small group behavior*, McGraw-Hill, New York

Showalter, J.T. (1974) 'Counsellor nonverbal behaviour as operant reinforcers for client self-references and expression of feelings' *Dissertation Abstracts International*, 35, 3435A

Shutes, R. (1969) 'Verbal behaviors and instructional effectiveness', unpublished dissertation, Stanford University, *Dissertation Abstracts International*, 30, 1970

Shuy, R.W. (1983) 'Three types of interference to an effective exchange of information in the medical interview', in S. Fisher and A.D. Todd (eds), *Social organization of doctor-patient communication*, Center for Applied Linguistics, Washington, DC

Siegel, J. (1980) 'Effects of objective evidence of expertness, nonverbal behavior and subject sex on client-perceived expertness', *Journal of Counseling Psychology*, 27, 117–21

Siegman, A.W. (1976) 'Do noncontingent interviewer Mm-hmms facilitate interviewee productivity?', *Journal of Consulting and Clinical Psychology*, 44, 171–82

Silver, R.J. (1970) 'Effects of subject status and interviewer response program on subject self-disclosure in standardized interviews', *Proceedings of the 78th Annual Convention*, APA, 5, 539–40

Simms, M. and Smith, C. (1984) 'Teenage mothers: some views on health visitors', *Health Visitor*, 57, 269–70

Simonson, N. (1973) 'Self-disclosure and psychotherapy', unpublished mimeo, University of Massachusetts

Sinha, V. (1972) 'Age differences in self-disclosure', *Developmental Psychology*, 7, 257–8

Skinner, B.F. (1953) *Science and human behaviour*, Collier Macmillan, London

—— (1957) *Verbal behavior*, Appleton-Century-Crofts, New York

—— (1969) *Contingencies of reinforcement*, Appleton-Century-Crofts, New York

—— (1978) *Reflections on behaviorism and society*, Prentice-Hall, Englewood Cliffs, NJ

Slobin, D., Miller, S. and Porter, L. (1968) 'Forms of address and social relations in a business organization', *Journal of Personality and Social Psychology*, 8, 289–92

Smith, P. (1974) 'Aspects of the playgroup environment', in D. Canter and T. Lee (eds), *Psychology and the built environment*, Architectural Press, London

Smith, V. (1968) 'Listening', in O. Hargie (ed.), *A handbook of communication skills*, Croom Helm, London/New York University Press, NY

Smock, C. and Holt, B. (1962) 'Children's reaction to novelty: an experimental study of curiosity motivation', *Child Development*, 33, 631–42

Solano, C. and Dunnam, M. (1985) 'Two's company: self-disclosure and reciprocity in triads versus dyads', *Social Psychology Quarterly*, 48, 183–7

Solomon, M. and Schopler, J. (1982) 'Self consciousness and clothing', *Personality and Social Psychology Bulletin*, 8, 508–14

Sommer, R. (1969) *Personal space*, Prentice-Hall, Englewood Cliffs, NJ

Spooner, S.E. (1976) 'An investigation of the maintenance of specific counselling skills over time', *Dissertation Abstracts International*, February, 5840A

Stenstroem, A. (1984) *Questions and responses in English conversations*, Liber Forlag, Malmo, Sweden

Stewart, C.J. and Cash, W.B. (1985) *Interviewing: principles and practices*, W.C. Brown, Dubuque, Iowa

Stewart, D.J. and Patterson, M.L. (1973) 'Eliciting effects of verbal and nonverbal cues on projective test responses', *Journal of Consulting and Clinical Psychology*, 41, 74–7

Stewart, J. (ed.) (1977) *Bridges, not walls*, Addison-Wesley, Reading, Mass.

Stewart, R., Powell, G. and Chetwynd, S. (1979) *Person perception and stereotyping*, Saxon House, Farnborough

Stock, C.G. (1978) 'Effects of praise and its source on performance', *Perceptual and Motor Skills*, 47, 43–6

Stogdill, R.M. (1948) 'Personal factors associated with leadership: a survey of the literature', *Journal of Psychology*, 25, 35–71

—— (1950) 'Leadership, membership and organization', *Psychological Bulletin*, 47, 1–14

—— (1974) *Handbook of leadership: a survey of theory and research*, Free Press, New York

Stokes, J., Fuehrer, A. and Childs, L. (1980) 'Gender differences in self-disclosure to various target persons', *Journal of Counseling Psychology*, 27, 192–8

Stone, G. (1962) 'Appearance and the self', in A. Rose (ed.), *Human behavior and social processes*, Houghton-Mifflin, Boston

Strauss, A. (1977) 'Sociological theories and personality', in R.J. Corsini (ed.), *Current personality theories*, Peacock, Itasca, Ill.

Strong, S., Taylor, R., Bratton, J. and Loper, R. (1971) 'Non-verbal behavior and perceived counselor characteristics', *Journal of Counseling Psychology*, 18, 554–61

Sudman, S. and Bradburn, N. (1982) *Asking questions*, Jossey-Bass, San Francisco

Sullivan, H.S. (1953) *The interpersonal theory of psychiatry*, Norton, New York

—— (1954) *The psychiatric interview*, Norton, New York

Swann, J. and Read, S. (1981) 'Self-verification processes: how we sustain our own self-conceptions', *Journal of Experimental Social Psychology*, 17, 351–72

Tamase, K. (1978) 'The effects of verbal reinforcement combinations under double reinforcements upon verbal conditioning', *Psychologia*, 21, 192–6

Taylor, D. (1979) 'Motivational bases', in G. Chelune (ed.), *Self-disclosure*, Jossey-Bass, San Francisco

Thibaut, J. and Kelley, H. (1959) *The social psychology of groups*, Wiley, New York

Thomas A. and Bull, P. (1981) 'The role of pre-speech posture change in dyadic interaction', *British Journal of Social Psychology*, 20, 105–11

Thyne, J. (1966) *The psychology of learning and techniques of teaching*, 2nd edition, University of London Press, London

Tjosvold, D. (1984) 'Effects of leader warmth and directiveness on subordinate performance on a subsequent task', *Journal of Applied Psychology*, 69, 422–7

Tomkins, S.S. (1963) *Affect, imagery, consciousness*, Springer, New York

Trower, P. (ed.) (1984) *Radical approaches to social skills training*, Croom Helm, London

—— Bryant, B. and Argyle, M. (1978) *Social skills and mental health*, Methuen, London

Tubbs, S. and Baird, J. (1976) *The open person . . . self-disclosure and personal growth*, Merrill, Columbus, Ohio

Turk, C. (1985) *Effective speaking*, E. & F.N. Spon, London

Turkat, I.D. and Alpher, V.S. (1984) 'Prediction versus reflection in therapist demonstrations of understanding: three analogue experiments', *British Journal of Medical Psychology*, 57, 235–40

Turney, C., Owens, L., Hatton, N., Williams, G. and Cairns, L. (1976) *Sydney micro skills: series 2 handbook*, Sydney University Press, Sydney, Australia

—— Eltis, K.J., Hatton, N., Owens, L.C., Towler, J. and Wright, R. (1983) *Sydney micro skills redeveloped: series 1 handbook*, Sydney University Press, Sydney, Australia

Uhlemann, M.R., Lea, G.W. and Stone, G.L. (1976) 'Effect of instructions and modeling on trainees low in interpersonal communication skills', *Journal of Counseling Psychology*, 23, 509–13

Verner, C. and Dickinson, G. (1967) 'The lecture, an analysis and review of research', *Adult Education*, 17, 85–100

Verplanck, W.S. (1955) 'The control of the content of conversation: reinforcement of statement of opinion', *Journal of Abnormal and Social Psychology*, 51, 668–76

Vondracek, F.W. (1969) 'The study of self-disclosure in experimental interviews', *Journal of Psychology*, 72, 55–9

Wallen, J., Waitzkin, H. and Stoeckle, J. (1979) 'Physicians' stereotypes about female health illness: a study of patients' sex and the information process during medical interviews', *Women and Health*, 4, 135–46

Washburn, P. and Hakel, M. (1973) 'Visual cues and verbal content as influences on impressions formed after simulated employment interviews', *Journal of Applied Psychology*, 58, 137–41

Waskow, I.E. (1962) 'Reinforcement in a therapy-like situation through selective responding to feelings or content', *Journal of Consulting Psychology*, 26, 11–19

Watson, K. and Barker, L. (1984) 'Listening behavior: definition and measurement', in R. Bostrom and B. Westley (eds), *Communication yearbook 8*, Sage, Beverley Hills, California

Watzlawick, P. (1978) *The language of change*, Basic Books, New York

Weaver, C. (1972) *Human listening: processes and behavior*, Bobbs-Merrill, Indianapolis, Indiana

West, C. (1983) 'Ask me no questions . . . an analysis of questions and replies', in S. Fisher and A. Todd *The social organization of doctor-patient communication*, Center for Applied Linguistics, Washington, DC

Wheeless, L., Erickson, K. and Behrens, J. (1986) 'Cultural differences in disclosiveness as a function of locus of control', *Communication Monographs*, 53, 36–46

Whittington, D. (1986) 'Chairmanship', in O. Hargie (ed.), *A handbook of communication skills*, Croom Helm, London/New York University Press, NY

Willis, F. and Hamm, H. (1980) 'The use of interpersonal touch in securing compliance', *Journal of Nonverbal Behaviour*, 5, 49–55

Wilson-Barnett, J. (1981) 'Communicating with patients in general wards', in W. Bridge and J. MacLeod Clark (eds), *Communication in nursing care*, Croom Helm, London

Wolff, F., Marsnik, N., Tacey, W. and Nichols, R. (1983) *Perceptive listening*, Holt, Rinehart and Winston, New York

Wolpe, J. (1958) *Psychotherapy by reciprocal inhibition*, Stanford University Press, Stanford, California

Wolvin, A. and Coakley, C. (1982) *Listening*, Wm C. Brown, Iowa

Woodbury, H. (1984) 'The strategic use of questions in court', *Semiotica*, 48, 197–228

Woodworth, R.S. and Marquis, D.G. (1949) *Psychology: a study of mental life*, Methuen, London

Woolfolk, A. (1979) 'Self-disclosure in the classroom: an experimental study', *Contemporary Educational Psychology*, 4, 132–9

Worthy, M., Gary, A. and Kahn, G. (1969) 'Self-disclosure as an exchange process', *Journal of Personality and Social Psychology*, 13, 59–64

Wright, C. and Nuthall, G. (1970) 'Relationships between teacher behaviors and pupil achievement in three experimental elementary science lessons', *American Educational Research Journal*, 7, 477–93

Yukl, G.A. (1981) *Leadership in organizations*, Prentice-Hall, Englewood Cliffs, NJ

Zaidel, S.F. and Mehrabian, A. (1969) 'The ability to communicate and infer positive and negative attitudes facially and vocally', *Journal of Experimental Research in Personality*, 3, 233–41

Zander, A. (1982) *Making groups effective*, Jossey-Bass, London

Zimmer, J.M. and Anderson, S. (1968) 'Dimensions of positive regard and empathy', *Journal of Counseling Psychology*, 15, 417–26

Zuckerman, M., Spiegel, N., De Paulo, P. and Rosenthal, R. (1982) 'Nonverbal strategies for decoding deception', *Journal of Nonverbal Behavior*, 6, 171–87

Zuker, E. (1983) *Mastering assertiveness skills*, AMACOM, New York

Subject Index

acoustic confusion 170
age 201
aggression 174-5, 211-14
assertiveness
  and aggression 211-14
  components of 218-19
  contextual factors 222-4
  covert processes 219-21
  definition 210-11
  functions 214-15
  nonassertion 211-14
  nonverbal elements 221
  personal factors 222-4
  types of 213-14
attractiveness 119-20

barristers 129
beliefs 220
business executives 32, 140

careers guidance 68, 125
careers officer 130, 145, 150, 154
chairpersons 130, 132, 136, 246 247, 248, 249
clergymen 144
client-centred counselling 89
closure
  definition of 127-8
  factual 129-32, 140
  functions of 128-9
  motivational 133-5, 141
  perceptual 137-40, 141
  social 135-7, 141
cognitive restructuring 220
counselling 33, 130
counsellor 72, 117, 120, 122, 124, 129, 131, 132, 135, 145, 152, 158, 163, 186, 190, 193, 204, 241
cueing
  nonverbal 153
  verbal 153-4

deception indicators 194
demonstrations 132-4
dentist 49, 118, 177
detective 63, 77, 116, 120
doctor 13, 14, 15, 60, 61, 63, 102, 115, 118, 120, 137, 140, 144, 146, 148, 151, 154, 157, 170, 190, 193, 228, 232

emotions 174-5
empathic understanding 92, 103, 104
employment advisory personnel 99
environmental factors 13, 31-2
explanation
  aids to explanation
    demonstrations 148, 155, 158-60; illustrations 147, 155; verbal examples 155
  definition 143-4
  functions 144-5
  gaining feedback 157-8
  planning 146-7
  presenting 147-57
  types 145-6
extroverts 27, 49, 236
eye contact 52
eye-gaze 20-2, 249
eye-witness testimony 71, 76-7

fogging 217

gender
  and assertiveness 222
  behavioural differences 119
  listening differences 172
  self-disclosure differences 201-2
gestures 16-18
goals 2, 3, 124
greeting 108, 114, 115
groups
  conformity 233

definition 229-30
dyadic and group interaction 227
face-to-face interaction 229
functions 231
goals 230
groupthink 233, 234
intra-group communication 235-40
communication networks 237-40
task and psyche communication 235-6
leaders 136, 245-6, 247-8
norms 232-3
primary and secondary 229
roles 233-4, 239
size 229, 236
status 233-5, 236
types 228
see also leadership

head nods 19-20, 52, 53, 57
health visitors 14, 15, 18, 34, 47, 88, 114, 119, 130, 197

interpersonal attraction 43
interpersonal distance 54
interview 18, 29, 34, 132, 137, 138, 140, 145, 147, 158
see also research interview and selection interview
interviewers 17, 18, 29, 31, 33, 90, 131, 147, 157
introverts 27, 49, 236

johari window 200, 201
judges 129

kinesics 13, 15-24

lawyer 60, 69, 75, 120
leadership
definition 240-1
skills 246-52
styles of 245-6
theories of 241-4
learned helplessness 44
lecturers 132, 134, 136, 140, 149, 153, 154, 156, 157

listening
active 164-6, 181-5
and rationalisation 170-1
and reductionism 169-70
and reflecting 106
definition 162-3
facets of 171-7
functions of 164
obstacles to 177-80
passive 164-6
process of 168-9
types of 166-8
locus of control 44, 45, 49

memory 170
motivation 111-14

negotiators 61, 167, 197
nonverbal behaviour 5, 49, 51, 52-3, 94, 100, 183-4, 205, 221, 233, 235
nonverbal communication
definition 9
purposes 10-13
note-taking 169-70
nurses 13, 14, 15, 18, 34, 49, 102, 119, 120, 129, 130, 135, 155, 163, 170, 209, 228, 231

operant conditioning 36-40
orientation 27-8

paralanguage 13, 32-3
paraphrase — *see* reflecting
pausing 83-4
perception
first impressions 117-21
selective nature of 165-6
social perception 220
personality 172-3, 202
perspective taking 203
pharmacist 145, 170
physical characteristics 13, 27, 28-31
physical contact 13-15
physical therapy 186
politicians 33, 153
positive regard 92
posture 18-19, 54, 55

proxemics 13, 24-7
psychiatrist 116
psychologist 108, 111
public speakers 17, 33, 129, 153
punishment 37, 53
question
  affective 72-3
  and pauses 83-4
  closed 65-6
  definition 58
  distribution 84
  functions 61
  leading 73-7
  multiple 81-2
  open 66-9
  probes 92, 93, 96, 105
  probing 77-80, 182
  process 63-4
  prompting 83
  prosodic 58
  recall 62-3
  responses to 84-5
  rhetorical 80-1
  sequence of 67-9
  status differences 60
  structuring 82-3
  versus reflections 89-91

reality testing 219
reflecting
  definition 89
  empathic understanding 92
  factual and affective communication 93-5
  functions 95-6
  guidelines 105-7
  paraphrase 52, 53, 93, 96-100
  positive regard 92
  reflection of content 93, 96
  reflection of feeling 93, 100-5
  restatement 93
  versus alternative styles 91-3
  versus other reinforcers 50
reinforcement
  appropriate use 55-6
  assertiveness 221
  definition 36
  extinction 37
  frequency 56
  functions 40-5
  generalised 39-40
  genuineness 46
  listening 181
  negative 36
  nonverbal components 6, 51-5
  operant and respondent behaviour 36
  operant conditioning 36-40
  partial 57
  primary and secondary 38-9
  punishment 37
  reinforcing stimuli 36
  social 40, 41, 43, 44, 49
  variety 57
  verbal components 5-6, 45-51
relationship development 196
research interview 66, 70, 71, 74, 76, 85, 125
restatement 53, 93
see also reflecting

salesmen 17, 29, 61, 111, 116, 120, 129, 133, 167
selection interview 116, 189, 191, 223
self-concept 44
self-disclosure
  and reflecting 92, 93
  definition 187-8
  elements of 191-5
  features of 188-91
  functions of 195-200
  influencing factors 200-2
self-esteem 44, 45
set induction
  cognitive aspects 121-5
  definition 109
  functions 110
  motivational 111-14
  perceptual 117-21
  social 114-17
smiles 52, 53
social class 48, 93
social comparison 44, 231
social learning theory 4
social skill
  definitions 1-5
  example of 5-6
  features 2-4
  nature of 1

social workers 15, 18, 25, 34, 49, 123, 129, 131, 140, 144, 176, 197, 228
speech rate
  and thought rate 173-4
status 175, 192, 203
see also groups
stereotypes 179
stimulus variation 111-12
structuring 82
styles of interacting
  direct vs. indirect 90-3
summaries of content 107
summaries of feeling 107
summary 130-1, 140, 154-5, 248, 249
sustaining 174-5
teachers 14, 15, 17, 18, 24, 25, 29, 30, 33, 34, 38, 39, 42, 47, 48, 50, 51, 55, 59, 60, 62, 64, 65, 91, 102, 112, 113, 122, 124, 129, 130, 131, 134, 136, 144, 145, 147, 148, 153, 155, 157, 172, 192, 228, 241, 246
television presenters 19, 129, 134, 138, 146, 153, 248
therapist 14, 129, 136
trainers 132, 135
topic shifts 182

warmth 42, 51, 52, 104

Author Index

Abercrombie, M. 249
Abrami, P. 157
Adams, R. 84
Alberti, R. 210, 211, 225
Allen, D. 112
Allen, J. 187
Allen, V. 233
Alper, T. 13
Alpher, V. 92
Altman, I. 119
Anderson, S. 92
Applbaum, R.L. 227, 232, 235
Archer, R. 200, 201, 204, 205
Arenson, S. 49
Argyle, M. 2, 3, 8, 21, 22, 30, 121, 228, 231
Armstrong, S. 145, 146, 156
Aronson, E. 43
Arvey, 117
Aubertine, H. 122
Auerswald, M. 93, 99
Austin, N. 213
Authier, J. 95, 100, 158, 189

Baccus, G. 105
Backman, C. 232, 239
Baird, J. 196
Bakhtar, M. 149
Bakken, D. 127
Baldock, J. 90
Baldwin, J.D. 36, 40
Baldwin, J.I. 36, 40
Bales, R. 136, 229, 236, 237
Balsam, P. 38
Bandura, A. 4, 50
Banks, D. 54
Barker, L. 169
Barnabei, F. 105
Barnes, D. 29, 151
Bass, B. 242, 250
Bavelas, A. 237
Baxter, J. 26
Beattie, G. 20, 21
Becker, H. 151
Beezer, R. 74
Beharry, E. 92
Behling, O. 241
Bender, V. 201
Benjamin, A. 90, 98, 131, 135
Benne, K. 234
Berg, J. 188
Berlyne, D. 111, 113
Bermann, E. 231
Berne, E. 138
Bernstein, B. 151
Berscheid, E. 29
Bickman, L. 31
Birdwhistell, R. 8
Black, J. 59
Blackman, D. 118
Blanchard, E. 51
Bligh, D. 81
Bochner, S. 151
Boddy, J. 49
Bond, M. 23
Bondy, A. 38
Boore, J. 145
Boy, A. 91
Bradburn, N. 59, 85
Brammer, L. 54, 93, 95, 96, 102, 103
Bremer, N. 64
Brimer, M. 172
Brokaw, D. 43
Brooks, L. 203
Brooks, R. 54
Brophy, J. 42, 47, 48, 56
Brown, A. 228
Brown, G. 81, 145, 146, 149, 153, 156
Brown, R. 49, 50
Brundage, L. 203
Bruner, J. 122, 144
Bryman, A. 247
Buckwalter, A. 77
Bugental, D. 23, 140
Bull, P. 8, 20
Burger, J. 203
Burley-Allen, M. 162, 183

Burton, M. 118
Busch, P. 111

Cairns, L. 47, 48
Campbell, D. 230
Campion, J. 117
Cannell, C. 42, 67
Carkhuff, R. 107
Carlisle, J. 61, 197
Carnevale, J. 46
Cartwright, D. 246, 249
Cary, M. 239
Cash, W. 90
Chaikin, A. 188, 189, 191, 196, 205, 207
Chelune, G. 188
Cianni-Surridge, M. 233
Citkowitz, R.D. 99
Clark, C. 209
Cline, V. 93
Clore, G. 43
Coakley, C. 162, 166
Collier, G. 94
Conine, N. 186
Cook, M. 22, 27, 119
Cooley, C. 229
Corey, S. 59, 64
Cozby, P. 187
Crow, B. 182

Dabbs, J. 23, 174, 205
Danish, S. 93
Davis, M. 199
Davison, G. 125
Davitz, J.R. 100
Dawley, H. 219, 220
De Giovanni, I. 213
Delefes, P. 84
Del Greco, L. 213
Dell, D. 114
Derlega, V. 188, 189, 191, 196, 206, 207
De Vito, J. 198
Dickinson, G. 148
Dickson, A. 14
Dickson, D. 53, 89, 99, 105
Dillon, J. 59, 77, 84, 85, 91
Di Mattia, D.J. 99
Dimond, R. 202
Dohrenwend, B. 70, 71, 73, 74
Donohue, G.B. 46, 49
Douglas, T. 247
Duck, S. 120
Dudley, W. 51
Duncan, S. 12, 20, 23, 53
Dunnam, M. 205

Egan, G. 95, 177
Egan, K. 216, 218, 222
Ehrlich, R.P. 105
Eisler, R. 4, 223
Ekman, P. 8, 11, 15, 19, 20, 22, 100
Eller, B.F. 48
Ellis, R. 1, 135
Ellison, C. 92
Ellsworth, P. 31
Emmons, M. 210, 211, 225
England, G. 242
Ennis, R. 145

Falk, D. 189
Farson, R. 185
Feigenbaum, W.M. 92
Feldman, R. 230
Ferber, A. 108, 114
Ferris, S. 33
Fest, T. 247
Festinger, L. 231
Fiedler, F. 230, 243
Field, S. 114
Firestone, I. 92
Fisch, H. 19
Fish, M.C. 49
Fisher, D. 187, 189
Fisher, J. 14
Fiske, D. 12, 20, 23, 53
Flanders, N. 90
Floyd, J. 162
Fong, M. 193
Foot, H. 250
Foxman, R. 119
Franzoi, S. 199
Frederiksen, L. 4
French, P. 149
Frey, S. 19
Friedman, H. 29
Friedman, N. 16, 157
Friesen, W. 11, 15, 19, 100
Fry, L. 217

Furnham, A. 223
Furst, N. 148

Gage, N. 144, 147, 151
Galassi, J. 219
Gall, M. 64
Gallagher, J. 64
Gallois, C. 222, 224
Gardner, W. 246
Garramone, G. 111
Geller, D.M. 51
Glaser, R. 130
Gleason, J. 144
Gluckstern, N. 147, 152
Goffman, E. 9, 13, 108, 127, 138, 241
Goldfried, M. 125
Goldman, M. 49, 53, 54
Gordon, T. 250
Gormally, J. 52, 99, 224
Graesser, A. 59
Graham, J. 18
Green, R. 37
Greenbaum, P. 115
Greenspoon, J. 46
Gregg, V. 170
Grigsby, J. 201
Grzelak, J. 191
Guetzkow, H. 239

Haase, R. 99
Hakel, M. 19
Hall, E. 26
Halpin, A. 247
Hamm, H. 14
Hancks, M. 183
Hare, A. 229, 230
Hargie, O. 3, 5, 42, 62, 64, 71, 147
Harnack, R. 247
Harper, R. 22
Harrigan, J. 181
Harris, C. 155
Harris, J. 76
Hastorf, A. 31
Hatton, N. 146
Hauer, A.L. 93
Haviland, J. 172
Heimberg, R. 220
Hekmat, H. 46, 49
Hellkamp, D. 202
Helmy, K. 48
Henley, N. 119
Henry, S. 49
Heslin, R. 13, 14, 95, 100
Heywood, S. 18
Higgins, S. 36
Highlen, P. 105
Hildum, D. 49, 50
Hill, C. 52, 99
Hiller, J. 146, 148, 149, 151
Hirsbrunner, H. 19
Ho, H. 23
Hoffman, S. 16
Hoffnung, R. 46, 99
Holahan, C. 118
Holborn, S. 46, 52, 53
Hollander, E. 241, 244
Holt, B. 111
Honing, W. 40
Horan, J. 223
Hore, T. 29
Hosking, D. 241, 245
Hutcheson, S. 9
Hyman, R. 59, 145

Ingham, R. 21
Ivey, A. 84, 95, 100, 147, 152, 158, 189

Jackson, B. 84
Jaffe, J. 33
Jakubowski, P. 210, 215
Janis, I. 233
Jesudason, S. 71
Johnson, C. 205
Johnson, D. 247
Johnson, F. 247
Jones, B. 247
Jones, S. 54
Jones, W. 41
Jourard, S. 188, 207
Julian, J. 244

Kahn, R. 67
Kahn, S. 222
Kelley, H. 204
Kelly, J. 2, 42, 210
Kendon, A. 12, 16, 21, 22, 108, 114

Kennedy, J. 46, 99
Kennedy, T. 92
Kennedy, W. 47
Kennelly, K. 44, 45, 49
Kenny, D. 193
Kern, J. 220, 222, 224
Kestler, J. 59, 60, 69, 75
Kiefer, F. 59
King, G. 65
Kittell, J. 121
Kleck, R. 27
Klein, K. 53
Kleinke, C. 14, 43, 52, 115, 120
Knapp, M. 8, 20, 23, 114, 128, 131, 132, 137, 138, 139
Knapper, C. 157
Kolotkin, R. 212, 219
Krasner, L. 52
Krivonos, P. 114
Kuperminc, M. 220

L'Abate, L. 1
Land, M. 148, 151
Lange, A. 210, 215
Laver, J. 9, 139
Lazarsfield, P. 71
Lazarus, A. 210
Lee, Y. 49
Leenthal, L. 157
Levin, M. 199
Lewin, K. 230, 245
Lewis, P. 222, 224
Ley, P. 145, 148, 154
Likert, R. 246
Linehan, M. 216, 218, 222
Lippitt, R. 245
Littlejohn S. 235
Loftus, E. 71, 75, 76, 77
Long, L. 59
Lott, A. 43
Lott, B. 43
Lott, D.F. 26
Luft, J. 200, 235
Lundsteen, S. 163
Lysakowski, R.S. 47

Maguire, G.P. 114, 155
Maguire, P. 61
Malatesta, C. 172
Margalit, B. 223
Marisi, D. 48
Marquis, D. 109
Marshall, K. 130
Martin, J. 143
Martinko, M. 246
Maslow, A. 44
Massarik, F. 228
Matarazzo, J. 33, 46, 53
Mauger, P. 223
Mayfield, E. 29
Mayo, C. 119
McCartan, P. 5
McFall, M. 212
McFall, R. 2
McGrade, B. 48
McGregor, D. 250
McGuire, J. 2
McHenry, R. 29, 121
McIntyre, T. 209
McKeown, R. 131
McLemore, C. 43
Mehrabian, A. 19, 23, 27, 54, 140
Merbaum, M. 105
Metzler, K. 59
Michelson, 2
Milan, M. 1
Miller, D. 231
Miller, J. 48
Miller, L. 193, 203
Mills, M. 92
Miltz, R. 151
Mock, J. 53
Montagu, M. 13
Montgomery, R. 175
Morgan, T. 114, 130, 168, 249
Morley, I. 241, 245
Morris, D. 16
Morris, E.K. 36
Mortensensen, C. 250
Mount, S. 45, 49
Mucchielli, R. 91
Munro, E. 131

Nagata, D. 99, 105
Naifeh, S. 201
Nelson-Jones, R. 72, 93, 117, 124, 132, 163
Newcomb, T. 190

Newman, H. 33
Nicholas, R. 105
Nix, J. 222
Norton, R. 90
Novak, J. 122
Nuthall, G. 82, 130, 131, 147

O'Brien, J. 46, 52, 53
O'Donnell, P. 43
O'Leary, K. 48, 56
O'Leary, S. 48, 56
O'Neill, G. 196
O'Neill, N. 196
Oster, H. 20
Owens, R. 175

Palmer, J. 76
Pansa, M. 52
Paradowski, W. 111
Passons, W. 103
Pate, R. 64
Patterson, C. 90
Patterson, M. 15, 49, 95, 100
Pattison, J. 14
Pavlov, I. 35
Peeck, J. 112
Pendleton, D. 151
Perlmann, R. 144
Perry, R. 157
Phelps, S. 213
Phillips, E. 2
Pietrofesa, J. 95, 97, 101
Pine, G. 91
Pinney, R. 154
Pisoni, S. 46
Pope, B. 124, 136
Poppleton, S. 61
Porritt, L. 163, 209
Powell, W. 92
Priestley, P. 2
Prior, D. 90
Purvis, J. 203

Raben, C. 40
Rachlin, H. 37 , 40
Rackham, N. 61, 114, 130, 168, 197, 249
Rakos, R. 218, 219, 221
Rauch, C. 241
Raven, B. 43, 237
Read, S. 44
Reece, M. 46
Redfield, D. 65
Reid, L. 121
Resnick, L. 59
Reynolds, J. 130
Richardson, S. 3, 73, 74
Rierdan, J. 54
Riggio, R. 29
Riseborough, M. 17
Robinson, J. 114
Rogers, C. 17, 44, 60, 89, 124, 185, 212, 218
Rose, Y. 212, 218
Rosenblatt, P. 120
Rosenfeld, H. 115, 183
Rosenshine, B. 51, 124, 148, 149, 153, 155, 156, 181
Rosenthal, R. 29
Roth, H. 108
Rothkopf, E. 131
Rotter, J. 44
Rousseau, E. 65
Rowe, M. 80
Rozelle, R. 26, 194
Rubin, J. 43, 237
Russell, J. 48
Russo, N. 21
Rutter, D. 21, 115
Ryan, E. 65

Sacks, H. 128, 138
Saigh, P. 52, 56
Salter, A. 209
Salzinger, K. 46
Sarbin, T. 233
Saunders, C. 116
Schatzman, L. 70
Schegloff, E. 128, 138
Scherer, K. 8
Schlundt, D. 2
Schmidt, L. 114
Schneider, D. 31
Schopler, J. 31
Schuck, R. 124
Schulman, L. 132, 133
Schultz, C. 48
Schutz, W. 15, 231
Scofield, M. 53
Scott, M. 33

Secord, P. 232, 239
Seligman, M. 44
Shapiro, J. 11
Shaw, M. 229, 239
Sheats, P. 234
Sherman, R. 48
Shostrom, E. 54, 95, 96, 102, 103
Showalter, J. 52
Shutes, R. 157
Shuy, R. 115, 137, 150
Siegel, J. 19
Siegman, A. 46
Silver, R. 91
Simms, M. 119
Simon, H. 239
Simonson, N. 122
Sinha, V. 201
Skinner, B. 36, 39
Slobin, D. 192
Smith, C. 119
Smith, G. 201
Smith, V. 162, 170
Smock, C. 111
Solano, C. 205
Solomon, M. 31
Sommer, R. 26, 27
Spooner, S. 99
Staddon, J. 40
Stenstroem, A. 59
Stewart, C. 90
Stewart, D. 49
Stewart, J. 148, 187
Stewart, R. 119
Stock, C. 49
Stoeckle, J. 145
Stogdill, R. 240, 242, 246
Stokes, J. 202
Stone, G. 241
Strauss, A. 70, 241
Strong, S. 181
Sudman, S. 59, 85
Sullivan, H. 44, 116
Swann, J. 44

Tamase, K, 49
Taylor, D. 203
Thibaut, J. 204
Thomas, A. 20
Thyne, J. 143
Tjosvold, D. 247
Tomkins, S. 100
Trower, P. 1, 41, 135
Tryon, W. 46, 49, 212, 218
Tubbs, S. 196
Turk, C. 81, 122
Turkat, I. 92
Turney, C. 47, 65, 69, 79, 84, 112, 143, 148, 248, 249

Uhlemann, M. 104

Vartabedian, R. 203
Verner, C. 148
Verplanck, W.S. 52
Vondracek, F. 92

Wagner, P. 189
Waitzkin, H. 145
Walberg, H. 47
Wallblatt, H. 11
Wallen, J. 145
Walster, E. 29
Washburn, P. 19
Waskow, I. 99
Watson, K. 169
Watzlawick, P. 33
Weatherley, D. 201
Weaver, C. 163
Wenrich, W. 219, 220
West, C. 60
Wheeless, L. 202
White, M. 49
White, R. 245
Whitman, R. 46
Whittington, D. 1, 135, 247
Wiens, A. 46, 53
Willcutt, H. 47
Willis, F. 14
Wilson, D. 111
Wilson-Barnett, J. 145
Winer, B. 247
Wolff, F. 162, 163, 166, 173
Wolpe, J. 209
Wolvin, A. 162, 166
Woodbury, H. 58
Woodworth, R. 109
Woolfolk, A. 192
Worthy, M. 187
Wright, C. 82, 130, 131, 147

Yarbrough, A. 54
Yukl, G. 242

Zaidel, S. 23, 140
Zander, A. 246, 247, 249, 252
Zanni, G. 75, 76
Zimmer, J. 46, 92, 99
Zuckerman, M. 188
Zuker, E. 183, 219, 226